SHADOWS OF SUBSTANCE

SHADOWS OF SUBSTANCE

Indo–Russian Trade and Military Technical Cooperation Since 1991

HARI VASUDEVAN

MANOHAR
2010

First published 2010

ISBN 978-81-7304-849-4

Published by
Ajay Kumar Jain *for*
Manohar Publishers & Distributors
4753/23 Ansari Road, Daryaganj,
New Delhi 110 002

Printed at
Salasar Imaging Systems
Delhi 110 035

Dedicated to
the memory
of my father
METHIL VASUDEVAN

Contents

Acknowledgements

This book owes its existence to the support provided from a number of sources. Most important was the Peace Studies Group (PSG), Calcutta University, and its coordinator, Prof. Suranjan Das. The PSG, under Ford Foundation grants, financed the basic fieldwork in Russia. The Academy of Third World Studies, and its Director, Prof. Mushirul Hasan, provided me with time to develop my ideas. The Maulana Abul Kalam Azad Institute of Asian Studies, Kolkata, has arranged for the publication and Manohar Publishers & Distributors and Mr. Ramesh Jain have supported the venture. To Sri S.N. Menon and and Sri Satbir Singh I owe a debt for the interest they have consistently shown in my work. This has also been true of Nandan Unnikrishnan and the Observer Research Foundation, New Delhi, which provided a forum for me to discuss my views. Without the India International Centre, New Delhi, and its many seminars and lectures, to evolve a focus for this research would have been difficult.

Collecting the material for this book would not have been possible without the assistance at different times of the Embassy of India, Moscow and the South Asian Studies Program of the Institute of Oriental Studies, Russian Academy of Sciences, Moscow, and the Program Head, Tatiana Shaumian. Important also was the Maison Des Sciences De L'Homme (Paris) and the assistance rendered by Maurice Aymard, Jean Luc Racine and Jaques Sapir. Invaluable to pursuing the study have been interactions with members of the Centre for Strategic Forces, Moscow and the Department of Commerce, Government of India, New Delhi, and conversations with Sri Mahapatra, Smt. Anju Sharma and Sri Murthi, who have closely surveyed Russian trade over time in this Department. It has been possible to understand the working of the private sector in Russia due to conversations with Animesh

Basu—who, I must state, is in no way responsible for the limitations of understanding that I have shown in this survey. Both Sri Basu and the late Pranab Guha Thakurta taught me much about trade that I would otherwise never have understood. Sri Guha Thakurta also allowed me access to the papers of Industrial Export Services—which were an eye-opener concerning the problems of the early disintegration period.

What little I have come to understand of military-technical affairs is the product of long conversations with my father, the late Methil Vasudevan, former DSO (DRDO), India, and an excellent aeronautics expert and teacher. I have also benefited in this area from discussions with K. Santanam and seminars at the IDSA, New Delhi.

My colleagues at the Department of History, Calcutta University, especially Bhaskar Chakravarty, have held fort for me while I have been working on some of this project. I am indebted to them for this, as well as to Prof. J.K Ray for similar assistance at the Azad Institute. Those who have done the same at home—Tapati Guha Thakurta and Mrinalini Vasudevan—have always stoically borne the burden of a subject that is alien to them. Young colleagues have been important to completion of the project in different ways—and I must mention Madhumita Majumdar, Kingshuk Chatterji, Ramakant Dwivedi and Sreemati Ganguly in this regard. I have regularly tested ideas with Madhavan Palat and Arup Banerji to my benefit. This is equally true of Nirmal Chandra, Amiya Bagchi, Sunanda Sen, Barun De, Sudip Chatterji and Ranajoy Bhattacharya. My mother Sreekumari Vasudevan has valiantly attempted to understand what I do—and has encouraged me to do it. My brother Ravi has firmly stood by me in everything I have done.

Despite all these inputs, this work has finally been my own—and I hold myself wholly responsible for its many shortcomings. The reason I have chosen to publish it, with its many defects, is the hope that it may serve as an imperfect but useful introduction to a field whose value and scope is seldom acknowledged.

HARI VASUDEVAN

Abbreviations/Glossary

AO	Joint Stock Company
BHEL	Bharat Heavy Electricals Limited
BFTR	Vneshtorgbank
CEDB	The Central Engineering and Design Bureau
CEO	Chief Executive Officer
CII	Confederation of Indian Industry
CIS	Commonwealth of Independent States
CMEA	Council of Mutual Economic Assistance
CPSU	Communist Party of the Soviet Union
crore	ten million
DCM	Delhi Cloth Mills
DRDO	Defense Research and Development Organization
EMK	Energy Machine-Building Corporation
energos	electricity supplying units
EBRD	European Bank for Reconstruction
EPW	*Economic and Political Weekly*
FCEM	Foreign & Colonial Emerging Markets Ltd
FICCI	Federation of Indian Chambers of Commerce and Industries
FIG	Financial Investment Groups
FSUE	Federal State Unitary Enterprise
FTO	Foreign Trade Organization
FSU	Former Soviet Union
Gorispolkom	The city executive committee
GKI	Committee (later Ministry) for State Property
HAL	Hindustan Aeronautics Limited
HEC	Heavy Engineering Corporation
HIID	Harvard Institute for International Development

HMBP	Heavy Machine-Building Plant
HMC	Harvard Management Company
IDPL	Indian Drugs and Pharmaceuticals Limited
IRJC	Indo-Russian Joint Commission
JSC	Joint Stock Concern
JV	Joint Venture
lakh	one hundred thousand
LC	Letter of Credit
LDC	Late Developing Country
MAMC	Mining and Allied Machinery Corporation
MECON	Metallurgical and Engineering Consultants
MFN	Most Favoured Nation
MIC	Military Industrial Complex
MOU	Memorandum of Understanding
nomenklatura	Soviet Communist Party elite
OAOs	Open Joint Stock Companies
ONGC	Oil and Natural Gas Corporation
OOO	Limited Liability Company
PRC	People's Republic of China
PSU	Public Sector Units
SBI	State Bank of India
TPE	Tiazhpromexport
RSFSR	Russian Socialist Federated Soviet Republic
RF	Russian Federation
RCP	Russian Communist Party
SA	Strategic Analyses
USAID	United States Agency for International Development
ZAO	Closed Joint Stock Company

Introduction
The Problem and the Argument

This book presents a survey and an interpretation of Indo–Russian economic relations during 1991–2002, the formative period in India's connections with the Russian Federation. Stress falls on trade, with some attention to military technical cooperation. The last chapter traces developments of more recent times (to 2009) for readers curious about trends after 2002—but this short essay does not pretend to give the detailed information that is available in the earlier chapters.

My argument is pitted against the tendency to downplay the significance of the post-Soviet entente that took shape between the two countries during 1995–2000, and points to important strengths that developed in the connection during the post-disintegration decade. In stressing this, there is no attempt made to understate the fact that Russia's India policy bore marks of inconsistencies typical of the Federation's foreign policy in general[1] during the period under survey, or that Indo–Russian relations fell prey to the 'Western tilt' in Russia at the time. These aspects of Russian policy cannot be ignored and attract attention even in writing in India, which is inclined to be careful and equivocal[2]—and they also find assertion in literature in Russia on major aspects of foreign policy.[3] The argument here, however, shows that during this period cooperation and trade, even if prone to instability, evolved a foundation in private entrepreneurial activity and official interaction. While challenges were severe, the main actors in Indo–Russian economic relations showed resilience and evolved strategies to deal with them, though the instability of the Russian economy at this time and the behaviour of the bulk of Indian entrepreneurs—who did not establish a proper foothold in the Russian market—portended an uncertain future, which is even today the case.

The importance of the subject is well established. As most commentators acknowledge, despite contrary trends in bilateral relations, Indo–Russian military cooperation was crucial to the relationship between the two countries in the immediate post-Cold War period, and was pivotal to the military industrial complex in both countries. Meanwhile trade and economic collaboration, although limited in scale, maintained a steady pace, with major benefits to specific sectors. The independent strength of India as a regional power after the Cold War came of the potential of this special relationship with the Federation, even if the country's image as a prominent democracy and a global force was refurbished by US rhetoric and the country's fast-developing economy came to be deeply connected with trade in goods and services with the US and the European Union. The determination of the US to 'cap' military development in countries such as India, within the framework of a broad strategy for global security, made the connection with Russia exceptionally important for India. Economic collaboration and trade established India's interests in a major 'emerging market' at a time when her commercial relations elsewhere had not acquired a degree of solidity. In Russia, meanwhile, for a military industrial complex acting under severe financial constraints in the Federation, Indian orders were a lifeline.

In this survey and interpretation of what happened, I look beyond varying accounts of trade and Indo–Russian military cooperation. The argument works out from a critical evaluation of Indo–Soviet trade and military–technical cooperation in 1991, and how this had evolved under M.S. Gorbachev's perestroika. The evaluation takes stock of problems in Indo–Soviet economic collaboration during 1979–91, whatever the rhetoric of the time, and points out that by 1991, Indo–Soviet *druzhba* (friendship) had come down to arms purchases and oil business. Within the framework of a diplomatic entente, the post-1991 period witnessed a complex commercial and economic relationship with new dimensions. Here, despite the decade-long industrial recession in Russia, a modicum of bilateral trade (other than the trade in arms) was maintained, though India remained substantially less important to Russia than the USA, the EU, China, and Japan (and vice versa) and benefits to India of the relationship cannot be compared to that which prevailed in the Indo–Soviet relationship of the early 1970s and before. The geographical contours of the new Russian state gave advantages to commerce between the Federation and the CIS states, European Union states, and China. Access to the Russian market was easier for these countries than for India.

The agreement by India and Russia to settle India's debts to the USSR over a twelve-year period (ending 2005), in the form of annual repayments in goods, was central to this new relationship that evolved in these circumstances—but it was not crucial. Elsewhere, the post-1991 export of arms to India acquired significance for the Russian economy as it considerably exceeded what went before 1991—a point stressed in Euro–American and Russian literature. For the Indian armed forces, Russian supplies continued to be of decisive importance.

An important dimension to the Indo–Russian commercial relationship was that Indian middlemen acquired a crucial role because Russian government agencies were seldom active in organizing and directing Indian debt repayments and Russian industry was preoccupied with its own reorganization. In many cases, these 'Indian' middlemen were neither India-based, nor Russia-based, but represented a form of multinational organization with a heavily Indian profile (operating from Singapore, the Gulf states, or Europe). Their companies promoted trade, had major Indian commitments, but were not hide-bound by Indian regulations. They not only offered Russia the advantages of India trade and the means to mobilize India's old rouble debt to Russia, they also provided access to a larger world of commercial and investment connections at a time when this expertise was developing slowly in the Russian Federation. Indian entrepreneurs had advantages that were similar to those enjoyed by their European and US counterparts, while their Indian connections, and their reluctance to displease the Indian government, made them manageable through state-to-state relations. This is a characteristic that is not unknown in US and European business circles in Russia; but it was not replicated in the same way in the case of Indian business, since the relationship between the EU, the USA, and Russia was different from that which prevailed between the Federation and India.

A commitment to sustaining Indo–Russian commerce was also to evolve ad hoc among Indian businessmen. Indian enterprise that took shape was not fly-by-night for the most part. Crucial in drawing Indian companies into the trade were their long-established ties with Russia, their near monopolistic position in the area once government agencies were inactive, and the attraction of the repayments business—a business that guaranteed deals, with no international competition. In India, private actors received encouragement from a government to whom they provided alternatives to state channels for access to the post-1991 Russian economy. For their part, using the repayments business as the kernel of their activity, Indian businessmen developed a broader trade, in convertible currency, which promised to ensure healthy commerce after the end of the repayments scheme. The opportunities companies found elsewhere in the CIS reinforced these connections. After the Yeltsin period, business as a whole received a fillip when the Government of India began to encourage foreign investment in its own right (in the case of ONGC investments in Sakhalin oil, specifically). This was a major development of the Indian state's contribution to the development of the special relationship with Russia—a contribution that included official support for schemes for modernization by Russian companies of PSUs in the power, steel, and coal sectors.

True, during 1991–2000, uncertainties were rife concerning the future of trade and military technical links because of Russian economic problems and the circumspection with which some Indian companies assessed their involvement in Russia. Various factors also made the Russia trade precarious: social decay in Russia, the social status of Indo–Russian trade, and the Indian trader's eye to the Western capital and goods markets. But a degree of steadiness emerged in trade, and the gathering strength of the Russian economy promised intensification rather than a fall off.

Much of this steadiness was intimately linked with the dependence of trade and interaction on a community of students and business persons of Indian origin who were resident in Russia. Although seldom connected among themselves in any formal way—except through the various initiatives of the Indian Embassy in Moscow, which played an important if poorly acknowledged role in bringing them together—this community created an important link between Russian and Indian business. No equivalent existed in Russia, except in the case of Chinese migrants in the Russian Far East. Most other communities linked by nationality to countries outside Russia were from the CIS countries, whose economies were passing through a severe depression and whose international trade connections were limited.

In the case of the development of Indo–Russian military cooperation after 1991, there was greater flexibility for India than before. Even though Moscow may have been guilty of many of the great-power ambitions attributed to it, as the Russian state promoted its arms trade, there can no longer be out-and-out certainty about who the piper was in the military-technological cooperation, or what the tune was. As Russia did in the case of China, so also in the case of India, the Federation provided the means to improve an arsenal and a regional authority with few conditions attached. The mutual interests that were built up in the course of arms purchases were a spur to future intensification of trade between the two countries, this time in convertible currencies.

Changes in the terms used in the discussion of economic cooperation and commerce marked what happened, giving the course of events a major reorientation. Before 1986, almost all that was stated of Indo–Soviet economic and military–technical collaboration involved terms that meant somewhat more than they said. The language led into perspectives on 'development' and 'development strategy' that had a pro-Soviet bias in the Cold War context and stressed the importance of the USSR as a country that was focused on building a new international division of labour which did not involve imperialist exploitation of late-developing countries. Clearly, words such as 'assistance' and 'cooperation' had an idiomatic dimension. They threw up a picture of a great drama of development where the USSR played the benevolent patron, India played the independent client, and, in both instances, the state was the necessary broker. The importance of the public sector in what took place found support in the ascendancy in India of growth based on Planning.[4] The idiomatic usages led into images of economic development that were linked to a critique of 'neocolonialism' and 'capitalist' hegemony in international affairs—terms that had anti-NATO and anti-US reverberations during the Cold War. The images persisted in the terms that Soviet commentators came to use concerning international trade from the mid-1970s, where the division of the world into two economic camps received less stress and more was said about cooperation between countries within one world economy.[5] In all this, tensions in the Indo–Soviet relationship (and tensions in comparable Soviet relationships) were stated through riders which mentioned losses to the USSR, leaving the overall picture of closeness intact. In the late 1970s and early 1980s, in India, the benefits of the relationship came to be questioned, but 'collaboration' as much as 'development' became fixed reference points to the mutual satisfaction of both sides.

Post-1991, everything to do with economic relations came to be seen in terms of 'the market' and 'profitability'. Such a transformation emptied trade and economic collaboration of strategic meaning, providing them with their own area of focus. Cooperation on arms production and arms sale was a different matter, since it was necessarily a strategic issue. Cooperation between Russia and India on missile technology and nuclear technology were regarded as a threat to global arms proliferation control regimes, irrespective of the terms in which they were couched, even if the states concerned were considered worthy of regard as global/regional powers. A phenomenon that was empty of a language of threat, and that might even have been beneficial to regional security, was seen by NATO analysts as a potential problem in the global context and an irritant to close relations between NATO, Russia, and India, especially after the Indian nuclear tests of 1998. The situation was responsible for some of the tensions between NATO and its potential clients, even following the improvement in Indo–US relations from 1999.

To draw out the picture, this argument divides into five chapters. Chapter 1 provides an account of how, at the highpoint of the India–USSR strategic partnership, Indo–Soviet economic cooperation was significant to the USSR within an import–export strategy to supplement consumer goods and manufactured goods inputs into the Planned Economy, without a drain on convertible currency resources which were scarce. Trade provided a means of circumventing the exclusion from certain forms of technology that the USSR suffered as a result of NATO-country embargoes. In developing the relationship, before 1988 decisions were taken at the highest level, and they involved key institutions of the Planned Economy (mainly Foreign Trade Organizations [FTO] and the Military Industrial Complex [MIC]) that worked under close official supervision. Producer–consumer contact on a regular basis, though, was rare in such a situation, except at the mundane level of training programmes. And this led to poor foundations for the USSR's initial links with the Indian economy. These links included a range of initiatives in setting up heavy engineering and capital goods plants (e.g. Mining and Allied Machinery Corporation [MAMC], the Heavy Engineering Corporation [HEC], steel plants at Bhilai and Bokaro, etc.). The initiatives were seldom based on everyday expediencies or the requirements of consumers, making for sterile, one-off projects. M.S. Gorbachev's perestroika hardly altered this situation, even if it opened a number of opportunities.

Soviet disintegration and the Russian reforms, on the other hand (chapter 2) quickly threw almost all aspects of the relationship into confusion. Independent factory pricing policy in Russia destroyed Planning and severely undermined the FTO. Alternative routes had to be devised to define requirements and carry through transactions. Disintegration and the Russian reforms altered the means of exchange, changing the basis of the rouble and creating new currencies in the former Soviet Union. Enterprises were transformed by privatization. At a time when the politics of Indo–Russian relations was being reworked, this radical restructuring of the economy threw India's trade operations in Russia into disorder. As I point out in the following chapter 3, however, this disorder led to a revitalization of trade—this time dominated by the Indian private sector, with little direct state involvement. Those involved were substantially India-based; but there were crucial players who had a cosmopolitan, international character which placed them outside the controls of the Indian government.

In chapter 4, I briefly point out that persistent interest in India as an economic partner came from institutions and leaders of the old order in the Russian MIC, whose services were crucial to the country's new elite. In India, even while a strong interest evinced itself in the Russian manufacturing sector and the Russian market, a focus on the armaments industry was sustained throughout this period. The Asian financial crisis of 1997–8 and the August Crash of 1998 consolidated this interest on both sides—even if the terms of the new relationship were to work in different ways from earlier *druzhba*. The relationship took on a wholly new dimension. Clearly, India had greater flexibility in the relationship than was the case in the past. The development of the Indo–Russian partnership and cooperation within the framework of Russian and Indian engagement with globalization and liberalization made the phenomenon substantially different from the India–USSR connection. They advanced India's authoritative role in South Asia without the conditions that the USSR had invoked in the pre-1991 period.

THE APPROACH

In terms of methodology, this is a historian's examination of a contemporary problem—i.e. it attempts to determine the chronological and structural contours of a phenomenon and place it in a time continuum. Hence, it is more concerned with the perspective of the past and the anatomy of the prevailing relationship than with models of development and economic behaviour.

In this regard, it must be mentioned that the examination of Russia's cooperation with India cannot pinpoint specific regional and enterprise centres around which the relationship revolved, and so will appear general. Pre-1991, it is difficult to find the equivalents of Ford, Coca Cola, Enron, or Bethlehem Steel in the Russian case to establish points of reference. Soviet manufacture was gathered into all-Union Ministry-centred industry-wide monoliths, made up of large concerns that comprised a number of factories and enterprises. Within the framework, specific units had almost no flexibility or identity independent of the state departments that looked after their management. This changed somewhat after privatization and the emergence of Russia's 'oligarchs' as an authoritative force. But clear corporate identities took shape weakly, and, as in the case of middle-size steel units, flux and uncertainty were endemic. I have attempted to give some sense of the new geography of the Russian economy while tracing the Federation's Indian links, but a degree of sketchiness is unavoidable.

The essence of the argument here takes its orientation from the classification of Russian political development that I have followed elsewhere: post-1991, we witness a 'revolutionary' society (fixed on libertarian goals) where the force of the revolutionary impulse is weak, and a degree of validity still goes to pre-1991 agreements between stalwarts of the ancien regime and the new order. While Indo–Russian cooperation came to be shaped by the transformation of the Russian economy, 'hangovers' remained in the conduct of agreements and deals. In the case of armaments especially, traditional habits of interaction continued to be important.[6]

Such an interpretation goes against two trends in Euro–American literature. One of these divides the decade into a 'period of transition' and a revolutionary upsurge which overran the attempt at a smooth 'transition'. This understates the elements of continuity between perestroika and the Yeltsin regime. The second characterizes the period as a move into 'post-communism' and understates the revolutionary impulse of the new order. Russian research, pointedly, offers a mixed menu of approaches, focusing on the 'hard structures' of the economy as well as the mind set of the public and the corporate elite.

The perspective that is followed here picks up the literature on Indo–Soviet relations before 1990 and supplements it with explanations of why commercial links stagnated towards the end of the period. The argument reviews the statistical foundations of accounts of Indo–Russian trade post-1991, which take as their theme the decline of commerce and link this decline to Russia's economic crisis. Raising questions about this reading of the statistics, I explain the persistence of Indo–Russian trade, and note the capacity of such trade to build mutual respect and interaction, even if its future was uncertain. For this, I have used information from unpublished official documents and interviews taken in Russia and India. In taking this position, the argument does not endorse the policies of the post-1991 Russian government and its IMF/World Bank mentors, but it does agree with characterization of the late Soviet economy as stagnant and uninventive, and the portrayal of its successor as a major opening to innovation and economic expansion.

Since for India (and for many other countries), the former Soviet Union offered opportunities for trade and growth that were precluded by subsequent 'globalization' and 'liberalization' of the WTO, the argument has implications for the literature on globalization, even in more recent times. Clearly the rules of trading and economic policy are still in their formative period in Russia and the FSU generally, and 'public good' and mutual natural interest as much as narrow profitability attract sympathy—attitudes that have little place in WTO circles. Hence, given that early association with Soviet technology makes it possible for India to pick up threads in this market, as does the powerful rhetoric of Indo–Soviet friendship and Indo–Russian partnership, at a time of uncertain gains from association with the WTO,[7] the region remains a 'vital periphery' to India's developing economy. How this state of affairs may evolve or may be utilized in future, however, remains difficult to gauge. Driven by these concerns, the last chapter in this book advances the questions (and answers) of the earlier chapters into a more recent time and offers a lens for the present that may be useful.

REFERENCES, NOTES AND SOURCES

In drawing out this story, a fairly large literature has been consulted—albeit not all that might be regarded as essential. The Select Bibliography and the notes mention only a fraction of the writing—and this is especially true of the political background to what transpired. Almost every aspect of the Soviet/Russian and Indian economies of the period has a substantial literature attached to it. It was considered necessary, though, to draw out a focal narrative that may act as the foundation for discussion and debate—including material that may itself become the take off point for new directions in debates.

I have tried to give this narrative a body that it would otherwise have not had by going beyond the standard material available in statistical databases and standard websites to integrate unpublished material from government sources, private archives, and interviews. Clearly, the final product is not comprehensive in the slightest. If it acts as food for broader speculation than is customary, though, it would have achieved its intention.

NOTES

1. Various studies emphasize the inconsistencies in Russian foreign policy, however, and their implications cannot be ignored for the case of India. See R. Allison, A. Pravda, and N. Malcolm (eds), *Internal Factors of Russian Foreign Policy* (Oxford: Oxford University Press, 1996), K. Sorokin, *Russia's Security in a Rapidly Changing World* (Stanford: CISAC, 1994), D.K. Simes, *After the Collapse: Russia Seeks its Place as a Great Power* (New York: Simon-Schuster, 1999) or C.C. Menges (ed.), *Russia and Nato* (Washington 1999). Much Russian writing is prescriptive, but reveals the debates that gave rise to inconsistencies in policy. Examples are K.V. Sorokin, *Geopolitika sovremennosti I geostrategiia Rossii* (Moscow: Rosspen, 1996), N.P. Gusakov and N.A. Zotova, *Natsional'nye interesy I vneshneekonomicheskaia bezopasnost' Rossii* (Moscow: Kompaniia Evraziiskii region, 1998). Alexei Arbatov, *Bezopasnost': Rossiiskii Vybor* (Moscow: Science Foundation, 1999), A.S. Panarin, *Revansh istorii: rossiiskaia strategicheskaia al'ternativa v XXI veke* (Moscow: Lagos, 1999), Sergei Karaganov (ed.), *Strategiia dliia Rossii: Povestka dnia dliia Prezidenta - 2000* (Moscow: Vagrius, 2000), Alexander Dugin, *Osnovy geopolitiki. Geopolitichesoe budushchee Rossii* (Moscow: Arktogeya, 1997). Work on specific regions illustrates the tensions surrounding policy, albeit from a more narrow perspective. For East Asia and China see R.N. Montaperto (ed.), *Cooperation Engagement and Economic Security in the Asia-Pacific Region* (Washington: National Defense University Press, 1993), Gilbert Rozman, Mikhail G. Nasos, and Koji Watanabe (eds.), *Russia and East Asia* (New York: M.E. Sharpe, 1999), V. Larin, *Kitai i Dal'nii Vostok Rossii* (Vladivostok: Dalnaika, 1998), Vladimir Portyakov, *The People's Republic of China: Economic Policy of the 1990s* (Moscow: Institute of Far Eastern Studies, RAN, 1999). Valuable work on Central Asia is: *Postsovetskaia Tsentral'naia Aziia* (Moscow: Vostochnaia Literatura, 1998), and

A. Dzhekshenkulov, *Novye nezavisimye gosudarstva Tsentral'noi Azii v mirovom soobshchestve* (Moscow: Nauchnaia Kniga, 2000). On Russia and Europe, see *Rossiia I osnovnye instituty bezopasnosti v Evrope* (Moscow, St.P., 2000), Anatole Lieven, *Chechnya, Tombstone of Democracy* (New Haven: Yale University Press, 1997).

2. On the Indian side, scholarship is dominated by the names of various researchers of the Institute for Defence and Strategic Analysis (IDSA), New Delhi. The main contributors on Indo–Russian relations are Jyotsna Bakshi and Baidya Bikash Basu, but there are other important commentators. For recent writing see: Baidya Bikash Basu, 'Russian Military-Technical Cooperation: Structures and Processes, Strategic Analysis', *Strategic Analyses* (*SA*), June 2001; 'Russian National Security Thinking', *SA*, October 2000; 'Trends in Russian Arms Export', *SA*, February 2000; 'Reforms in Russian Defence Industry: Problems and Prospects', *SA*, January 2000; 'The Private Sector and Defence Production', *SA*, June 1997; Meena Singh Roy, 'Russia and Central Asia: Problems and Prospects', *SA*, June 2001. Jyotsna Bakshi has a book, *Russia and India: From Ideology to Geopolitics (1947–1998)* (Delhi: Dev Publications, 1999). She also has a range of articles: 'Sino-Russian Strategic Partnership in Central Asia: Implications for India', *SA*, May 2001; 'Russia's National Security Concepts and Military Doctrines: Continuity and Change', *SA*, October 2000; 'Russia-China Military-Technical Cooperation: Implications for India', *SA*, July 2000; 'Russian Policy Towards South Asia', *SA*, November 1999; 'Moscow Grapples with Political and Economic Crises: Implications for Foreign Policy', *SA*, May 1999; 'Russian Policy Towards Central Asia-II', *SA*, February 1999; 'Russian Policy Towards Central Asia-I', *SA*, January 1999; 'Russia's Post-Pokhran Dilemma', *SA*, August 1998; 'No Single Power or Power Centre Can Have Exclusive Sway Over Central Asia: A Geo-Political Analysis', *SA*, April 1998; 'India in Russia's Strategic Thinking', *SA*, January 1998. Important also is O.N. Mehrotra, 'Nato Eastward Expansion and Russian Security', *SA*, November 1998; P. Stobdan, 'Central Asia in Geo-Political Transition', *SA*, April 1998. Other work that is equivocal is Anuradha Chenoy, 'A Cosy Relationship', *Seminar* 1998. Devindra Kaushik follows a similar line from the Central Asian perspective, as do A. Shamsuddin and K. Warikoo, as indicated in K. Warikoo and M. Singh (eds.), *Central Asia since Independence* (Delhi: Shipra, 2005). For contributions from Calcutta, see Jyotirmoy Banerjee, 'Indo-Russian Relations: The Cryogenic Rocket Deal', *Jadavpur Journal of Inernational Relations*, 1995.

3. Russian perspectives on Russian foreign policy towards India are dominated by the work of T. Shaumian, although a number of other contributions have been of importance. Shaumian follows a cautious position in her assessments of Russian foreign policy, adhering to a factoral approach, without taking into consideration the imbalances that have been created by the instability of government. For a typical example of her work, see her *Rossiia I regional'nye problemy Iuzhnoi Azii* in *Vostok I Rossiia na rubezhe XXI veka* (1998, Moscow: Institut Vostokovedeniia RAN and Rossiiskaia Ekonomicheskaia Akademiia

im. G.V. Plekhanova). See also A.S. Iurlov, *Rossiia I Indiia* (Moscow: Institut Vostokovedeniia RAN, 1998). In his copious writing on Russian foreign policy, some of which is reflected in his *Rossiia v poiskakh identichnosti* (Moscow: Mezhdunarodnye Otnosheniia, 1997), Andrannik Migranian explains many of the inconsistencies of Russian foreign policy in terms of problems of governance.

4. Bhabatosh Datta, *Indian Economic Thought* (Delhi: Tata McGraw Hill, 1978), chapter 16.
5. The new trend in Soviet thinking is neatly covered in Elizabeth Kridl Valkenier, 'The USSR, the Third World and the Global Economy', *Problems of Communism*, July–August 1979.
6. I have established this argument following a reasonable consultation of the literature on the Soviet Revolution, and 'transition' in the country. See M. McFaul, *The Troubled Birth of Russian Democracy* (Stanford: Hoover, 1993), 'Russian Centrism', in *Post-Soviet Affairs*, 1993, *Post Communist Politics* (Washington: Center for Strategic and International Studies, 1993); M. Stevan Fish, *Democracy from Scratch* (Princeton: Princeton University Press, 1995); P. Schmitter, and Terry Karl, 'The Conceptual Travels of Transitologists: How Far East Should They Go?', in *Slavic Review*, 1994, 'From an Iron Curtain to a Paper Curtain', *Slavic Review*, 1995, V. Bunce, 'Paper Curtains and Paper Tigers', *Slavic Review*, 1995, 'Should Transitologists be Grounded?', *Slavic Review*, 1995, Gavrill Popov, *Opiat' v opozitsii* (Moscow, 1994). The most recent addition to the literature, which bears out my model is Valerie Bunce, *Subversive Institutions* (Cambridge: Cambridge University Press, 1999), and A.V. Shubin, *Ot zastoia k reformam. SSSR v 1917-1985* (Moscow: Rosspen, 2001).
7. Many of the issues here were discussed in the literature on the Uruguay Round. While relaxation of trade restrictions is treated positively in Alan Oxley, *The Challenge of Free Trade* (New York: Harvester, 1990) and *Trade Policies for a Better Future: The Leutwiler Report, the GATT and the Uruguay Round* (The Hague: Martinus Nijhoff, 1987), the problems find a place in W.P. Avery, *World Agriculture and the GATT* (Boulder, Colorado: 1973), K.A. Ingersont, A.J. Rayner and R.C. Hine, *Agriculture and the Uruguay Round* (New York: Macmillan, 1993), Jagdish N. Bhagwati, *The World Trading System at Risk* (New York: Harvester, 1991).

CHAPTER 1

Indo–Soviet Economic and Military Cooperation Until 1991

BALANCE SHEET OF INDO–SOVIET ECONOMIC RELATIONS IN 1991

In 1986, at the time of the onset of perestroika in the Soviet Union, the trends that marked India's economic collaboration, trade, and military cooperation with the USSR differed sharply from those of the heady days of 'friendship' (1955–73). Over the period 1974–86, trade remained steady, but the character of economic cooperation changed, so that while Indian public-sector units (PSU) maintained close links with Soviet enterprises, and obtained technology updates, the interaction made little difference to trade figures. Imports of machinery fell off and cooperation centred on the management of enterprises or the servicing of plants. Meanwhile, India's acquisition of Soviet military hardware developed new dimensions, as the USSR competed with French producers and outdistanced them. But military cooperation did not extend to a crucial area that the Indian side wished to evolve—i.e. nuclear technology. The USSR's commitment to global arms restriction meant that approaches to military cooperation with India were more circumspect. Pivotal Indian PSUs, meanwhile, that operated with Soviet aid, witnessed a decline in productivity and a desertion of personnel for private companies.[1] In an important area of early collaboration—steel production—Indian mills had an eye to global trends and moved to benefit from them without reference to Soviet prototypes. The tone of collaboration altered, with changes in Soviet perspectives on trade, which now stressed the necessity to obtain greater benefit to the USSR. Throughout this, features of the Soviet establishment reinforced the decline in the intensity of cooperative ventures. Soviet Planning practices that dominated management of the link between the USSR and LDCs (including India) worked sluggishly with designs for future collaboration.

The onset of perestroika under M.S. Gorbachev did not alter this situation, although in the course of reviews of economic programmes, new agenda for collaboration were advanced and greater flexibility was developed in the operation of the Soviet economy. The Indian private sector asserted its presence in Moscow vigorously; but changes in the nature of Indo–Soviet interaction began to appear by 1991.

Significantly, these trends in the Indo–Soviet economic relationship seldom attracted alarm among officials in India or in the USSR, pre-1991. Bureaucrats did not conceive of what was happening as a problem—and characterized the relationship as healthy, albeit in need of adjustment. At the time of Soviet disintegration, India's trade with the USSR compared poorly with a buoyant commerce with the USA and Western Europe, but seldom was it stressed in public circles in Moscow or New Delhi that it was a phenomenon that unsettled 'friendship' between the two countries.

ECONOMIC AND MILITARY COLLABORATION BEFORE THE ONSET OF PERESTROIKA

The Achievement of Indo–Soviet Friendship and the Understatement of the Problems of Technology Transfer and Trade until the mid-1970s

Understatement of the 'plateau' in the Indo–Soviet economic relationship was linked in part to the early story of Indo–Soviet friendship and the emotions it generated immediately before and after 1947.[2] More specifically, when functionaries, politicians, and the press understated the roots of eventual decline in Indo–Soviet economic collaboration even when these showed themselves during the early phase of development assistance (1955–72), their attitude was related to the impressive consequences of Indo–Soviet cooperation. The technology transfer that took place from the USSR to India generated respect; officials and technocrats were thus disinclined to discuss its problems. Technology transfer had brought India Soviet know-how and plant and manufacturing machinery for large-scale steel production. Transfers also gave India the means to manufacture heavy electrical equipment, coal-mining and steel-making machinery, as well as other heavy engineering and power-generating material. Collaboration established the foundations of the Indian capacity for bulk drugs production. The build-up of military hardware production in India with Soviet assistance[3] was a further concomitant of aid at a different level. The construction of townships at Ranchi, Durgapur, Bhilai, and Bokaro was a testament to the scale of collaboration. Tables 1.1a and 1.1b indicate the several enterprises that were set up under the aegis of collaboration—a substantial addition to the meagre production network the Indian nation-state inherited in 1947 (primarily the Tata and Burn units in steel production and small units for machine manufacture scattered through the country).

Specific indicators of the consequences of the Soviet 'contribution' to India's industrialization were impressive. As late as 1985–8, Bokaro and Bhilai, the Soviet aided steel plants, accounted for about 75 per cent of the output of the public sector in steel manufacture. The Heavy Machine Building Plant at Ranchi manufactured 77 per cent of the equipment for steel-making industries in India; the Soviet-built mining equipment works at Durgapur produced 43 per cent of the mining equipment made in India; and the heavy electrical equipment plant at Hardwar (part of the BHEL enterprises) made 47 per cent of the power-generating equipment in India.

Certainly, important problems showed, even as ventures got under way and attempted to sustain themselves during the period before the mid-1970s. In some cases, Soviet plants in India had installed capacities that could not be utilized. This meant a waste of the resources used for payment as well as in the endeavour to run the enterprises. In other cases, the technology that came to India was below par. In MAMC and HEC, there was no call for machinery on the scale the plant could produce: and diversification into consumer goods production did not come to much.[4] In oil refining, the processing that could be done was limited to Soviet imports and Indian production and the costs were high compared to other refineries set up by international companies.[5] In pharmaceuticals, owing to the technology, productivity was poor by world standards.

A policy of 'make do' was followed in the cases of heavy engineering units, though, and criticisms were dismissed as inappropriate since the

TABLE 1.1a: INDO-SOVIET COOPERATION IN HEAVY ENGINEERING

Enterprise	Status	Focus	Path of development (collaborations)
Bharat Heavy Electricals Ltd.	State enterprise set up in the late 1960s	Power generation	Develops Soviet technology to manufacture 210 m-w units which depend on indigenous R&D. Export of technology to the USSR was a consequence. More than 20 separate agreements with firms from east and west. All later collaborations, 1970–89, with Western firms (primarily Siemens)
Mining and Allied Machinery Corporation	State enterprise	Coal-mining machinery	Plant severely underutilized, since most coal units based on Western models: techniques unsuitable for MAMC machinery. Only some ranges in underground coal mining equipment in demand. Consequently, diversifies into tractors, railway wagons, equipment for coal washeries, and coal benefication plant. All collaborators Western
Heavy Engineering Corporation (established 1958)	State enterprise	Steel equipment	No development of design capacity for technological processes or specific equipment. Focus on plant creation (building) and manufacture. Subsequent large-scale collaboration with Western firms
Metallurgical and Engineering Consultants	State enterprise. The Central Engineering and design Bureau (CEDB) set up before Soviet collaboration initiated, in association with German (Rourkela) and British (Durgapur) experts (in the 1950s). Renamed MECON in 1973.	Consultancy (primarily steel related)	Involved in Soviet projects in India (including Bhilai, whose Design Cell was merged into MECON). Major international operations from the late 1970s.

TABLE 1.1b: OTHER MAJOR AREAS OF COOPERATION

Area	Results	Focus	Path of development
Steel Making	Construction of steel plants at Bhilai (commissioned in 1959), Bokaro (first furnace commissioned in 1972) and Vishakhapatanam (commissioned 1982).	Steel production	On a par with most steel units in the United States and Europe. Much greater capacity than ever used. Easily maintained using units such as HEC
Oil and Oil Refining	Assistance to ONGC, and construction of refineries	Oil exploration and refining	Poor standards in international comparison. But gave access to refining of Soviet crude, which was cheaper than the standard international product
Pharmaceuticals	Assistance to Indian Drugs and Pharmaceuticals Ltd. (established 1961) and Hindustan Anti-Biotics Ltd. (established 1954)	Crucial or life-saving drugs	By 1988, IDPL produces 28 per cent of the capital and technology-intensive bulk drugs produced in India, as against 11 per cent for other foreign concerns, who draw their profits from the high end of the market. Almost wholly India-based in personnel and inputs. Well behind West in standards, pharmacoepia, and profitability.

Source: Santosh Mehrotra, *India and the Soviet Union: Trade and Technology Transfer* (Delhi: Oxford University Press, 1991).

future might present a different situation. In the case of oil refining, Soviet assistance, although relatively expensive, saved foreign exchange, and provided the wherewithal to develop new plants.[6] In pharmaceuticals, despite the limitations of technology transfer, there were good grounds for taking the Soviet option. International manufacturers set high prices for technology transfer for the production of bulk drugs in India. High royalties were required, whereas the Soviet deal did not stipulate this.[7] After technology transfer, IDPL and HAL acted as major training grounds for the Indian industry. Their presence had a spin off effect:

international manufacturers began the manufacture of bulk drugs locally—both because this was the only way of retaining a hold in India, and because IDPL and HAL could provide important inputs into their enterprises. Upgrade and innovation became possible.

In the case of steel manufacture, the benefits of the Soviet collaboration were palpable. Soviet production via blast-furnace and open-hearth processes had integrated most well-known techniques at the time when Bokaro and Bhilai were set up: and non-Soviet accounts of the Soviet industry do not question its rolling and pelletizing methods. Some Soviet plants worked with updated technology of early industrialization (primarily German and British). But the main Soviet designing agency (Gipromez) and the Soviet plants that developed the Indian mills had a different pedigree. They took shape in collaboration with major enterprises in the US in the 1920s and 1930s: McKee of Cleveland (Ohio), Freyn Engineering (Chicago), Perrin and Marshall, and Bassert & Co. were the main partners. Freyn remained under contract to the Soviet government through the 1930s. Soviet enterprises benefited from contact with the United States during the Second World War; and they imported machinery from Eastern Europe after 1945,[8] and licensed breakthrough technology from firms such as Krupp-Kopp of West Germany.[9] Major innovations were introduced, and new processes were patented. In some areas, such as blast-furnace equipment and coke-oven technology, Soviet industry was a global leader and sold licenses to major steel manufacturers such as the Japanese producers, standing up to German competition.[10]

The Soviet steel industry's response to the processes that threw up major improvements in productivity were muted. These were the extensive use of the electric arc process for steel production and the (related) focus on the minimill as the unit of production. The electric arc process was used on a small scale in the USSR,[11] but the minimill found no takers. Opting for the Soviet tie-up and using Soviet 'giganticism' (focus on large integrated production plants) as a reference for the public sector, India took a course that made it difficult to take advantage of comparatively low costs of production that come with the electric arc/minimill technology. Since, however, the innovation has, in general, been linked to use of scrap or scrap substitutes among steel producers in established steel producing centres, it is questionable whether criticism of the Indian choice would be valid. For India, where decisions were made bearing in mind foreign exchange constraints, the focus on scrap would have been inappropriate, since it required sizeable imports. When local scrap became available on a scale that made a difference to the industry, the technology became appropriate. In fact, after the construction of Bokaro, Bhilai, and other public sector units, the value of an alternative technology, and the reputation of that technology turned attention away from further Soviet collaboration except in terms of minor additions to existing plant. Experiment took place with electric production and minimills in the 1970s, when the GOI briefly relaxed its licensing system to allow small-scale units to emerge. But the new thrust in the industry did not acquire the importance it came to have in Japan,[12] faced as it was by limited supplies of scrap and the problems of power supply. Experiments did not undermine the importance of traditional forms of production and their improvement, even if the technology's international standing gave this side of the industry a reputation for being passé.[13] The persistent importance of basic steel production led to preservation of the Soviet connection in the area—and to a sense among public sector technocrats that the downturn in the vitality of cooperation was not important.

Analysts considered the benefits of the Indo–Soviet relationship to be mutual.[14] India fitted into an overall scheme of Soviet bilateral relations with a number of countries, including Syria, Iraq, and Egypt which met deficiencies in the Soviet (and CMEA) economies. If most Soviet industry and commerce was directed towards internal consumption, or towards Eastern Europe, Indian companies like Syrian or Egyptian gave a glitter to the economy by way of high quality consumer goods (such as Darjeeling tea), and ballast by way of cheap garments, or machinery that was compatible but different from products available in the USSR. Barter for capital goods that the Soviet Union could not sell in the West brought the USSR and Comecon countries goods that were sold for convertible currencies within the form of 'switch trade'. For this, agreements were made in Western markets, and the barter-rupee was sold at a discount, much to the chagrin of Indian observers who recognized the process as a loss to India of payments in convertible currency. Such operations cannot however be held to have been the norm. Calculations by Deepak Nayyar have established that the volume of activity here was small.[15] Elsewhere, as in the case of Soviet relations with NATO-friendly Yugoslavia, the Indian link gave access to technology that the US and its partners seldom made available to the Soviet Union—but the scale of this transfer is unknown.

Benefits to the USSR (and India) from cooperation came from the method of settling accounts. Payments were made in rupees/roubles according to a rupee–rouble exchange rate, initially based on the value of the gold component in the currencies,[16] but which came to vary with other factors over time. No reference existed to the prevailing rate of exchange of the currencies to gold or hard currencies; and no transfers of either gold, hard currencies or SDRs were required for trading operations. Convertible rupees and convertible roubles existed for purposes of exchange; but since most trade was conducted on an account book basis, involving goods exchange, and currency was issued in the form of bankers' cheques/drafts/travellers' cheques, actual transfer of rupees or roubles seldom occurred. The arrangement was of value to both countries who possessed limited stocks of hard currency. Again, if by the time of perestroika in the USSR, India had accumulated a sizeable rupee debt to the Soviet Union, mainly as a result of arms imports, this was comfortably balanced by a regular trade balance in India's favour.

Problems and Limitations of Technology Transfer and Trade: The Perspective of the 1980s

Indicators

By the 1980s, though, critiques of collaboration drew strength from the consequences of the limitations mentioned above and from other sources—ignoring the bonhomie that officials were inclined to stress. Statistical indications of Soviet trade in Tables 1.2a and 1.2b point to the limited importance to the USSR of exchange with a range of developing countries, including India by the 1980s, by which time, as George Sokoloff has noted, Western Europe and the United States had become the Soviet Union's primary trading partners. Information concerning where Soviet statesmen attempted to 'improve' their performance in the 1970s and 1980s: i.e. in the West or in the 'Red Market'[17] reinforce this picture of the declining significance of the developing world for Soviet trade. Important strategies[18] that were attempted in Eastern Europe to improve production and research were never applied in 'the Third World' until the advent of perestroika, except, perhaps, tangentially,

TABLE 1.2a: USSR EXPORTS AND IMPORTS 1982–6

(*totals in billions of roubles*)

	Exports	Imports
1982	63.1	56.4
1983	67.9	59.6
1984	74.4	65.3
1985	72.5	69.1
1986	68.3	62.6

TABLE 1.2b: USSR EXPORTS/IMPORTS 1982–6, BY COUNTRY GROUPS

(*billions of roubles*)

	Exports			Imports		
	Socialist bloc	Capitalist countries	Developing countries	Socialist bloc	Capitalist countries	Developing countries
1982	34.1	18.8	10.2	30.8	18.9	6.7
1983	37.7	19.7	10.5	33.7	18.7	7.1
1984	42.1	21.3	10.9	38.3	19.6	7.5
1985	44.2	18.6	9.6	42.2	19.3	7.6
1986	45.6	13.1	9.6	41.9	15.9	4.9

TABLE 1.2c: SOVIET EXPORTS TO AND IMPORTS FROM INDIA 1982–6

(*millions of roubles*)

	Exports	Imports
1982	1040.2	1473.8
1983	1271.6	1537.4
1984	1537.5	1272.0
1985	1574.9	1509.5
1986	957.6	1233.6

Source: Vneshnaia Torgovliia SSSR (Moscow: Finansy I Statistiki). Volumes for 1983, 1984, 1985, 1986.

in Vietnam and Cuba. A comparison of Tables 1.2a and 1.2b shows that by the time of the onset of M.S. Gorbachev's perestroika (1986), exports to the developing world as a whole accounted for *c.* 15 per cent of the USSR's total exports, while exports to 'capitalist' countries came to over half the value of exports. Import figures speak of an equal lack of dependence on the 'developing world' and a high level of involvement with the 'capitalist' bloc.

The India–USSR relationship was marked by a lack of mutual understanding where business and economic matters were concerned. In the arena of technology transfer, almost all operations were worked out within the framework of strict bilateral agreements and government/semi-government agencies were involved, and where the work followed an inter-government agreement. Individual Soviet associations and enterprises in no way acted as the initiators of the operation, which took place within the framework of the Soviet Planned Economy, whose priorities were decided by a combination of technocrats, bureaucrats and Communist Party functionaries. Complications concerning matters such as customs and local taxes did not figure on the Soviet or Indian sides in the course of operations (except in the case of private Indian operators bringing goods into India). Hence, in the course of collaboration, neither did the Soviet side come to acquaint itself with the complexities of the Indian economy, nor vice versa. Transfers of technology were of undoubted value to the Indian economy, but mutual understanding of economic behaviour remained poor. This even as Soviet operatives working in India accumulated some experience and enterprise-to-enterprise acquaintance was established by technocrats and professionals. General academic studies betrayed a lack of awareness of economic practices in India. No major study of Indo–Soviet economic relations exists that demonstrates an intimate acquaintance with negotiations about agreements or the problems of plant upgrade, plant maintenance, or the management of collaboration.

Scholars sympathetic to socialist economics identified other problems with the relationship. Whether India was paying dearly for technology transfer was the focus not only of major US commentators,[19] and Indian economists of decided political opinion—notably Padma Desai and Asha Datar who indicted Soviet transfers as sluggish and of poor quality. It was a question raised (albeit in a more nuanced argument) by the socialist economist Nirmal Chandra,[20] who doubted the reading of statistics that was common within the pro-Soviet establishment of the Indian Left.[21] That there was some problem by the late 1970s cannot be doubted. The rouble was overvalued against the rupee by the rupee–rouble exchange rate, so that prices of Soviet goods in India were excessive, compared with what they would fetch in Europe or the US. It was this phenomenon that attracted Chandra's attention when he claimed that India might gain from the relationship, but the USSR would gain more.

Elsewhere, in the course of Moscow's initiatives in India, Soviet experts trained and used Indian operatives to provide crucial resources at home and to prepare exports to Eastern Europe and the Soviet Union. In the case of the steel plants, Soviet operatives managed the plant well into the 1980s, even though, apparently, they were present in a consultative capacity. They also evinced a clear sense of superiority. Indian operatives, consequently always felt that they worked in a context of 'tutelage', despite assertions to the contrary from their Soviet colleagues. And, differences surfaced at another level also. B. D'Mello found, as late as the early 1980s, in interviews in Bokaro, that whereas various senior staff were not dissatisfied with Soviet attitudes, some would complain about a lack of innovation in Soviet practice: 'Soviet specialists have incorporated very little if any modifications. They are too narrow in their specialization. For instance an OH specialist will be found lacking in his knowledge of LD steelmaking.'

The Problem of the Soviet Planned Economy

It is not surprising therefore, that for reasons other than machine costs, following the initial collaboration with Soviet industry, developments in plant in new directions did not proceed with Soviet collaboration, except in a few cases, indicating an implicit critique of collaboration. Most departures occurred with the involvement of US/European companies. Partly this was because of a direct interest shown in India by foreign firms: as in the case of Luigi Chemie which specialized in sintering and palletizing, formed Luigi (India) and came into active collaboration with HEC.[22] In pharmaceuticals, companies such as Hoechst set up limited operations in India.

But there were other factors at work: factors reflected in the tensions over the Soviet capacity for innovation that D'Mello noticed. Unlike units within the USSR itself, where innovations took place within the framework of the Plan within a limited range, no such allowances were made for plant in the case of technology transferred to India. In rare cases, information concerning breakthroughs came to be known on the Indian side and taken up.[23] But, as a norm, the USSR did not pursue this kind of collaboration, stressing consolidation, for instance, in the 1970s, following the period of construction. Nor did the Indian side seek other arrangements, at a loss as it was most of the time *vis-à-vis* the vagaries of the Soviet Planned Economy. Possibilities were aired during the meetings of the working groups of the Indo–Soviet Joint Commission: but implementation and payment required reference to professionals and technocrats in India, and a long drawn-out process of decision-making. In this respect, the Soviet involvement in India was unimaginative if authoritative. Soviet planners were slow to envisage long-term improvements of any scale, based on on-going research and development, when they evolved links with countries outside the purview of their standard activity. Activity also failed to adapt to ad hoc needs and requirements. Pivotal bodies dealing with India were focused on a goal rather than an opportunity.

Important here was Soviet managerial behaviour. Jaques Sapir argues that a particular culture of technology and enterprise organization made Soviet units only open to change of a very specific type—where innovation was limited to changes which retained most existing superstructure. True, Soviet work on innovation presents a different picture—a good record of improvements and encouragement of innovation, using case studies' information. The latter is drawn from a number of enterprises: the Gorkii Automobile Works, the Krasnaia Etna Plant, the Gorkii Milling Machine Works, the Zavolzhskii Engine Works, the Nizhnii Tagil Iron and Steel Works, the Urals Heavy Engineering Plant and other units of the Sverdlovsk region. But the research does not include instances of quick implementation of innovation on a large scale in the case of foreign trade, and leaves Sapir's arguments fundamentally unchallenged in this arena. A number of incidents highlighted by Stephen Kotkin and others further indicates that the smooth surface of the Plan, its targets and their refinement were a legend that hid a harum-scarum rush to deal with quotas and, where there was outright subterfuge to cover up corruption and diversion of resources—as in the case of failed investment in the northern fields in the case of the oil and natural gas industry, and Central Asian cotton. The final product might have had quality, but the efficiency of its production left much to be desired. To think of plans for development abroad was often difficult.

Overall, innovation was encouraged within the framework of a Plan primarily, and broader perspectives were discouraged except in times of emergency. The hope of the time was that decision-making and the transmission of decisions could be made with greater rapidity with the use of new information technology. Hence the great Soviet interest in cybernetics in the 1970s. A different approach to management seldom received attention. Indian public sector behaviour followed suit, and cannot be excused. This lay at the heart of the 'bureaucracy' in India and in the USSR, which, Mehrotra suggests, was the main brake on development. Such habits, as much as the political preoccupations of Soviet technocrats or their professional conditioning[24] was responsible for the fall away in economic collaboration. In general, whatever the refinements introduced into the system of planning in the USSR in the realm of foreign trade, managers acted according to the principle that initiatives were made for the economy as a whole by its prime functionaries, keeping vast goals in mind: the forays were not to be made by specific enterprises.

The very size of industrial conglomerates and networks that developed in the Soviet Union, and the manner of their operation, made local departures difficult. The conglomerates and networks were gigantic in scale, their production systems operating *in tandem*, for economic and political reasons. Under the Ministry of Machine-Tool and Instrument-Making Industry of the USSR, a number of heavy engineering networks functioned, such as the Urals Association. Under the Ministry of Coal came mining *kombinaty* such Novomoskovskugol, Tulskugol, and Ramenskii Gornoobogatelnyi Kombinat. The Ministry of Steel was divided into a Central Administration, and Chief Directorates and Trusts: where major *kombinaty* at Magnitogorsk, Tula, Lipetsk, and in the Urals (Nizhnii Tagil, Novyi Tagil, etc.) came under the Central Administration and others were part of the Directorates and Trusts. The combines included a number of factories or workshops ('enterprises' or *predpiiatiia* with many 'sections'). They enjoyed the advantages of the integrated unit—immediate accessibility of each process. But they also suffered disabilities—an incapacity to implement innovation with least possible hindrance. The long distance of the early 'giants' from centres of consumption, moreover, impelled the Plan to explore a variety of resources in the Union. Hence there were major investments in an array of coal resources: not only in the established Urals (Kizel Coal Basin), Donbass, and Kuzbass of the pre-Revolutionary and early Plan development, but also in Karaganda, in the Pechora Basin in the far north (Vorkuta), in Cheremkhovo in Eastern Siberia, on the Bureia River in the Far East, at Tkvarcheli and Tkvibali deposits in Georgia, and at the Kok-Iangak and Angren deposits in Central Asia.[25] Iron deposits were exploited alongside: in the north-west at Ensk and near

Lake Imandra; in Central Asia at Chimkent; and in Eastern Siberia at Petrovsk Zabaikalskii. Steel plants were duly set up in an integrated network: Amurstal in the Far East, Begovat in Central Asia and Petrovsk Zabaikalskii for Eastern Siberia.[26] Ultimately all were interlinked by the heavily-subsidized Soviet rail system, which made innovation yet more difficult, for it required reference within a vast network.

Again, despite relative flexibility in making low-level appointments—which were made after advertisement and/or interview—ministries or departments of ministries were decisive to senior appointments and production decisions. They often acted as the *de facto* collective managers of the conglomerates, working mainly with plan quotas in mind. For distribution, they contacted or were contacted by trading organizations. Even where Soviet conglomerates or enterprises did deal with Indian enterprise (such as Bhilai) or authorities (such as SAIL) directly, after work began on plant design or plant construction, they could not take initiative but had to refer to FTOs in their dealings (organizations such as Tiazhpromexport[27] and Promashexport[28]).

The framework within which Indian industry took shape consequently is exemplified by the way the Ranchi plant (of the Heavy Engineering Corporation) came into being and developed. Its construction followed the 1955 visit of Jawaharlal Nehru to the Ural Engineering Works in Sverdlovsk—which impressed the prime minister and which he wished to make the point of reference for Soviet assistance in India. However, when the Ranchi plant was eventually begun in 1961, it was without direct reference to the Urals plant. It was designed by the elite unit Giprotiazhmash. And 82 different engineering units supplied the 27,000 tons of equipment and 18,000 tons of steel structural elements that went into Ranchi. In such a situation, neither the Urals factory which inspired it nor any specific plant could act as a reference point for the future. The only direct link was with FTOs designed to liase with the unit and the educational and research unit that was crucial for training the personnel—Vnimetmash (All-Union Scientific Research and Design Institute of Metallurgical Equipment). Here, and in other cases, the matter was made even more complicated by the involvement of other Eastern European countries: as in the case of the Czechoslovak assistance in the construction of a foundry, a forge plant, and a heavy machine tool plant at Ranchi.[29] This vast range of connections made the planning of the plant by itself almost impossible. Anything that happened had to wait for directives within the structures of the Planned Economy.

As those who handled everyday problems testify and scholars later discovered, there was a pivotal role that the state played in what followed, and plant-to-plant contacts were kept to a minimum. This has been well described by Bernard D'Mello[30] in his account of the activities of Tiazhpromexport (TPE) in supplying a steel plant.

> Differences at the firm to firm level are resolved at the intergovernmental level. The typical procedure for transactions, after an overall inter-governmental agreement, is as follows. The Indian public sector firms and TPE together prepare a division list which sets out the scope of equipment supply between Soviet, Indian and third country sources. TPE is then given an invitation to tender. The detailed technical specifications for Soviet supplies are generally prepared by the Soviet side itself. After receiving the Soviet quotations . . . bargaining gets under way. Unresolved differences are referred to the intergovernmental level. Typically, the ministry concerned then issues directives to the public sector enterprise concerned. . . .

Maitreyee Chowdhury, who worked for many years at senior levels with the Barauni Oil Refinery remembers that when everyday requirements in India required advice from Russian engineering advisors about possible manoeuvres, the Russians would listen stonily and would state point blank that they could do nothing and that reference had to be made to agencies in Moscow.

The FTOs themselves acquired a pivotal position in this process, but their case indicates the lack of flexibility and poor mutual understanding within the system of bilateral relations. They were specialized, as the nature of those who dealt with India testify: Energomasheksport (energy industry machinery exports), Avtopromeksport (motorized machinery exports), Mashinoimport (machine imports), Tiazhpromeksport (heavy industrial machinery exports), etc. Both within the Soviet Union and outside, they were the points around which producer and distributor concerns operated. They exercised the authority of choice (i.e. they set priorities of when to give what) in a limited fashion, even if they were constrained by the Plan. They also possessed property (warehouses, etc.). Yet their authority did not run to guiding production or planning. They were influential middlemen, and ultimate decision-making fell to the Planning officials and high functionaries in the Party or the government. This raised serious problems in the long run for ad hoc diversification. It must be noted that Soviet initiatives with the Indian private sector followed similar institutional arrangements. The FTO made specific arrangements with a number of concerns: AGIO Trading, Menon-Impex, and Chinar Exports, to cite a few. FTOs also occasionally intervened directly in tea auctions, when off-take was quite substantial. Proper and regular reassessments of the market were notoriously unusual, however: which went to the great detriment of the Soviet consumer.

The Independent Perspective of the Indian Public Sector

Significantly, as the GOI engaged with this system of cooperation, it did so on terms that indicated a clear self-possession—an awareness of standards set through close self-analysis and introspection. The government was heir to a series of elaborate economic initiatives taken in economic affairs, initiatives taken both before and after the period of the World Wars. A degree of public ownership over various enterprises (such as the railways and ordnance factories) was already in place before engagement with the USSR. Policy-makers as well as technocrats worked from a regime of how to handle this. Evidence given to the Committee on PSUs indicates the existence of such a regime and a degree of self-awareness where statist impulses for the organization of development were concerned.

Post-1947, Indian practices did not follow those of the Soviet state (or any state for that matter). Rather, they fitted into a system of public management inherited from the railways and now generalized to fit other enterprises. Those who were to work with public sector units referred across enterprises to each other, occasionally transferring from oil or coal to steel as administrators.

True, in the case of Indo–Soviet cooperation, when transfer of technology took place it involved 'transfer' of practices to the most minute detail. Hence, the townships and support systems that came with collaboration involved the implantation of the integrated plant that was most appropriate to Soviet circumstances, and of the settlements that went with them. Much that was set up during these years came to be shaped by Soviet practices, ground up as it were. Hence, organizational manuals were prepared for the Soviet-sponsored units (such as the HEC) by Soviet and Czech consultants, based on practices followed in their own countries. And again, the Lok Sabha Committee on Public Sector Units noted:

> . . . in the case of the Heavy Power Equipment Plant and the Boiler Plant of the HEL, the consultants M/S Techno-export (Czechoslovakia) prepared, besides the outlines of the main sections of the plants, the outlines for all auxiliary shops (e.g. carpenter shop, oxygen house) and wood storage and coke yard, garages, and fire stations, locomotive sheds, kitchen, dining room, cycle stand, car parking garages, parking places and bus stand. . . .[31]

Yet a close integration of Indian development strategies with those of the USSR or Comecon nations was prevented by no 'follow through' of other aspects of strategy. Hence, in the case of proper follow up to the establishment of IDPL, Soviet experts stressed the necessity to integrate research programmes around the Fuel Research Institute, Dhanbad, the Central Food Technological Institute, Mysore, and the School of Tropical Medicine, Calcutta. They also suggested close links between the Research Pharmaceutical Institute of India and Russian bodies. But as late as the Fourth Lok Sabha, nothing was done on these lines. This was partly the consequence of Indian circumstances themselves, i.e. the problems of organization. Partly, there were also important preferences at work that had an eye to other priorities. Hence, the Lok Sabha Committee on PSUs pointedly noted that in developing pharmaceutical industries, it should be borne in mind that:

> . . . the country possesses a great tradition in the field of Ayurveda which has specialized in the use of medicinal plants and synthesizes their properties into drugs and medicines. Unless raw materials of Indian origin are used, our dependence on foreign manufactures will not cease. . . .[32]

In keeping with this drift away from the recommendations of the Soviet consultants, specifically Indian practices took shape. Planning worked with its own priorities in India. The GOI evolved elaborate recommendations on a variety of themes as far as the public sector was concerned: marketing, finance management, administration, personnel, etc. Technocrats and parliamentarians evolved codes of behaviour in all these areas through recommendations and cross-reference year after year concerning whether these recommendations were carried out. This formed the framework of reference within which the Indian public sector came to function by the end of the 1960s. Hence, not only did the compulsions of the Indian economy generate their own thrust to the way the public sector evolved—away from the Soviet 'vision'—everyday priorities and language too evolved a space of their own.

Consequences

The result of the narrow focus of cooperation, and the self-focused perspectives of Indian enterprise, was a fall off of contacts between Indian organizations and the Soviet technology network by the 1980s. This is evidenced not only by the cooperation sought by such filials with Western firms in the 1980s (Table 1.1a, Column 4), but also by trade figures, which indicate a precipitous decline in technology imports. The situation took an important turn where, at plants constructed according to Soviet design, links were preserved primarily because the transfer of technology had been imperfect and assistance was still required[33]—not because the links were beneficial for future development. Improvement according to Soviet innovation was sometimes considered beneficial, and it was hoped that maintenance of links would preserve opportunities for this. Equally, though, it was well known that bureaucracy made such opportunities remote. A plant could be altered with assistance from European concerns, and even through import of US equipment.[34] This phenomenon was a comment on the international character of the steel/machine tools industry as well as the capacity of the Indian public sector to innovate.

In fact, with time, the USSR used Indian plants to set off the limitations in the productivity of its own resources. The Soviet Union was heavy-industry oriented where machine-tools were concerned, and focused on steel-making machinery, coal mining machinery, etc. Machinery for the production of useful consumer articles was in short supply. Within the framework of cooperation under the Long Term Programme of Economic, Trade, and Scientific and Technical Cooperation signed between the USSR and India on 14 March 1979, various contracts were made for such material as well as for back up for Soviet heavy industry. The Soviet Union placed orders for 10,000–12,000 tons of equipment with engineering units at Ranchi, Durgapur and Hardwar. This was followed up with further orders to such enterprises (for 50,000 tons of equipment) during 1980–6.[35] Elsewhere, the Soviet Union bought printing machinery from India.

Increasing exports from India clearly became a phenomenon of the time. Although there were variations, the equipment went not only to the Soviet Union but also to a range of countries to whom the USSR supplied aid.[36] In addition, some level of activity continued in goods such as spices, tea, and ready-made garments, making up a steady trade

TABLE 1.3: COMPOSITION OF INDIA'S IMPORTS FROM THE USSR, 1970–1 TO 1984–5 *(percentage)*

	1970–1 to 1972–3	1973–4 to 1975–6	1976–7 to 1978–9	1979–80 to 1981–2	1982–3 to 1984–5
Petroleum and petroleum products	5.7	20.5	49.8	76.8	74.8
Raw materials	5.4	3.1	4.1	0.5	0.3
Food	-	23.3	-	-	-
Manufactures	77.3	42.8	37.5	15.0	11.8

Source: Santosh Mehrotra, *India and the Soviet Union: Trade and Technology Transfer* (Delhi: Oxford University Press, 1991), p. 173. Mehrotra uses the statistics provided by the DGCI&S, cited below.

surplus in India's favour in the 1970s and 1980s. This balanced the heavy debt to the USSR incurred by arms imports. The capacity for further expansion, though, was clearly limited until the death of L. Brezhnev. Soviet institutional structures lacked the imagination to generate areas of cooperation that would give a fillip to trade. The preponderance in Indo–Soviet trade of the public sector made the expansion of consumer goods exports from India increasingly difficult.

Significantly well before perestroika began, attempts were made to break the syndrome of poor communications between Soviet and Indian partners. Andrei Muravyov, who was involved with Soviet economic affairs in India at this time, for instance, noted a range of connections established between enterprises by a 1983 agreement. This dealt with working cooperative programmes between HEC and the Uralmash Association (Sverdlovsk); MAMC (Durgapur) and the Donetskgormash Production Association (Donetsk), and BHEL and three production associations (Leningrad Metallicheskii Zavod, Kharkov Turbinnyi Zavod and Elektrosila of Leningrad).[37] The upshot of such agreements was that in 1983–5, the Uralmash production association passed on information on improvements in processes of building excavator parts to HMBP (Ranchi). However, such interaction was not regular, as indicated in the broad-ranging research of Mehrotra and Bernard D'Mello.

Cooperation in the Area of Nuclear Technology

The shortfall in assistance to India in the field of nuclear energy was a result of these factors as much as the commitments of the Soviet Union to regimes of non-proliferation. Despite the existence of an important nuclear energy programme in India in the period before 1985 and the developed nature of the Soviet nuclear energy programme at the time, the USSR did not provide significant assistance to India in this arena. An agreement existed on cooperation in this sphere from 1979, but there were no tangible consequences. Finally, perestroika witnessed the decision to cooperate on the construction of nuclear power plants (1988).

Arms Supplies[38]

Soviet initiatives in armaments sales followed a slightly different pattern from that which prevailed in technology transfer in steel production and machine tools production. An edifice as important as the Soviet contribution to heavy industry was involved—an achievement that took Indian military hardware and defence production in a direction very different from that established in the decade after Independence.

At that time the Indian armed forces had close links with British and US munitions technology—links forged during the Second World War, and maintained through control by London over how defence expenditure took place after 1947. These were marginal in the sphere of production for the infantry—where there was persistent dependence on the country's ordnance factories and minor imports of hardware—and in the case of the navy, where purchases were only a little more substantial. The links were more substantial in the case of the air force, where, despite official homilies concerning budgetary restraints, between 1947 and 1956, a large air fleet was acquired: French Dassault MD 450 fighter bombers, and various generations of Vampire (F3 fighters, FB9s, NF 540s). After 1956, the fleet was supplemented with Canberras (B(1) 58 light bombers, PR57 photo-reconnaissance aircraft, T4 dual-control trainers), additional Ouragans and a number of Mystere IVA interceptors. Hawker Hunter Mk.56 FGAs (ground attack fighters) and Mk.66 trainers were acquired. A major possibility existed for a close link between technical cadres in India and the British–American–French design board at this time—as Indian personnel were drawn in to the licensed production in India of the US Vultee Vengeance bombers, Vampire jets, Tiger Moth trainers, and, later (in 1960) the Gnat. However, as indicated by those who observed the crucial production centre of the time, Hindustan Aeronautics Ltd. (HAL) at Bangalore, 'licensed production' here meant little more than assembly and maintenance. And the attempts to produce Indian aircraft did not get off the ground under specialists at the Indian Institute of Science, Ghatake and, later Kurt Tank.[39] So when the time came for purchase, the commitment to Anglo–US technology was surprisingly thin and depended on inertia and the habits of the air force. As the Indian arsenal looked to new generations of weaponry in the 1960s, the US proved reluctant to sell F-104 Starfighters and C-130 transport aircraft to India.

The USSR offered the Indian government weapons from 1955, and supplied India with hardware during the 1965 war with Pakistan, when the US suspended supplies. Thereafter, during 1967–77, 81 per cent of Indian arms imports came from the Soviet Union. The only major attempt to vary the trend came when the Janata government (1978–80) concluded the Jaguar deal (initiated by the Congress government during the Emergency) for purchase of deep penetration aircraft that had a greater range than the Soviet MiG 23. Again, post-1980, the Congress government decided on the acquisition of Mirage-2000 fighters. This last was part of a broader plan of diversification of the Indian arsenal, and West German submarines, British Harrier jump-jets and Sea King helicopters were also obtained. A major alteration in India's military-technology foundation was envisaged: through licensed production of the Mirage in India, whereas hitherto only Soviet aircraft had been produced in this manner. Some consideration was also given to purchase US TOW missiles and howitzers.

In the event, no licensed production of Mirages took place, and India kept to purchases and production of MiGs: MiG 27 ground-attack fighters, MiG 29 Fulcrums, and MiG 31 Foxhounds. The result of Indo–Soviet military interaction was such that by 1991, its impact was clear in all sections of the armed forces. Soviet craft dominated a navy that had once been British. There were now destroyers (Kashin 2), submarines (F-class and later Kilo class), missile boats (Osa, equipped with Styx missiles), frigates (Petra-2), corvettes ('Nanuchka'), cruisers (Krestiia II), large patrol craft (Poluchat), ocean minesweepers (Natia), and landing craft (Polnochnyi). The importance of cooperation to the air force is well known, leading to the move away from Canberras and Gnats to a range of Soviet-made craft. These included the MiG 21 defence craft, MiG 23 BM ground attack aircraft, MiG 25 reconnaissance interceptors, MiG 29 interceptors, MiG 27 fighter bombers, Tu 142M naval reconnaissance and anti-submarine turbo props. The AN72 became the main transport aircraft of the air force. The Il-76 became the equivalent of the AWAC. In the army, in preference to British Chieftain Tanks and West German Leopard Tanks, Soviet T-72s and T-80s became the core vehicles, following on the Indian Vijayanta and the older Soviet imports.

Much of this acquisition was linked to a development of national production and maintenance capacity. In the case of the navy, this meant close links with the Soviet Union, which constructed the naval dockyard at Vishakhapatnam; but this was balanced by close ties with the UK, with the British developing the Leander Class frigate facility at Mazagon Docks in Bombay, leading to the construction of India's Godavari Class frigates. In the case of aircraft production, Soviet collaboration dominated, centred on HAL production at Koraput, Nasik, and Lucknow and on R&D at Bangalore. It came to have the lead over various other production (at Hyderabad and Kanpur), which focused on the manufacture of aircraft of Western European companies. The Soviet collaboration led to results that went far beyond the licensed production of British and US aircraft that featured in the 1940s, 1950s and early 1960s—although there were complaints that it could have gone further.[40] Production of the MiG 21 was crucial here. Following initial full import and local testing, all components were assembled and tested in India, some assembly undertaken and finally production was based on Indian raw materials. Seventy per cent of tools and equipment were finally indigenously produced. The Indian Aluminium Company provided a part of the aluminium required, and HAL was responsible for the construction of a factory in Hyderabad that manufactured various materials required for the aircraft.

To establish the problems and tensions in this interaction is difficult, except that it is certain that there were some, otherwise the determination to vary the arsenal in 1978–80 would not have been taken. Certainly, the supply of spares (rubber items, brake pads, adhesives, etc.) was a major difficulty since the complexities of the Soviet Planned Economy made difficult regular acquisition of what India needed. Great secrecy surrounded such issues and what transpired is difficult to trace. The HAL reports are bald, and there are no memoirs available from HAL staff. By the time of perestroika, changes in the defence production establishment (DPE) in India added to sources of tension between the

Indian and Soviet sides. The changes had begun in 1970, until when the acquisition and maintenance of equipment was the domain of the armed forces. From then, the Defence Research and Development Organization (DRDO) and its various laboratories were better integrated into the system, as were many universities[41]—making Indian demands and requirements a degree sharper. They also took a direction that varied with consensus among the nuclear powers regarding non-proliferation after the test of the nuclear device at Pokhran in 1974. Following hard investment in the Integrated Guided Missile Project from 1983—where indigenous design and production clearly dominated—Indian needs also ran the likelihood of running counter to the interpretations of the Missile Technology Control Protocol that was underwritten by the United States and the USSR.

Trade surpluses to India's benefit were used to deal with payments for arms in the 1970s, but the mechanics of this are not always clear. Certainly, Indian organizations received standard LCs and payment via the Reserve Bank in payment for exports, so it must have been at such an apex-level that arrangements were made. Again, the entire operation was finalized at the highest levels of government with intervention between the ministries concerned. It is impossible to speak of enterprise-to-enterprise exchange, or open competition within the international market for military hardware.

Within such a framework, minimum independent contact characterized the involvement of Indian Ordinance Factories, HAL, with their collaborating producer agencies in the USSR at a time when Indian defence production was increasing in its sophistication and demands. Rather, FTOs of the MIC (such as Oboroneksport) had to field questions, and the Ministry of Defence arranged for specialist visits, once the main computer blueprints of process and production technology had been transferred to Nasik and Koraput (the main HAL producer units). This ran alongside normal arrangements for training, where the Indian side sent personnel to the Soviet armed forces. Three confidential sources agree on this picture of the procedure: one source attached to the Embassy of India before 1971; a group of sources for 1986, which dealt with several aspects of technological training, educational exchange and Soviet politics (again attached to the Embassy);[42] and a source from the Koraput plant of HAL, whose evidence holds good for the period up to 1984. A degree of interaction between private agencies and Soviet MIC factories through the FTO network cannot be ruled out at this time, but these were marginal to the entire operation of production and training before 1991.[43]

The Private Sector

Against such a background, the private sector had some significance in Indo–Soviet collaboration before 1982, but it did not show itself in Moscow directly. A senior member of the Indian Foreign Service stationed in Moscow at the time of the Indo–Soviet Friendship Treaty (1971), who supervised economic affairs at the Embassy for a brief while, is straightforward about this. He states that it was seldom considered worthwhile to look into the activity of Indian businessmen, except in so far as it created problems for the Consular Department when they visited the country. In Moscow, there were no independent entrepreneurs (Soviet or Indian) who dealt with Indo–Soviet business at this time (other than shuttle traders who dealt in black market activities on a small scale). Various producers in India had Soviet connections, but this did not lead to an Indian presence in Moscow. This was true in the area of arms manufacture, where 20 per cent of India's 70 per cent indigenization of aircraft output was under sub-contract to PSUs and independent agencies at the end of the 1970s. It was certainly true in the case of Soviet assistance to heavy industry, where Soviet specialists provided assistance to Indian companies that serviced the PSUs that took shape in India—as in the case of the Khemka family.

Besides functioning as ancillaries to Indian PSUs, Indian businessmen involved themselves in the Soviet market from India or Singapore or Hong Kong, as suppliers of a variety of products. In India, as repayments in kind of the debt to the USSR took off, the Soviet Embassy in Delhi looked into possible purchases from local suppliers. And on occasion this led to further discussions in Moscow (as in the case of jute exports to the USSR for instance) and the appointment of representatives.

A major break in the pattern came at the beginning of the 1980s when a small group of private firms established a skeletal presence in Moscow. This followed permission by the Soviet government to such entrepreneurs to open offices in Moscow in 1981. Those who opened Moscow units included Chinar Exports, Bremco (under the leadership of Dr. Dharam Vir) and Larsen and Toubro (represented by the Soviet-trained Anil Agarwal), all of whom were concerned with trading or agency work for Soviet operations in India. Rohintan Aga of Thermax, on the other hand, came to the USSR in 1983 with M.P. Rao (of Thermax's International Division) and explored possibilities of production for the USSR outside the standard FTO chain without ignoring the profits of trading. Thermax thereafter developed a Moscow office. It began to work with Gazprom and also acted as agent for a number of companies, Bharat Fitzwarner, HMT, and Dr. Beck. On the eve of perestroika, and in response to Soviet stimuli to breathe life into a declining economic relationship with India, such Indian business expanded offices and activity in the Soviet capital. Firms acquired accommodation through the UPDK and they extended projects. Thermax Ltd. continued to export containerized boilers from India for Gazprom's use in remote drilling sites where the large standard Soviet boilers were inappropriate. Gagan Patwardhan, who had been trained in the USSR, managed this work. In this line, the corporation acted as a marketing assistance channel for other machine tools producers such as Span Overseas of Pune. For some time, HMT exported printing machinery to the USSR through the company.

The AGIO group emerged out of a link between Dr. Dharam Vir and Ravinder Chamaria at this time, and it extended its prominence systematically, forming a large network of connections in FTOs and the production units that normally worked with Indian PSUs. Vir was seasoned in Soviet economic life and Ravinder Chamaria had begun Soviet operations from a base in Singapore in the 1970s. Other entrepreneurs upgraded operations. These included the Khemka family (in whose case Nand Khemka had focused on machine imports from the USSR into India), the Agarwal family of Bombay (the family of the latter-day Texcuna tycoon, Prakash Agarwal), and the trader K.V. Gopinath, who was consulted on a number of business deals by Soviet officials. Some enterprises had become involved in the USSR by virtue of connections with the Communist Party of India or the left in the Congress party. But this was not the standard pattern at the onset of perestroika. A more general interest in Soviet trade was evolving by 1986, as represented by Thermax and the Torrent pharmaceutical company. (Firms such as Kirloskar attempted to breach the market but failed.)

INDO–SOVIET ECONOMIC COLLABORATION AND THE VISION OF A NEW GLOBAL ECONOMIC ORDER: VARYING PERSPECTIVES

The understatement of the problems of Indo–Soviet technical collaboration on the eve of perestroika was the upshot not only of the known benefits that had accrued to the Indian economy, but of a focus in both countries on the evolution of a new global economic order. This common commitment was severely qualified in the 1970s in the USSR, but had considerable authority until the onset of perestroika and even thereafter up to Soviet disintegration. In India, the commitment was strongly tinged by nationalism and often did not include any serious attention to global issues.

The common ground is ascribed to Soviet propaganda in India (the output of the World Peace Council or the Afro–Asian Solidarity Group, for instance) and the political clout of the Communist Party of India and the pro-Soviet Left in Indian politics before and after 1947. This, though, merely strengthened the coincidence of Soviet anti-capitalist, anti-NATO Cold War rhetoric and India's official non-aligned anti-imperialist stances, which had a great following among bureaucrats and the public. The coincidence was marked in the discussion of 'development' strategy in both countries, a discussion which had distinctly anti-Western overtones. The terms had theoretical implications, which were expounded and debated at length in left-wing circles, which included many Indian economists, Euro–American economists and Soviet economists.[44] The key focus was a socialist idea of the international division of labour, but the range of the terms ran much further than academic discourse on the economy. They also emerged as something more than a standard motif of the large pro-Soviet literature that was circulated in India by Soviet agencies operating in the country.

The ideas were a normal reference among Indian and Soviet politicians and professionals when they met during summits and ordinary meetings, and they were accompanied by grand images. The terms used by Indira Gandhi during her visit to Moscow in 1976 gives a sense of the interplay of enthusiasm, issues and implications:

> 'Darkness is dispelled . . . by lighting lamps. . . . For our part, we specially appreciate the quantum and scope of assistance from the Soviet Union for it has enabled us to establish heavy industries in our public sector and has reinforced our self-reliance.

The same rhetoric was evident elsewhere also, in the public statements of technocrats who worked at Bokaro, Bhilai, Ranchi, etc.

The specific points of reference in this rhetorical posture were indicated by I. Kulev, Deputy Chairman of the State Committee of the USSR Council of Ministers for Foreign Economic Relations in 1977, in a statement where the oratorical projection of the socialist vision is evident and where stress fell on three points: that the relationship was beneficial to the developing world (the 'Third World' in the terminology of the time) in that it placed the resources of the socialist world at its disposal; that the relationship conserved 'convertible currency' (which was of value to both); and that it was of some value to the socialist bloc, providing them with important commodities. A broader implication that was drawn was that such relations indicated the rise of a new division of labour worldwide: a theme that was a frequent refrain when the Soviet approach to economics was discussed, and which clearly had political and strategic significance in the context of the Cold War.

> It should be noted first of all that all the material and financial resources provided by the socialist states in the course of the cooperation are placed entirely at the disposal of the developing countries and can be used to meet the needs of their economic and cultural development. The developing countries also derive considerable benefits from their reciprocal deliveries to the socialist countries. These deliveries, made in accordance with long term trade agreements, the export of goods as a means of repayment of credits advanced by the socialist states, have a stimulating effect on the production of these goods in the developing countries. Participation in a new type of international division of labour—that between the socialist and the developing countries—opens for the new nation states the opportunity of exchanging their commodities for those of the industrialised countries on a truly equitable and just basis, while the clearing arrangements between them enable the developing countries to conserve their resources of convertible currencies.[45]

This perspective clearly referred to Soviet aid and exports to the socialist bloc of manufactured goods that came of such aid. The perspective developed from the notion that the USSR and its allies stood against a (Euro–American and capitalist-inspired) idea of an 'international division of labour' based on prevailing strengths and weaknesses, and market forces (i.e. strengths in primary goods production in the developing world and manufactured goods in the developed world). Instead the socialist bloc encouraged the statement of alternate visions of the future (expressed by the national government) and adequate representation for such visions in the organization of international trade—a stand that had created a genuinely global economy. Benefit to partners within the overall framework of international trade had to be worked into this respect for the long-term national perspective.

Interaction itself generated raw enthusiasm, independent of ideological and theoretical perspectives—enthusiasm that figures such as I.F. Goldin, who worked with Indian cooperation would carry on to the highest ranks of Soviet government as they rose to be major technocrats in the USSR. The unqualified enthusiasm is evident in an interview with Igor Petrovich Sakharov, the Head of Soviet specialists at Bokaro, a graduate of the Moscow Steel Institute and a former member of staff at Cheliabinsk steel plant. At the beginning of the interview, he said, 'Have you seen the plant? It's beautiful isn't it'. And later, when asked to assess his work, he went on

> What is there to tell, my blast furnaces are on their feet, functioning. Bokaro you have seen. The plant will become still better. The MECON will design its expansion up to seven million tonnes and afterwards to 10 million tonnes. It will be something like a dream.[46]

In arguments in the USSR by the late 1970s, though, there was increasing stress that a new approach to collaboration was necessary. Soviet specialists were not satisfied with the benefits accruing to the Soviet bloc from the prevailing system of Comecon–LDC trade.[47] This approach would involve a firm development of policies already followed by the USSR for simple national benefit, i.e. long-term agreements with LDCs for investment in extractive industries to supply the Comecon with important raw materials. Soviet economists called for such policy to be stepped up into a system of cooperation that considered strengths and weaknesses as much as national goals, and that would function within a system of greater rapprochement between the Soviet bloc and the capitalist world. The approach would coincide with the integration of the socialist economies. The new thrust was a necessity, according to analysts, since the capitalist world was establishing strong links with the LDCs on the basis of the latter's strengths (oil exports primarily): a situation that had led in turn to industrial development of the LDCs themselves. Response to such a view cast a different light on trade agreements with LDCs, according to E.K. Valkenier. Here the burden for project development fell more squarely on the LDC and the profitability of the enterprise was to be fixed before the project got going. The period 1976–86 witnessed a number of border projects, where the USSR had common frontiers with LDCs (power plants, oil extraction and refining enterprises, etc., in the case of Iraq and Syria), a major agreement with Morocco that involved phosphate mining,[48] and a host of similar projects elsewhere.

These new demands coincided with differences in Soviet and Indian approaches to collaboration. When Russians and Indians evinced their enthusiasm for ideas of global development, and for projects of technology transfer, important distinctions were clear in their approach. Those who staffed the new projects on behalf of the USSR were clearly proud of their work;[49] but they were equally certain that what they created could not compare with what existed in the Soviet Union. Hence, the enthusiasm cited of Igor Petrovich Sakharov, the Head of Soviet specialists at Bokaro, must be seen in the perspective of the views expressed by workers from Uralmash, who had experience in India. The latter made it clear, following praise of the achievements of Ranchi, that there was no comparison ultimately with what existed in the Soviet Union, i.e. that Ranchi was 'nothing compared with our Uralmash Plant, which is at least ten times bigger'.

On the Indian side, meanwhile, as indicated earlier, the public sector had a sense of self-possession, direction, and achievement. Managers and executives stressed the importance of the Soviet contribution to the making of plant; but they were equally mindful of the contributions of Indian engineers and workers. The balance is evident in the comments of D.R. Sastri, Executive Director of HMBP (Ranchi), who gave due credit to the USSR:

> The Heavy Machine Building Plant, Ranchi, which was set up with Soviet technical assistance . . . started from small beginnings and has continued to grow in stature year after year.
> The Heavy Machine Building Plant had to grow virtually from green fields, but with the ever-willing advice and guidance of Soviet experts attached to the plant. . . .

Again:

> The sincerity of our Soviet friends in making it possible for the HEC and the HMBP to enter the world market is evident from the selection of the items they proposed for such exports—not choosing items new or difficult for the HEC, but those in respect of which adequate experience and confidence have already been gained.

But elsewhere Sastri proceeds in a different vein:

> Today the design engineers are very much on their own and are now in search of the 'know-how' for attaining an even higher level of self-reliance. Technologists and shop engineers have likewise acquired the capability for converting even the most complicated designs into reality, not to speak of the confidence acquired by the workers whose zeal, enthusiasm and determination form the backbone of the Heavy Machine Building Plant.[50]

A.K. Khosla, Executive Director and group Manager BHEL and Heavy Electrical Equipment Plant, was equally balanced in his stress on his unit's achievement at Hardwar.

> Products of the Hardwar Plant add to the total effort of the Bharat Heavy Electricals Ltd., in meeting the vital need of our economy. Today, India has achieved self-sufficiency in this sector and in the sphere of power generating, transmission and utilisation equipment. All this has been possible by the utmost dedication of our people and the assistance received from friendly countries like the Soviet Union.[51]

The stress on collaboration between the USSR and India served to reinforce the strength of the blinkers that impeded recognition of the limits of collaboration. Together with the strong Soviet bent in India's foreign policy (especially after the Indo–Soviet Treaty of Friendship of 1971), commitment to the Indo–Soviet projects for nationalist reasons served to prevent policy makers from acknowledging that the relationship was going through a rough phase. Equally, in a manner comparable to the new Soviet perspectives on international trade, which made for a break with the past, national self-assertion had a further angle. It provided a good springboard to initiatives outside the Soviet network when the search for technological improvements began.

INDO–SOVIET ECONOMIC AND MILITARY COOPERATION DURING THE 'TRANSITION' OF PERESTROIKA

The Implications of Perestroika

The 'transition to democracy' that began under M.S. Gorbachev in 1988 had few *major* economic implications for this situation. In the Soviet Union, attempts were made to establish the grounds for associative initiative independent of the CPSU and the state (by measures of 1986 and 1987) and to encourage cooperative and individual enterprise (1987); greater flexibility was given to state corporations in the way they managed their affairs. The 'Enterprise Law' of 1990 and a statute on Joint Stock Enterprises (1990) permitted some degree of privatization. As far as 'reformers' and influential technocrats of the *nomenklatura* (Communist elite) were concerned, this was the bottom line of the agreements which they evolved mutually as they undertook the task of solving the international economic crisis of the Soviet state. Excessive concession to private production was ruled out, as was privatization of state corporations in a manner that altered their social and administrative standing.[52]

Equally, reform did not (as in the past) rest solely on exhortation and discipline by the Party. The Soviet government acted to allow independent associations and cooperatives to function so that such enterprises would not be stillborn. The future oligarchs Mikhail Khodorkovskii and Kaka Benukidze, like many others, began their work in such units: Khodorkovskii in youth organizations—'youth centres for scientific and artistic creativity' or NTTMs[53]—and Benukidze in cooperatives. Their activities during this time are indicators of how entrepreneurship developed. Khodorkovskii (b.1964) represented the Komsomol activists who came into entrepreneurship. He was a graduate of the Mendeleev Moscow Chemical Technological Institute, and took courses at a law institute and the Plekhanov Economic Institute, while actively involved in Komsomol work at the Mendeleev. After 1986, he formed a youth association (which ran a disco and a café) and later one of the numerous NTTMs. He invested the funds of this organization in various forms of consultancy that employed over time some 5,000 people in a number of sub-centres. The sub-centres were transformed into cooperatives, which then suffered from inadequate capital, leading Khodorkovskii to form the Menatep bank, which then grew spectacularly during the currency speculation of 1991 and after. From this base, he invested in oil and a range of other industries during privatization.[54]

The case of Kakha Benukidze (b. 1957) is somewhat more *sui generis*, and indicates that *nomenklatura* (party elite) entrepreneurship was not the sole form of entrepreneurship at this time. A geneticist by training, Benukidze completed studies at the Faculty of Biology of Tblisi State University, came to Moscow in 1977, and finished his M. Phil. at MGU. He then worked in the Institute for the study of the Biochemistry and Physiology of micro-organisms, went into cooperatives in 1987, and established units concerned with the preparation and distribution of various biochemical compounds. Benukidze then went on to form the network that became the Joint Stock company 'Bioprocess' (where he was the President of the Board of Directors). This was a holding company, which had some interest in biochemical compounds initially but which then ventured into a number of companies including the merchant marine enterprise *Morskie i rechnye perevozki* and the gasoline-oriented enterprise NIPEK (*Narodaia neftianoi investitsionno-promyshlennaia Evro-Aziatskaia korporatsiia*). Bioprocess founded the Moscow Petrol Exchange and worked closely with the Most Group and the Industrial-Commercial Bank.[55] It eventually diversified into machine-tools and, in the 1990s, came to be a major player in the Urals, controlling Uralmash.

Following the victory of 'democrats' in the Russian Federation elections of 1990, serious enclaves of disinvestment and deregulation were formed, especially in the Moscow region within the framework of the new Soviet laws on enterprise. Boris Yeltsin (President of the RSFSR) gave permission to Gavrill Popov, head of the Moscow Executive (*gorispolkom*) and his lieutenant, Iurii Luzhkov, to undertake experiments to improve the economy of the city. Under their initiative, and the participation of Zaslavskii, the deputy for the October Region of Moscow, the Board for Public Property of the October Region was set up (*Upravlenie kommunal'noi sobstvennosti na territorii Oktiabrskogo Raiona* or UKOSO) under Iu. Gusev. Large amounts of property were transferred to the charge of the new body; and this property in turn was concentrated in the hands of a number of Joint Ventures and Joint Stock companies that the Board formed to make the property more profitable. The companies included OOO Roza Co. Ltd. (which received the Vanda store on Bol'shaia Pol'ianka), the joint venture (Cypriot-Russian-Dutch) 'Peter the Great' (which received space in a building on Bol'shaia Pol'ianka), the joint venture 'Okean' (which received land on Kadashevskaia Naberezhnaia), a Soviet–Austrian joint venture 'Kamennyi Most' (which received land on the Naberezhaia M. Toreza), and the Yakimanka Bank (which received building space on Donskaia). Land was granted on a 99-year lease to such bodies (and elsewhere to a number of foreigners) for joint ventures. Comparable ventures, which were also given land at concessional rates included the international tourist company 'Moskva', which received funds from various city bodies. This enterprise set up the Joint Stock Company,

'Mosintur', which then created the 'Intourist Holding'. In real estate development of a different type, the nest of the *nomenklatura*, Serebianyi Bor now witnessed the construction of 'cottages' where there had once been only the dachas of KGB officials; and apartment blocks were built by the Joint Venture 'Pergamon-Moskva'.[56]

In parallel with what occurred in Moscow and the Russian Federation, changes took shape in the Baltic states, which demanded their independence after 1990, and in Georgia, where the authority of Gamsakhurdia acted as an umbrella for various initiatives of economic reform.

The significance of such 'enclaves', as well as enterprise flexibility, grew during and after the budget war of 1990 August, when republican governments, led by the RSFSR, demanded that tax revenues be concentrated in their hands, and refused to transfer funds to the Union government. The position was accepted by the Gorbachev administration and this led to an increase of opportunities in a number of republics—primarily the Baltic states, Russia, and the Ukraine—even though it led to crises in the Central Asian republics whose economies were dependent on Union subsidies.

Within such a framework, state enterprises were given a non-Plan domain for action. Cooperative commercial banking also became permissible; and many state enterprises used their funds to set up such organizations. Both developments led to a drift into sharp inflation during 1991. State enterprises hoarded stock that they obtained at low prices. This led to artificial shortages and blackmarketing, and encouraged price inflation. Such inflation was accentuated by the inclination by enterprises to price their non-Plan products exorbitantly high. The new commercial banks provided credit for such operations, and refused to accept any serious regulation by the State Bank. The rouble depreciated rapidly.[57]

Privatization of a sort took place with the declaration of large groups of state industry as independent juridical entities, even though their structure and personnel were hardly altered. Here, for example, the Ministry of Machine-Tool and Instrument-Making Industry of the USSR was transformed into a 'state joint-stock association' (called *Stankoinstrument*). But its industrial leaders were untouched, and the former Minister became the President of the entity. The reorganization affected a large portion of Russian production by 1991 (over 30 per cent of the industrial workforce). But it is worth noting that it took place within the framework of the so-called Ryzhkov plan of reform (1990), which wished to maintain the rudiments of the Planned Economy. It also took place against the background of a determination within the Communist Party to avoid loss of authority in the same way Eastern European communists had lost out. A concentration of economic power in the hands of *nomenklatura* (the communist elite) was duly set in place through the form of privatization just outlined.[58] In general, some flexibility was introduced into planning and pricing: but this hardly changed enterprise structures and their links and hierarchies before August 1991.

Changes in the Idiomatic use of 'Assistance' and 'Cooperation': Implications for Indo–Soviet Collaboration

Changing Terminology and Changing Assumptions

The period immediately before perestroika and the time of perestroika itself did witness important changes in the way in which notions of 'development' were treated in Soviet debates. Possible variations in strategy for the Soviet Union and the socialist bloc were stressed, including methods such as 'compensatory cooperation' as existed with Iraq and Syria, where the latter undertook the fulfilment of Soviet commitments in exchange for services. An argument was also noticeable that the USSR had 'lost' in the way in which it had conducted programmes of cooperation, and changes needed to be made in the system that prevailed. Attention was now paid to the extension to the 'Third World' of the principles of collaboration that had been recommended in dealing with Eastern Europe since 1971. Commentators on the Soviet Union's relations with developing countries alluded to the importance for future reference of the Complex Programme of 1971 as well as the 'Statement on Guidelines for the further development and deepening of economic, scientific and technological cooperation of the CMEA member countries' (Moscow 1984). Concern with the necessity to pass on to 'joint ventures' for future cooperation was repeated frequently, and this became a standard principle of government action after the Soviet Presidium issued a decree on 13 January 1987 that permitted joint ventures with developing countries. The change in emphasis was linked to the new stress on the 'market' at this time: a stress which, as Abel Aganbegyan (a popular 'reform' economist of the time) noted, did not forego the intervention of the state in economic affairs, but attempted to give greater flexibility to individual actors in the planned economy.[59]

Attempts to Initiate a New Phase of Collaboration with PSUs

These developments coincided with a reexamination of the character of Indo–Soviet collaborations at governmental level. A decision was taken at the IXth Meeting of the Intergovernmental Soviet–Indian Commission (April 1985) to form a Working Group for Industrial Cooperation and Engineering. The Group first met in January 1986, and the work of a sub-group for supervision and coordination of industrial cooperation (that met every four months) accompanied its activities, to examine where projects for expansion could be undertaken. Thereafter, in April 1987, the Indo–Soviet intergovernmental commission for economic, scientific, and technical cooperation discussed the decree of the Soviet Presidium of January 1987, and agreed to work on the basis of it. The long-term programme of industrial cooperation (until 2000) that was then formulated was an indicator of the stress on joint ventures to resuscitate collaboration in the manufacturing sector and trade in manufactured goods.

Andrei Muravyov, who was a close observer of the process from the Soviet Embassy in New Delhi, provides a detailed account of the projects and plans that evolved from these discussions. His information provides the basis for comparison of what was said and what was done, although it does not include information on the 1989–91 period, when a number of projects did take shape, including a major power project in the Bakra area contracted to Gidroenergoprom. A grand vision was at work: this is clear from the range of collaboration envisaged. Much of it was directed at building on earlier areas of cooperation, where Soviet technology was already in place in India. Hence, among the areas Muravyov mentions as the focus of special attention were: machine tools; joint production of mining, metal making and power-generating equipment; joint manufacture of excavators, pipe layers, heavy bulldozers, truck-mounted and tower cranes, rigs for deep drilling (beyond 3,000 metres); the production of rigs capable of drilling over 8,000 metres; joint manufacture of plasma, thermal and electric welding equipment, semi-conductor instruments, including thyristors and computer tomographs; joint production of tractors, cotton pickers, sowers and cultivators. The last indicated a departure, even if they were new avenues of cooperation linked to standard lines of machine tools production. More significant, a commitment was stated to investigate a range of new possibilities: joint manufacture of products on the basis of the exchange of technology, drawings, production forms and records, as well as deliveries by both sides of raw materials, semi-finished products, and manufactured units; and again, joint research on and development of innovative machinery, components, materials, and technology through exchange of consultants and specialists.

Steps were also envisaged in yet a different direction—in the very means of cooperation, which had been associated with government-to-government agreements. Departures in the character of cooperation were suggested according to Muravyov: contracts for manufacturing purposes; product assembly; production sharing; consultancy, in association with units in the CMEA, for the evolution of programmes for developing nations; further comprehensive long-term agreements for cooperation; the use of temporary consortiums for developmental programmes.[60]

The result of the evolution of such new principles of cooperation were a number of specific plans and suggestions for extending and developing existing collaboration between the USSR and India. Not surprisingly, as Muravyov's information indicates, the target areas were limited. Soviet organizations associated with lead, zinc and copper production indicated their interest in helping India to design and construct lead, zinc, and copper making units. This would work on the standard format of supplying equipment and training specialists. Specialists produced a comprehensive programme (ending 1989) for retooling and expanding the Ranchi HMBP. A project for 1986–90 for modernizing the foundry and the forge plant was also developed. An extensive plan for development was devised for the Durgapur mining equipment plant. Collaborative ventures were worked out for the supply of equipment to Janjra coal pits, and Nigakhi and Mukunda open-cast collieries. An extension of the Durgapur line of products was also envisaged, with the Soviet Union supplying the works with a list of 210 types of equipment and 26 processes towards this end.

By October 1987 (the time of the fourth meeting of the Soviet–Indian sub-group for supervising and coordinating industrial cooperation), some ten projects of this type had been concretized, under the general coordination of the State Planning Committee of the USSR and the Indian Ministry of Industry.

As Muravyov indicates, these measures were accompanied by close interactions between specific production units in the Soviet Union and India—a feature which was not typical of earlier cooperation, even if it had been projected in 1983, and some cooperation had taken place between Uralmash and HMBP (Ranchi). Ties between these bodies were extended in 1987; in addition, some specific arrangements took place, though Muravyov's list of deals that came to this stage is still shorter than his earlier list of projects and plans. The Donetskgormash association gave the MAMC about 80 projects for the manufacture of new products. In 1987, the HEC and the Uralmash Association took measures to produce the Esh/20/90 walking excavator, making parts, creating improved welding techniques and computing equipment (such as automated design systems). In 1987, BHEL and Elektrosila agreed to work on aid to Hardwar Heavy Electrical Equipment Plant for the production of 300–500 megawatt turbogenerators (on the basis of Soviet forms and records), and improved forms of 210-megawatt turbogenerators and super-cooled turbogenerators. This included schemes for upgradation that would save fuel and increase productivity. The accord was the foundation of the agreement between the Ministry of Electrical Engineering Industry of the USSR and BHEL in 1987 to broker the links between Elektrosila and Hardwar Heavy Electrical Equipment Plant which took form during 1987–90.

Trade figures do not indicate any revitalization of dealings in heavy engineering goods at the public sector level, despite these projects. Even if perestroika generated hope and planning, the results had not begun to show in actual commerce by 1991.

Responses from the Indian Private Sector

Indian entrepreneurs in Moscow at this time spoke of a sudden increase in opportunities as a result of the reforms.[61] The rupee–rouble arrangement gave Indian entrepreneurs an advantage. As the rouble fluctuated against hard currencies in 1991, its purchasing power in India remained steady, stimulating imports from India. Officials encouraged

Indian connections in the circumstances, especially since the volume of Soviet exports to India (mainly oil) remained high. Again, since a volume of barter payment was always expected by the Soviet government (against India's debt to the USSR), the latter encouraged its enterprises to look into the possibility of imports from India without waiting for permission from planning bodies. This provided an opportunity for the use of rupees in various import-export dealings by private parties. The relaxed plan mechanism and the flexibility given to enterprises allowed a diversification of ways and means to use the opportunities. The decentralization of revenues that followed the budget war of August 1990 between Union and republics provided opportunities for a different kind of commerce outside Moscow and the projects of the Union government.

In the circumstances, Thermax Ltd. made a decisive bid to expand operations. Animesh Basu was brought in to strengthen the team. He had been schooled in Russia and had Indian marketing experience with Tega (a Finnish company operating in India). Another addition was Shankar Mukherji, who had been on the engineering side of the organization. The latter was put through a three-month course of Russian in Tallin and then set to work from Moscow. By 1991, Thermax had begun work in Podol'sk, Krasnodar, Nizhnii Novgorod, St. Petersburg, and in the Tiumen (where it set up with Union Tiumen and Sibkomplet Montazh).[62] Elsewhere, in pharmaceuticals, Torrent expanded its sales considerably during the period, and drew competition from Cadilla, which entered the Soviet market in 1989. NRI Indian traders, such as the AGIO group, acted as agents for sales of Indian goods in Russia. Businessmen in India began to size up the potential market. Significantly, Indian students in the Soviet Union, who could act as a bridge between India and the USSR, responded with enthusiasm to the opportunities that perestroika offered. A typical example was the future tyre tycoon Sudhir Gupta, who had completed his studies, and, instead of returning to India, went into business. Gupta began rubber-exporting operations from Singapore through his small company, Amtel, which became a major supplier of material from South-East Asia to Russian enterprises by 1991. Amtel maintained Indian operations also, dealing in everything from fruit juice to tea, and the situation was encouraging, as Gupta recently remembered:

> After defending my doctoral thesis I was planning to go back to India and find a

suitable job, but then came Gorbachev's perestroika that opened new opportunities for doing business, including by foreigners . . . I seized the opportunity to try my luck in business and plunged into trading. Those were the days when everybody was trading in everything, and I was not an exception . . . I was making good money in trading. . . .

Even at this time, though, the vitality of the FTOs meant that much of this commerce was negotiated in India itself (via figures such as K.V. Gopinath). Businessmen sometimes focused on the opportunities provided by the new budgetary prosperity of republican administrations in the Ukraine and the Baltic because of such constraints, often recruiting Indian students to make the running with their local contacts.

Although there were also no serious alterations in the workings of the MIC, in the relaxed atmosphere, there were collaborations between private units and Soviet public units. A unit of the Kothari Group, for example, worked with a range of Soviet defence units: Gorky Aviation, Tashkent Aviation, Irkutsk Aviation, the Ufa Engine Factory, etc. There is, moreover, evidence that indicates this was not a unique case. Implications of 'transition' in trade affairs clearly meant the preservation of ascendancy by old managers and old styles while contending with new techniques and a range of new economic actors. In 1988 and thereafter, FTOs and specific enterprises worked to engage the private sector in India, as much as put life into bilateral collaboration[63] through the public sector.

THE SOVIET AND EASTERN EUROPEAN COMPONENT IN THE COHORT OF INDIAN TECHNICAL PERSONNEL

An important consequence of transfers of technology from the Soviet alliance to India, and the sale of crucial military supplies by the USSR to India, was a change in Indian technical personnel. This should not be overstressed, since the development of the national education system (especially in science and technology) had a momentum of its own, especially after 1947. Also, important inputs came from the West, which trained Indians under various programmes. Seldom did Indian scientists of distinction of the first post-1947 generation look to the USSR as a significant partner in research collaboration.[64] The Soviet and Eastern European component in India's technological profile, however, is easily ignored since it was only celebrated within a limited set. Soviet institutions never had the same cachet in Indian social life that US, British or French and German educational bodies possessed, even if their significance was as great. In the long term, this link was important to why Russian technology continued to be viewed with sympathy by Indian professionals.

Before 1947, Indian technical personnel were trained on the basis of British approaches to technology (at Engineering Schools at Shibpur and Guindy, for instance). They were oriented towards the United Kingdom in terms of the texts they used and the machinery they knew. Where exceptions existed, the link was with European or US centres of training. After 1947 this tradition was consolidated. Economic collaboration with the USSR in different fields, however, introduced a new dimension into the way Indian technologists and scientists worked. Initially such training centred around the units themselves. The construction of a Soviet plant in India was accompanied by a large training programme in different fields. At the time of the construction of the Ranchi Heavy Machinery Building Plant, 250 engineers were sent to the USSR to train in various manufacturing units. In connection with the construction of the power plant at Hardwar, 600 workers were trained locally and 200 engineers at the Elektrosila Plant in Leningrad (a major power engineering unit). Similar programmes were devised for the Bhilai and Bokaro steel plants. Important training programmes centred around the IDPL units and Hindustan Antibiotics.

The pivotal role of Soviet technology in the Indian economy during the 1960s and 1970s took the situation further. It required that all technical training in higher institutions and practical courses take into consideration the character of Soviet technology. Hence, the implications of technology stretched well beyond the workplace. Minor adaptations were made to technical courses. Soviet textbooks became well known in India, and came to be used in colleges and universities. Training in the ordnance factories, the Air Force, and the Navy was also directed at Soviet production, after personnel were trained in Soviet institutions. A steady inflow into industry of Indian technical personnel trained under Soviet aegis followed from the extensive recruitment of Indians by the Patrice Lumumba Friendship University after 1965. Other centres also trained and repatriated Indians: Moscow and Leningrad Universities, Tashkent University, various institutes of the Academy of Sciences, etc.

NOTES

1. This is true of MAMC, HEC and IDPL (Indian Drugs and Pharmaceuticals Ltd.).
2. A picture of 'friendship' has to be assembled from a variety of sources. The basic interest in the USSR in India and vice versa before 1947 has to be put together from several sources: Purabi Roy, S. Datta Gupta, and Hari Vasudevan (eds), *Indo-Soviet Relations 1917–1947: Select Documents from the Archives of the Russian Federation*, 2 vols. (Calcutta: The Asiatic Society, 1998, 2000); T.R. Sareen, *Russian Revolution and India, 1917–1921* (Delhi: Sterling Publishers, 1977); Hiren Mukherjee, *Time-tested Treasure* (Delhi: Allied Publishers, 1975); B.R. Nanda (ed.), *Socialism in India* (Delhi: Vikas, 1972); S.R. Chowdhuri, *Leftist Movements in India, 1917–47* (Calcutta: Minerva Associates, 1976); V.S. Budraj, *Soviet Russia and the Hindustan Sub-continent* (Bombay: 1973); Mohit Sen, *The Indian Revolution* (Delhi: PPH, 1970); S.G. Sardesai, *India and the Russian Revolution* (Bombay: Communist Party Publ., 1962); Zafar Imam, *Colonialism in East-West Relations* (Delhi: Patriot, 1967). Memoirs crucial to this literature are Muzaffar Ahmed, *Myself and the Communist Party of India, 1920–29* (Calcutta: National Book Agency, 1970); Sampurnanand, *Memoirs and Reflections* (Bombay: Asia Publishing House, 1962); Shaukat Usmani, *Peshawar to Moscow* (Benaras: Swarajya Publ. Hs., 1957); and *I Met Stalin Twice* (Bombay: K. Kurian, 1953).
3. The best (and most rigorous) overall accounts of Indo–Soviet economic relations is Santosh Mehrotra, *India and the Soviet Union: Trade and Technology Transfer* (Delhi: Oxford University Press, 1991). Useful articles appear in *Indo-Soviet Cooperation* (Delhi: ISCUS, 1971), where there are informative contributions by O.P. Mehrotra ('Two Decades of Fruitful Economic Contacts'), K.N. Aiyar ('Indo–Soviet Economic Relations'), S.C. Patnaik ('Indo–Soviet Economic Co-operation') and R.N. Chopra ('Indo–Soviet Economic Relations'). This literature is supplemented by other writing which provides data on points of cooperation. Some of this is mundane [as in Girish Mishra in P.N. Haksar et al., *Studies in Indo–Soviet Relations* (Delhi: Patriot, 1986)], while some are tightly argued if insubstantial [sections of Peter J.S. Duncan, *The Soviet Union and India* (Chatham House Papers, RIIR, RKP, 1989)]. On the equitability of Indo–Russian trade, see Nirmal Chandra, 'USSR and Third World, Unequal Distributions of Gains in Trade', *Economic and Political Weekly*, February 1977.
4. For MAMC and HEC problems, see Mehrotra, op. cit., pp. 96 ff.
5. Mehrotra, pp. 116 ff. Non-Soviet suppliers did their refining before dispatch of the product to India. Soviet imported crude was refined in India, and technology was transferred for this and to extend the facilities for refining Indian oil (all owned until then by foreign companies). This was the basis for Soviet (and Rumanian) assistance for the construction of refineries at Barauni, Koyali, and Mathura. Mehrotra deals with the debate concerning the costs of these refineries when compared with the private sector refinery at Cochin.

6. Ibid. See also early chapters of S. Chaudhuri, *The WTO and India's Pharmaceutical Industry* (Delhi: Oxford University Press, 2005).
7. Mehrotra, pp. 121 ff.
8. Especially from Skodo Export of Czechoslovakia and Sket Export-Import of East Germany. See B. D'Mello, 'Foreign Collaboration in the Public Sector Steel Industry', unpublished Ph.D. dissertation, Indian Institute of Management (Calcutta), December 1986. A more general monograph is William Johnson, *The Steel Industry of India* (Cambridge, Mass.: Harvard University Press, 1967). This has some minor references to the overall global standing of the technology that India imported.
9. B. D'Mello, op. cit., p. 74.
10. Ibid., p. 65.
11. C. Zumbrennen and Jeffrey P. Osleeb, *The Soviet Iron and Steel Industry* (New York: Croom Helm, 1986), pp. 150–6 for an analysis of the data on Soviet use of electricity in steel production.
12. S.S. Sidhu, *The Steel Industry in India* (Delhi: Vikas, 1983). Minimills are discussed extensively pp. 81 ff. See also N. Srinivasan, *The Iron and Steel Industry in India* (Jamshedpur: TISCO, 1982).
13. A good resume of the advantages of both traditional processes of steel production and the new focus on scrap and scrap substitutes is to be found in R. Ranier and J. Aylen, *The Steel Industry in the New Millennium* (London: IOM Communications, 1998). See especially P.F. Marcus, 'Ironies in Steel' and J. Aylen and K. Albertson, 'The World Market for Scrap and Iron'. Marcus points out the continued prosperity of standard production. And he is supported by S. Moonan, *Technology Transfer: Rejuvenating Matured Industries* (New York: Garland, 1997). The discussion of minimills is also taken up in A. Da Costa, *The Global Restructuring of the Steel Industry* (London: Routledge, 1999), which deals with the organization of the steel industry. Da Costa touches on the minimill and evaluates it against other production units. More general accounts are Kent Jones, *Politics vs. Economics in the World Steel Industry* (London: Allen Unwin, 1986), A. Nayar, *The Steel Handbook* (Bombay: Tata McGraw Hill, 2001) and J. Szekely, *The Future of the World Steel Industry* (New York: Marcel Dekker Inc., 1976), Sidhu, op. cit. and Srinivasan op. cit. indicate the commitment to standard production in India until the early 1980s.
14. See Deepak Nayyar (ed.), *Economic Relations between Socialist Countries and the Third World* (London: Macmillan, 1977) where the introduction is the most sober articulation of this position.
15. The calculation compares figures for Indian exports to the Comecon countries and figures for imports in the countries themselves. See Nayyar (ed.), op. cit., pp. 105 ff.
16. A good analysis of the mechanism of the rupee–rouble exchange rate is Pronab Sen, 'Rupee–Rouble Exchange Rate', *Economic and Political Weekly*, 24 March 1990.

17. Vladimir Sobell, *The Red Market* (Aldershot: Gower, 1984) gives a good idea of institutional trading patterns in Eastern Europe.
18. Ibid. The principles of such strategies were framed in the Complex Programme for the Further Extension and Improvement of Cooperation and the Development of Socialist Economic Integration (1971) adopted by the Comecon in 1971. The strategies themselves developed thereafter in various areas, using specially created international economic organizations (IEOs): the International bank for Economic Cooperation, the International Investment Bank, and research and development coordinating centres. A resume of the fate of such collaboration is also to be found in Michael Ellman, *Socialist Planning* (Cambridge: Cambridge University Press, 1987).
19. J.R. Carter, *The Net Cost of Soviet Foreign Aid* (New York: Praeger, 1971), J. Berliner, *Soviet Economic Aid* (New York: Praeger, 1978), M. Goldman, *Soviet Foreign Aid* (New York: Praeger, 1967).
20. Chandra, op. cit.
21. For a sample of this work, see S.M. Sebastian, 'Gains from Indo-Soviet Trade', in R.K. Sharma (ed.), *The Economics of Indo-Soviet Trade*. See also Vinod K. Mehta, *Soviet Union and India's Industrial Development* (Delhi: Manas, 1975) and Sumitra Chishti, *India's Trade with Eastern Europe* (Delhi: Indian Institute of Foreign Trade, 1973).
22. B. D'Mello, op. cit., p. 67.
23. In the case of coke oven plant equipment, the technology was dominated by a number of West German firms, Firma Carl Still Gmbh. & Co, Dr. C. Otto & Co., Gmbh. Krupp-Koppers Gmbh, and Didier Engineering Gmbh. US and UK firms licensed the technology from these. However, Giprokoks, the Soviet design institute for coke oven plants, developed a coke dry-quenching technique around 1972 which was quickly taken up by Japanese firms (the Nippon Steel Corporation and Ishikawajima Harima Heavy Industries). Eight years later, Mecon licenced the technology from Giprokoks. B. D'Mello, op. cit., pp. 62–6.
24. See Jaques Sapir, *Les bases futres de la puissance militaire russe* (Paris: EHESS, Groupe de la sociologie de la Defense, Cahiers d'etudes strategiques, no. 16, 1993). He has made a speciality of such work and has encouraged it. See J. Sapir, *La culture technologique: le cas des materiels militaires sovietiques*. Compiegne, UTC, Cahiers de Recherches, no. 3, 1990, and T. Malleret, 'Les transferts de technologie non negocies de l'ouest a destination de l'URSS et leur contribution au potentiel militaire sovietique' (Ph.D. thesis, September 1992, EHESS, Paris), J. Sapir and T. Malleret, 'Soviet Military Policy: from Restructuring to Reform', in R. Allison (ed.), *Radical Reform in Soviet Defence Policy* (London: Macmillan, 1992). Sapir restates his arguments in *Feu la systeme Sovietique* (Paris: La Decouverte, 1992), in an excellent analysis of how the failure to innovate placed considerable strain on the Planned Economy, leading into the crisis of 1991.

    For specific details of what innovation took place in Soviet industry, see G.V.

Osipov (ed.), *Industry and Labour in the USSR* (London: Tavistock Publications, 1966). This has important articles: B.I. Yeremyev, 'Social Conditions for Creative Activity among Workers', provides the information from the Gorkii Automobile Works, the Krasnaia Etna Plant, the Gorkii Milling Machine Works and the Zavolzhskii Engine Works; M.T. Yovchuk, 'Improvement of the Cultural and Technical Standards of Workers', has information from the Nizhnii Tagil Iron and Steel Works, the Urals Heavy Engineering Plant, and other units of the Sverdlovsk region. There are, however, few instances of quick implementation of innovation on a large scale, backing up Sapir's arguments. For the preoccupation with decision making and information technology, see V.G. Afanasyev, *The Scientific and Technological Revolution: Its Impact on Management.* (Moscow: Progress, 1975). American and British scholars have examined and stressed the political preoccupations of technocrats, but with little assessment of how this affected the results of their work. This is true of J. Azrael, *Managerial Power and Soviet Politics* (Cambridge: Harvard University Press, 1967). Revisionist work by Kenneth Bailles and Nicholas Lampert represents a new trend, as does the work of Stephen Kotkin. The trend is taken up in Harley Balzer, *Russia's Missing Middle Class* (New York: M.K. Sharpe, 1996). The historical perspective has not been drawn together to form perspectives on Soviet management.

25. Clark, op. cit., pp. 113 ff.
26. Ibid., pp. 144 ff.
27. FTO concerned with steel plant equipment.
28. FTO concerned with blast furnace equipment.
29. Andrei Muravyov, *Soviet Indian Economic Relations* (Delhi: Panchsheel Publishers, 1988), pp. 79–92.
30. D'Mello, op. cit., pp. 109–10.
31. Committee on Public Sector Units, 3rd Lok Sabha, 13th Report, *Management and Administration of Public Undertakings* (New Delhi: Lok Sabha, 1965), p. 33.
32. Committee on Public Sector Units, 4th Lok Sabha, 30th Report, Action taken on 22nd Report of 3rd Lok Sabha. *Indian Drugs and Pharmaceuticals Ltd.* (New Delhi, 1968), pp. 8–9.
33. See D'Mello, op. cit., p. ii. Both D'Mello and Mehrotra point out that while indigenization of equipment took place in the case of Soviet technology transfer, plant and engineering portfolios were retained by the Soviet side, and this required more long-term interaction. See D'Mello, op. cit., p. 59. Technology transfer did not always allow total waiver of patents. Hence, some process patents may have expired in the case of plant/equipment transfer, but various improvements and changes related to them remained patented and proprietory. The USSR adhered to these notions as much as did the West or Japan in the 1970s and 1980s.
34. At the Barauni Oil Refinery, adaptation of equipment using imports from the US and Europe was not unknown. This was the direct result of the Soviet

incapacity to come up to immediate requirements fast enough. This was communicated to me by Maitreyee Chowdhury, a senior staff member at Barauni during the period 1959–85.

35. Ibid.
36. Under initial agreements, the Ranchi plant produced machines for an alumina plant in Yugoslavia, for a nickel works in Cuba, and for metal making units in Turkey, Hungary, Bulgaria, Sri Lanka, and Egypt (where, in 1976, orders went to the Heavy Machine-Building Plant, Ranchi, and the Mining Equipment Plant, Durgapur, for 22,000 tons of equipment for projects that ran with Soviet assistance). See Muravyov, op. cit., p. 85.
37. See Muravyov, op. cit., pp. 88–9. Muravyov points out that the programmes 'Provided for joint work in designing, the development of new designs, modernisation, conduct of service tests, organisation of the production at Indian engineering plants of various types of metal-making, mining and power-generating equipment for projects being built in India' and elsewhere. That they 'provided for the manufacture of equipment to Soviet designs for subsequent delivery to the USSR'; and that they 'paid attention to improving the performance of the equipment installed at the engineering works in Ranchi, Durgapur and Haridwar and to introducing the latest technologies at these plants.'
38. The best account of defence production in India is C. Smith, *India's Ad hoc Arsenal* (Delhi: Oxford University Press, 1994), from which the bulk of the information in this section is drawn.
39. Testimony of Methil Vasudevan who worked at HAL in 1945 and 1952–6.
40. See Smith, op. cit., p. 157 for the complaints of the Subramanian Committee (1968).
41. The story of how laboratories of the DRDO (before 1967 the Defence Science Organization) were marginal to production and how they came to lend a sophistication to the production establishment is drawn out in Air Vice Marshal Samir K. Sen's *Military Technology and Defence Industrialization: The Indian Experience* (Delhi: Manas Publications, 2000). This is a subtle critique of the best scholarship on the subject, provided by Raju G.C. Thomas, whose perspectives are neatly summarized and updated in his 'Arms Procurement in India: Military Self-reliance versus Technological Self-sufficiency', in Eric Arnett (ed.), *Military Capacity and the Risk of War* (Oxford: Oxford University Press, 1997).
42. Interviews in 1986, March June with Rajiv Sikri and Veena Sikri (Councillor Political and Councillor Cultural, Embassy of India, Moscow), Sri Kulasresta (Councillor Scientific, Embassy of India, Moscow) Sri. Ranganathan (Minister, Embassy of India, Moscow), S. Nurul Hasan (Ambassador, Embassy of India, Moscow).
43. Jaques Sapir considers the Soviet military system possessed characteristics that made it behave differently from other systems. It was, he argues, characterized

by 'paradoxal militarism', which involved symbolic strength, and an avoidance of dynamic military vision with an eye to conflict. Such a perspective, if extended to the MIC, might explain its limited horizons in collaboration with India. The latter could also be explained by the culture of the Soviet enterprise, which Sapir discusses elsewhere (see n. 5). For 'paradoxal militarism', see Sapir, *Les bases futures*, op. cit. Also, J. Sapir, *The Soviet Military System* (Cambridge: Polity Press, 1991).

44. See, for instance, on the socialist idea of the international division of labour, Imre Vajda, *The Role of Foreign Trade in a Socialist Economy* (Budapest: Corvina Press, 1965).
45. I. Kulev, 'Economic Cooperation between USSR and Developing Countries', *Soviet Land*, no. 5, 1977, p. 9.
46. See E. Alexandrov's extension of K.C. Mohan, 'Mecon's Role in Building Heavy Industry', *Soviet Land*, no. 1, 1976.
47. The main literature on this is E.K. Valkenier, 'New Trends in Soviet Economic Relations with the Third World', *World Politics*, April 1970; 'The USSR, the Third World and the Global Economy', *Problems of Communism*, July–August 1979; *The Soviet Union and the Third World: An Economic Bind* (New York: Praeger, 1983). The Soviet economists who took this stand were associated with the Institute for World Economy and International Relations (IMEMO), and a major representative of the new perspective is N.P. Shmelev, who discusses it in 'Sotsializm I Mirovaia Ekonomika', MEMO, no. 10, 1976.
48. Mehrotra, op. cit., pp. 50–3. Mehrotra clearly disagrees with the Valkenier notion (restated in various CIA documents) that the approach was 'new'. And he proves this with material from the Indian case. It is likely, though, that if the habit was not new, the conceptualization of it was—paving way for the overall decline in fixation with socialist orthodoxies in the USSR during the 1980s.
49. See Alexandrov, op. cit., and Anatoly Filatov, 'Uralmash: India's Partner', *Soviet Land*, no. 2, 1976, pp. 3–8.
50. 'Expanding Cooperation for the Well-being of the Peoples of Two Countries', *Soviet Land*, no. 22–3, pp. 62–3.
51. Ibid.
52. For perestroika generally, *Cambridge Encyclopaedia of Russia and the Former Soviet Union* (Cambridge: Cambridge University Press, 1995).
53. These were used to spawn small enterprises. The centres were some of the many bases used by young entrepreneurs associated with the Komsomol to accumulate capital that was later invested in companies and privatization.
54. See *Biznesmeny Rossii* (Moscow, 1994), pp. 170 ff. Also Sapir, *Le krach russe*.
55. Ibid., pp. 25 ff.
56. V. Kucherenko, *Moskva—Imperiia T'my* (Moscow: Paleia, 1995), pp. 13ff. and 27 ff.
57. Jaques Sapir, *Feu le systeme sovietique?* (Paris: La Decouverte, 1992), pp. 106 ff.
58. Roman Frydman, Andrezej Rapaczynski and John S. Earle, *The Privatization*

Process in Russia, Ukraine and the Baltic States (Budapest: Central European University, 1993), pp. 15–26. By December 1991, there were just under 4,000 forms of such associations in the Federation. Of them, 53 comprised 4,162 enterprises. The 'concerns' were unions which exercised a monopoly over sectors of the economy: Rosneftgas controlled 99.8 per cent of oil production, Gasprom 93 per cent of natural gas production, Ugol Rossii 97.7 per cent of coal production, Stankoinstrument 88.7 per cent of machine tools production and 81.6 per cent of forge presses. Avtocelhozmash-Holding controlled 87.6 per cent of tractor production and 99.8 per cent of combine harvester production, while Norilskii Nikel controlled 87 per cent of nickel and cobalt production.

59. See Abel Aganbegyan, *The Challenge: Economics of Perestroika* (London: Hutchinson, 1988). Hence, prices would only be controlled for a specific range of goods, within a system of 'coordinated prices', where 'Plans are being implemented by proportional norms and contracts and not by commands' (p. 133).
60. Leon Zevin and Tadeush Teodorovich, *Soviet Union and Developing Countries: Economic Cooperation, Principles and Practice* (Delhi: Allied, 1988), pp. 114 ff.
61. Interviews with Animesh Basu of Thermax, Calcutta, 1991.
62. Interview with Shankar Mukherji in Moscow, December 2002. Mukherji stressed the considerable vision that Aga had at this time for development of Russian operations. Aga brought in Mukherji as a professional engineer to give a degree of rigour to Soviet operations that were dominated on the ground by marketing men with some professional expertise (such as Narain Apte). Both in Mukherji's and Basu's case he was attempting to vary his team to develop new directions, guided as he was by considerations that Indian potential had to be borne in mind as expansion took place. Basu was trained at Kanpur IIT, and, even though he had done schooling in Russia when his parents were attached to the Embassy in Moscow, his professional life had been spent in Indian units. Mukherji had no Russian experience, but he was thoroughly trained on the ground, beginning with a course in Russian which would have made the CIA proud. [The course involved morning to night study and conversation, with no exchanges in English or any Indian language for a period of three months.]
63. Santosh Mehrotra, *India and the Soviet Union: Trade and Technology Transfer* (Delhi: Oxford University Press, 1991).
64. This is true of Meghnad Saha, Krishnan and Homi Bhabha, who all sought their prime inspiration from the West. Despite sympathy for Soviet technological achievements, Soviet science seldom attracted Indian respect until the 1960s, when satellite technology drew some attention. I am grateful to Methil Vasudevan for his impressions of the various individuals with whom he worked in and around the Defence Science Organization during 1949–57. Vasudevan was acquainted with units in Delhi and Bangalore, and participated in several discussions concerning defence science possibilities at the time.

CHAPTER 2

Indo–Russian Relations After 1991: Background—The post-Soviet Dispensation in the Russian Federation

Following the disintegration of the USSR in December 1991, the Soviet republics emerged sovereign, albeit linked in the CIS, and all-Union FTOs and producer units that had handled Indian cooperation were thrown out of gear. The GOI and Indian businessmen were required to adapt to a fast-changing situation if trade was to be preserved and the interests of Indian defence production assured. Different trajectories marked the connections of new states with India, where some framed their links within priorities that had marked the USSR's Planned Economy (in the case of Belorussia and Uzbekistan), while others permitted regimes of reform to recast cooperation with India.

It was in the Russian Federation (the former RSFSR, now RF)—if the Baltic states are not considered—that officials reformed enterprises most radically, avowedly to remove impediments to innovation that were associated with the Planned Economy but also guided by the most narrow self-interest. Fundamental changes were made in the economic environment. India's adjustment to the dispensation was crucial to her economic relationship with the FSU as a whole. While the technology that bound India to the Soviet Union was now available in a string of successor states (especially the Baltic states and the Ukraine)—not to mention the Eastern European states that had moved out of the Soviet orbit in 1989–90—the Russian Federation was in a pivotal position in the new dispensation as far as India was concerned.

Not only was the Russian Federation the most powerful and well-endowed of the successor states of the USSR, networks of personal contacts and links between India and the FSU were focused on Moscow, the capital of the RF. The Federation inherited India's debt to the USSR, and the Federation had the bulk of the enterprises with which Indian manufactories did business. The other successor states of the Soviet Union were almost *terra incognita* to Indian entrepreneurs. Diplomatic relations were established and opportunities explored, but it was with the Russian Federation that the GOI and Indian businessmen dealt primarily to reset the trade.

The principles that determined the scope of the relationship with the Federation differed from those that guided Indo–Soviet relations. Economic performance was now the consideration; notions of planned development and a 'socialist' international division of labour were out. This turn of events followed partly from the changes of the perestroika era, partly from the political associations of the process of Soviet disintegration in Russia—i.e. the collapse of the Communist Party of the Soviet Union (CPSU) after the putsch of August 1991, the ban on the CPSU and the Russian Communist Party (RCP) on 22 August 1991, and the formation of an independent Russian Federation in December 1991. Endowed with special powers from November 1991, the Russian President Boris Yeltsin set to carry through economic reforms to move the Federation towards 'a market economy'. He was supported by the Democratic Russia Movement and operated with the course begun before Soviet disintegration, following Democrat victory in the republican elections in Russia in March 1990. This course had involved close work with neutral members of the Communist Party, and pursuit of strategies to dismantle the planned economy in the Russian Federated Soviet Socialist Republic even when the USSR had existed. Such strategies involved disinvestment, privatization, and the creation of a market rather than a command economy. The strategies were evolved and extended after the grant of special powers to Yeltsin in November 1991 and further after the disintegration of the USSR in December 1991.

India–Russia trade and collaboration had to face the disastrous consequences of the course: economic dislocation, fall in industrial and agricultural production, inflation, capital flight, and underemployment —a picture indicated by the fate of Russian GDP, which fell steadily from year to year (along with industrial and agricultural production) until 1997.

Trade however stood to benefit from opportunities for foreign capital and Russian entrepreneurship to explore avenues for commerce

TABLE 2.1: GDP IN THE RUSSIAN FEDERATION 1992–9

	GDP as % of the previous year at constant prices	Industrial Production as % of the previous year	Agricultural Production as % of the previous year
1992	85.5	82.0	91
1994	87.5	79.1	88
1995	95.9	96.7	92
1996	96.6	96.0	95
1997	100.9	102.0	102
1998	95.1	94.8	87
1999	103.2	108.1	102

Source: *Statisticheskii Ezhegodnik 2000* (Moscow: Mezhdugosudarstvennyi Statisticheskii Komitet SNG, 2001).

and to recast Russian manufacturing industry. Russia's India trade and military cooperation adapted the links of the past to new circumstances, exploiting the possibilities presented by the 'emerging markets' and the new corporate entities, albeit constrained by problems of social decay and confusion. Certain nodal points in the economy were crucial: government institutions that were powerful in a new way, as regulatory factors in policy and as the owners of shares in the newly corporatized private sector; 'oligarchs' such as Berezovskii, Potanin, Gusinskii, Abramov, and Khodorkovskii; and 'holding' companies or their equivalents, which held shares in a number of enterprises, keeping them together within the new corporate structure. Such nodal points gave access to enterprises of other states that grew out of the former Soviet Union since many governmental agencies and 'oligarchs' networked the economies of the Soviet and Eastern European region as a whole.

CONSEQUENCES OF DISINTEGRATION

The immediate aftermath of the disintegration of the USSR witnessed only a marginal economic reorientation within the Russian Federation. Borders in the FSU were 'soft' well into 1993, and almost all successor states were concerned to maintain some form of 'common economic space' to replace the Economic Union that had briefly existed in the USSR during September–December 1991. The rouble continued to be standard currency throughout the region, though shortage of rouble stock led to issue of 'coupons' in the newly independent Ukrainian Republic in 1992. Where companies faced shortages of technical staff as a result of migration of national minorities, the problem had begun well before December 1991, both in Central Asia and the Baltic, which were most affected. Trade within the FSU on lines comparable with the past was wholly possible. Significantly, the RF encouraged such trade. Bilateral agreements with FSU countries established 'obligatory' and 'indicative' off-take for various goods from March 1992. Governments were to broker the manner of the off-take and its distribution among enterprises both in the supplying countries and the receiving countries. The authority of the state among enterprises at this time, before privatization was completed in 1995, made such arrangements important in the RF.[1]

However, the Commonwealth of Independent States (CIS), the main umbrella organization of the FSU, in keeping with its general inchoate and underinstitutionalized character,[2] did not generate a planning mechanism similar to the old planning bodies of the Soviet Union—bodies which would provide 'command' references for production, and arrange distribution. Trade became the concern of enterprises and individual governments. Here, the determination of various republics to make their sovereignty meaningful through drastic measures undermined the link among enterprises. For the Black Sea states, Ukrainian control over Odessa (and its imposition of restrictions on non-Ukrainian vessels) affected trading patterns. Elsewhere, issues of ethnicity created tensions between states. This was true both of Russia's relations with the newly independent countries as well as relations between the countries themselves. In Central Asia, conflicting territorial claims undermined Russo–Kazakh amity[3] and cordiality between Kazaks and Uzbeks,[4] Kyrgyz and Kazakhs,[5] Turkmens and Kazakhs,[6] Turkmens and Uzbeks,[7] Tajiks and Kyrgyz,[8] Kyrgyz and Uzbeks,[9] and Tajiks and Uzbeks.[10] The same was true of the Caucasus, where there were not only conflicts between South Ossetia (of the Russian Federation) and Georgia and Azerbaijan and Armenia over Karabakh, but also claims and counter-claims between Azerbaijan and Georgia,[11] Azerbaijan and Armenia,[12] and Georgia and Armenia.[13] A common consequence of all this was inescapable: trade became the victim of dissension among officials and politicians. Coordination of economic policy within the FSU became difficult.

Disintegration became economically disruptive with the growing momentum of reforms in Russia. After January 1992, Russian prices followed their own path. Tariff reform in the railways hit freight and passenger traffic from Russia to the old Republics and increasing road freight favoured commerce within the Russian Federation.[14] Federation policy concerning restrictions on rouble stock in Republican Central Banks made it difficult for FSU states to remain within the rouble zone, compelling republics to begin the issue of their own currency.[15] This in turn further undermined intra-CIS trade, since exchange was not always a straightforward business and the clearing house system that was established ran into trouble. The situation became complicated by quarrels between the states and Russia about settling debts for electricity, oil, and gas, where payment for services was a point of tension. The Ukraine wished to establish a levy on the Russian oil and gas that passed through its territory to Europe. The Russian electricity supplying units (*energos*), still linked into a Soviet-era grid, with links into Eastern Europe, served the Caucasus and Central Asia, but did not know how to extract payments and often had to resort to threats of closure of essential supplies.[16] This led to retaliation of various sorts. In Russia, this gamut of little upsets threw production processes out of gear where they relied on inputs from (and demand in) other republics. National self-assertion within the Federation added its bit to dislocation, since authorities within Bashkortostan and Tartaristan 'favoured' their own industries.

THE YELTSIN REFORMS AND THEIR IMMEDIATE CONSEQUENCES

The distinctly 'Russian' economy that evolved against this background was associated with the Yeltsin reforms in the Russian Federation. These were the motif of the economic transformation in the area at this time, and were fundamental not only to Russia but also to the CIS.[17] To establish a relationship with the Federation, the GOI and Indian businessmen had to come to terms with the new dispensation that the measures had created.

The prime focus of the reforms was the Soviet Planned Economy and its system of targets, directives, and closed networks. Reformers reduced subsidies, permitted foreign competition, and encouraged private enterprise to give a market orientation to 'kombinaty', 'associations', and smaller 'enterprises' of the old dispensation. The steps originated in Stanislav Shatalin's '500 days' programme for making a market economy in the USSR (and taken as a reference point for the RSFSR in 1990). This presented an optimistic vision of market reform that had conceived of a fourfold process:[18]

1. An initial 100 days when a programme of extraordinary measures was implemented.
2. A second 100–50 days when there would be liberalization of prices and tight financial restrictions.
3. A third period of 100–50 days when stabilization of the market took place.
4. And a fourth 100-day period when an economic upswing was anticipated.

Little was achieved as the plan was developed and elaborated during 1990–1 in the RSFSR. Thereafter, from November 1991, policy focused on changes in enterprises and on a drastic alteration of the economic environment.[19] The latter was carried out through the following steps:

a. liquidation of the planning structure in the Russian Federation.
b. permission to enterprises to set their own pricing levels (in January 1992).
c. 'floating' the rouble.
d. The 'Western' tilt in the Russian economy after 1991.
e. The state abandonment of the monopoly on foreign trade and the reform of the country's customs regime.

Enterprise restructuring was worked through

a. privatization of distribution outlets in January–June 1992 on a large and intense scale.
b. privatization of producer units, outside a list of exceptions,[20] by the voucher method after December 1992, following Parliamentary approval on 11 June 1992.[21]
c. intensification of the banking reform.

Changes in the Economic Environment

Liquidation of the Planning Structure in the Russian Federation

The first Yeltsin reform Cabinets dispensed with planning. Various institutions of planning survived after 1992 (e.g., the habit of gathering statistics in the Goskomstat). But the Gosplan itself was scrapped[22] and the planned economy, where pre-1992 planning directed 80 per cent of production and distribution, was abandoned by Yevgenii Gaidar, Finance Minister in the Burbulis Cabinet and Acting PM to December 1992. Enterprises did not cease to follow past practices; but other measures in the reform package made the pursuit of such practices difficult.[23] Official decisions to scrap economic subsidies, which were a part of the liquidation of planning, led to the collapse of infrastructural arrangements in remote areas of the Russian Federation (such as the Sakha Republic).

Permission to Enterprises to Set Their Own Pricing Levels (in January 1992)

Enterprises were permitted to set their own price levels after 1 January 1992. Although 'freeing' prices was regulated by 'norms' set out by the Russian government (which included the introduction of 'indexation' of prices for certain goods), this led to sharp increases in prices that went well beyond anticipation. The credit that was available to most enterprises with state banks did not provide for loans to tide over temporary indebtedness. Consequently, enterprises evolved a debt economy where firms balanced debts they owed with debts owed to them. In much of industry, the use of money was expressly forbidden in 1992 as part of monetarist policy. Viktor Gerashchenko at the State Bank supplied subsidies (by way of soft loans) to some industries from June 1992 as shortage of capital became a problem, but this provided limited relief in a situation where inflation was growing and the rouble steadily depreciating. Out and out resort to barter arrangements within a network was a better solution to the problem, but large scale retreat into such arrangements was impossible since this required government back-up.

'Floating' the Rouble

In 1991, poor availability of goods and inflation had come to mark the Soviet economy, as had currency depreciation. To attract foreign direct investment into the country, and to improve productivity and industrial efficiency at a time of funds shortage, the Soviet government sought assistance from the World Bank and the IMF. In return for aid, the USSR was required to make adjustments in its currency rate, even if curbs on convertibility were permitted. The RF, even before the disintegration of the Union, decided to work within this framework. From January 1992, therefore, following the course adopted in the last months of perestroika, the government auctioned convertible currency, and allowed the rouble to find its own value against such currencies.

The intensified depreciation of the rouble that followed was linked to a considerable rise in prices after January 1992, revealing a drastic decline in the purchasing power of the currency. Continuing shortages of goods (in keeping with the tendencies of 1991) compounded this internal inflation and depreciation. The shortfall in rouble stock within the rouble zone (the CIS) led to the unregulated issue, on a greater scale than before, of local 'currencies'—linked to the rouble in the case of the Ukrainian coupon or 'karbovanets' for instance—a phenomenon that pushed the depreciation still further. Demand for foreign currencies, as a hedge against inflation and to obtain goods at reasonable prices, became noticeable everywhere. Lifting of the state monopoly of foreign trade led to easier movements of goods and encouraged dealers who were willing to trade in foreign goods to work with convertible currencies. The US dollar gained strength as a currency that could be used locally, despite a brief 'rallying' of the rouble during February–August 1992, when control of currency emission and (from June 1992) state intervention to buy roubles was most marked. The government turned a blind eye initially to the proliferation of moneychangers—a common sight to all visitors to Russia in early 1992. It then made the rouble internally convertible in mid-1992—that is, change into convertible currencies was permitted within the country as long as the currency was not exported. Demand for the dollar and the German mark was greatest in these circumstances—a phenomenon that grew after June 1992, when issue of currency by the State Bank increased, intervention to steady the currency failed, and the gamut of inflation and dollar-demand hastened rouble depreciation further.

From early 1992, the exchange rate of the rouble against the dollar changed from the official 27 in early 1991(as against an auction value of 110 in November 1991) to 180 (January 1992), to 175 (February 1992), 125 (June 1992), 226 (September 1992) to 353 (October 1992) and 414 (December 1992). Fall in production, overpricing, increasing government debts, and currency speculation by the new commercial banks intensified the trend over the next three years. By 1995, the value of the rouble was over 5000 to the dollar. To provide some stability to the situation, the government continued to permit free trade in currency and quotations of prices in such currencies became regular, even in shop windows. The dollar was clearly used as a 'support currency', and helped to preserve savings. The significance of this 'strategy' among the public only declined after Prime Minister Viktor Chernomyrdin introduced profit controls and focused subsidies for industry in January 1994. The scale of inflation declined—a trend that continued after the establishment of a 'corridor' for the rouble, from 1995 (i.e. creation by the Central Bank of a financial situation where the value of the rouble would vary within fixed limits) and strict requirements that goods must be bought in roubles even if the rouble continued to be internally convertible.[24] By this, savings came increasingly to be retained in roubles and rouble depreciation was checked. This solution was given a jolt by the crash of August 1998. But the situation thereafter did not revert to what it was during 1992–5, and the rouble has been the main currency of saving and everyday use for most Russians.[25]

The 'Western' Tilt in the Russian Economy after 1991

Close links between 'reformers' and US/European financiers, and the widespread use of the dollar as a support currency were among the factors that led the process into a 'Western' tilt. Moreover, a range of official European and US initiatives were set afoot post-1991 to 'retrain' Russians in capitalism and to rework Russian institutions to make them enterprise friendly. Both the European Union and the EBRD set out funds for this. Under the Freedom Support Act, the US Agency for International Development (USAID) and other bodies received funds to retrain Russians.

Different organizations undertook seminars and training programmes, culminating in ventures such as the Rand Corporation's Russian–American Business Leaders Forum, founded in 1997.[26] The latter came to be very high profile, although it allowed the representatives of small units to be present. On the Russian side, the founder members included delegates of the new corporate structures that emerged from the privatization of Russian industry in 1992–4: Lukoil, Tostelekom, Uralmash, Gazprom, GAZ, Aviacor, the Siberian Aluminium Group,

Novoship, and Transaero. Members of other major enterprises also participated: SBS-AGRO, MediaMost, the Berezovsky group, and the Alfa Group. On the US side, the Forum included representatives of Lockheed, Boeing, Kellogg, Enron, Whirlpool, Procter and Gamble, the Chase Manhattan Bank, General Motors, and J.P. Morgan. The focus included on-running problems such as Russia's economic future, governmental and popular attitudes towards business, the business community, and civic responsibility. On the surface, the association was intended to promote understanding between Russian and US businessmen; but clearly, a further concern was forming a common code of reference.

Networks of entrepreneurs grew up in the catchment area of such schemes, often drawing in major privatized units. Under each scheme, funds were tied to specific projects (housing, heating, health, etc.) which drew enterprises concerned with these areas to team up with Euro–American corporations/agencies, and work according to their principles. Encouraged by the opportunities provided by privatization, many Euro–American enterprises bought into Russia, leading to management changes. The more outrageous relationships of the reform era, such as those that existed between Anatolii Chubais and crucial members of the Harvard Institute for International Development—Jeffrey Sachs, David Lipton and Jonathan Hay[27]—placed a number of US personal networks in pivotal positions in Russian government and policy-planning throughout the 1990s. True, large areas of Russian industry remained unaffected by what happened, but the image of Euro–American style business caught on and became a model for economic activity, just as it became the acknowledged fact of life that, to get on, American friends were useful.

Abandonment of the Monopoly on Foreign Trade and Reform of the Customs Regime

Previous to 1992, under an economic regime where the state had a monopoly of foreign trade, 'customs' meant an instrument for regulation of state enterprises working under the general directives of the government. With perestroika, a customs levy that constituted an independent reference point was established. In practice, this levy was the difference between the price of the product abroad and its price in

Russia.[28] But the meaning of such a reference point was limited, since enterprises worked with a system of export quotas and import licensing. From November 1991, the Russian government, even as it moved towards abandonment of the monopoly of foreign trade, adhered to the prevailing system of import duties, and continued to use these as well as export quotas, export duties, and import licenses as its main lever for control of foreign trade for the RSFSR.

After January 1992, the practice of import licensing fell away. Hence, before the introduction of VAT in mid-1992, there was a general free-for-all when it came to imports, arbitrary levies being imposed at customs posts, often with no reference to Moscow. After the introduction of VAT, those goods that did not attract VAT (a large number initially) were free of import duties which continued to be applied in an unsystematic manner. Goods that had to pay VAT were required to pay the tax at the time of their entry into the Federation. A regulatory mechanism for imports of such goods was set up in July 1992, with the promulgation of a Tariff Law.[29] which was often amended thereafter. This introduced systematic levies—a basic rate of 5 per cent, nothing more for CIS states, 2.5 per cent for developing countries and MFNs and 10 per cent for imports from elsewhere. Amendments gradually introduced import duties of over 100 per cent for some groups of imports.

A large loophole was that imports from other CIS states were guided by special trading arrangements that worked outside tariff laws. From March 1992, bilateral agreements established lists of 'obligatory', 'indicative', and 'free' goods to be traded, where only goods on the 'free' list attracted tariff. The Kazakh–Kyrgyz–Belorussia–Russia Customs Union of 1996 also allowed scope for avoiding the Russian customs regime.

Crucial to the ineffectual working of this entire system of duties was that the creation of an apparatus to inspect and levy duties took time, as did the evolution of an ethos for the customs service. The situation permitted great corruption, especially since import duties could be waived if officials intervened at the ministerial level. A degree of stability developed in the control of trade after the regularization of the rouble within a 'corridor' of rates during 1995–8, and as a consequence of the crash of 1998, after which the demand for non-CIS goods fell sharply.

Important sectors were subject to little or no duty for long periods. These included foodstuffs and pharmaceuticals. Before July 1995 an extensive list of drugs and substances for their production were exempt from customs. The list for free import was then narrowed, and 10 per cent duty introduced for some—revised, according to item, on 11 April 1996, to anything from 5 per cent to 30 per cent. Imported registered pharmaceuticals, though, were even then exempt from VAT until 2000.[30]

CHANGING ENTERPRISES

Privatization of Distribution Outlets in January–June 1992

To stimulate independent enterprise initiative, the Federation government embarked on privatization that followed the steps already taken during perestroika. Initially focus fell on distribution outlets and the first sales took place in April 1992 in Nizhnii Novgorod (under the patronage of the Sakharovite Boris Nemtsov). Auctions were held for the purpose. Other cities followed soon.[31] In the course of this, the State Committee for Property (the official privatization agency headed by Anatolii Chubais) encouraged the privatization. The World Bank's International Finance Corporation assisted, handing out booklets to municipalities concerning how to go about the auctions, and so on.[32] Private trade emerged as a standard feature of Russian life, after years of restriction to the margins of legality or to the limited ambit of the *kolkhoz* market. By 1994, hawkers were a well-regulated unit of the Russian distribution system. Most food producers worked through *tonary* (mobile units parked at street corners). Municipalities provided some space for the hawker: either on a grand scale, as in the Moscow and St. Petersburg Metro, or on a small scale, around railway stations in provincial towns such as Tver, Vladimir, etc.

The process was marked by a concentration of ownership of prime real estate and distribution centres in the hands of individuals—a development marked by the involvement of organized crime. The coming of a major political and social force in Russia, the 'oligarchs', was visible in what happened. However, the real significance of this group was established through its grip on sections of manufacturing enterprise—a grip that came in the course of the privatization of producer units.

Privatization of Producer Units, Outside a List of Exceptions,[33] *by the Voucher Method after December 1992, Following Parliamentary Approval on June 11 1992:*[34] *The Emergence of the 'Oligarchs'*

Reformers took a more circumspect approach in the case of the privatization of manufacturing enterprise. Many producer units associated with energy and the military industrial complex continued to be state property long after 1991, and came under the Committee (later Ministry) for State Property (GKI). But the Yeltsin government was committed to privatization of large producer units, in the spirit of abandonment of the command economy, and it proceeded with its agenda, centering its activities around the State Committee on Privatization or its local branches and equivalents, which were to supervise the process. Enterprises in light industry (food processing, textiles, etc.) were slated for 'mandatory privatization'. Others had to be approved for privatization by the GKI.

This added a major dimension to the privatization already begun during the months before disintegration, when some state enterprises and parts of ministries turned themselves into shareholding companies, taking advantage of Soviet and Russian Federation laws of 1990. The process affected some 4,000 concerns with assets of over 50 million roubles, employing over 1,000 persons.[35] Some 2,000 concerns of this size were specifically excluded from privatization, but many later followed suit. 'Exit' from the status of state property followed two steps. Companies had to register as Joint Stock Companies, OAOs or ZAOs (Open and Closed Joint Stock Companies respectively). The terms of this were established by a Presidential decree of June 1992. Their equity, for the most part, would then be auctioned for vouchers with the caveat that *c.* 29 per cent must be available to the general public and some portion would be retained by the state for future 'investment tenders'. Here, tenders were to be a means of raising funds for the enterprise in future.

All adult members of the public received vouchers that were pivotal to this process and could potentially be traded for shares. In a number of cases, vouchers were traded for shares in the units in which individuals worked: a development that was reinforced by management policy to give local staff preference. Three 'variants' were followed, where Variants 2 and 3 had to be voted by a two-thirds majority in the enterprise.

Variant 1 was where workers received 25 per cent of preferred stock (but no voting rights) without payment (and the management had the right to purchase an additional 5 per cent at the nominal price). Variant 2 was where there were no free shares for enterprise staff, but the workers were permitted to purchase up to 51 per cent of stock at the nominal price. Variant 3[36] was where some free allocation to the enterprise staff took place, but where there were also privileges to 'groups' of 'insiders' if they undertook certain duties and responsibilities. The privileges could be permanent if the groups fulfilled their commitments.

The public could buy shares, therefore, in all enterprises destined for privatization, and here, as well as in instances where there were quotas or restrictions in favour of local management and workforce, the shares were 'auctioned'.[37] Auctioneers set a possible book value for the enterprise, based on a mark up for the 1991 value, and decided the number of shares to be issued. They then invited voucher owners to present themselves for bidding at a specific place and time. The face value of the voucher was irrelevant in the prevailing conditions of runaway inflation. The number of shares a voucher could demand was set on the basis of the number of vouchers presented (if 5000 were presented for 5,000 shares, one per share, if 500, ten per share). To take advantage of the opportunity, and following the example of Eastern Europe, 'investment funds' developed (such as 'First Voucher'). These took on vouchers and guaranteed to invest them. But unlike the case in Eastern Europe, organizers often decamped with the vouchers. In many lucrative industries, managements bought up shares from cash-starved workers, leading to a transfer of authority in corporations from the *nomenklatura* as management to the *nomenklatura* as lead shareholder.[38] It is this that has been described as the takeover of industry by 'red directors'. It was at this time that individuals who had made their name in the dealings of new Russian enterprise came into their own—the so-called oligarchs. These were persons of great political and economic influence: Vladimir Potanin,[39] Vladimir Gusinskii,[40] Boris Berezovskii,[41] Roman Abramovich,[42] etc.[43]

Privatization of producer units was given a scandalous twist by these entrepreneurs in the 'loans for shares' scheme of 1996, where Vladimir Potanin and his associates were beneficiaries. By this scheme, suggested by Potanin in March 1995 and authorized by Boris Yeltsin on 31 August 1995, a consortium of banks agreed to lend the government about

$2 billion for shares in a number of major companies. The shares would be held in trust for the government, and the banks would attempt to restructure the companies and 'turn them around'. If the government did not pay back the loan by September 1996, the banks could sell the shares, keeping 30 per cent of the proceeds, the government getting the rest. Eventually, the shares passed on to the banks concerned (Onexim Bank, Inkombank, Menatep, Stolichny Bank, and Imperial Bank) for auction among a limited group. The Banks bought the controlling packet of shares for a number of companies at a ridiculously low price.[44]

Concentration of privatized public property in the hands of individuals often occurred in a more straightforward manner—as in the St. Petersburg pharmaceutical company, Farmakon. Following privatization, 51 per cent of shares in the production unit went to employees. The company was not able to make ends meet from government orders, however, debt and arrears of wage payment followed and employees had to sell their shares. By the end of the 1990s, the employees had only 10 per cent. Twenty per cent went to Baltic Insurance Fund, which was controlled by Promstroybank, which gave loans to Farmakon and which was an operation in which oligarchs had great influence. Additional funds came from other private sources, whittling worker control over the organization to a legend.[45]

Elsewhere, board-room battles and stock purchase on the market marked concentration of property. The manoeuvres gave oligarchic practice and privatization a reputation for harshness. Seizure of authority in an enterprise could follow from 'summary bankruptcy' where debts were bought up, the offices of the management were forcibly seized, additional shares were issued and the register of shareholders rewritten; or from 'long drawn out bankruptcy', when a weak company became the site of collusion between an oligarch determined to buy and local management who were willing to help through the emission of shares at intervals. It could also follow from the removal of capital into offshore holdings; additional share issues to alter the complexion of the ownership; the use of political influence to bring a case against an enterprise's management or its owners, and have the property sequestered and passed on to others. Such tactics, apparently, have been linked to Oleg Deripaska's control of the aluminium industry and the Abramov-Mahmudov group's influence in the metallurgical industry and the MDM Group's hold over mining and pipes.[46]

Classification of Oligarchs

The oligarchs who came to do well out of the privatization were a mixed group and have been described in different ways. References to 'old' and 'new' are to federal actors. 'Regional' actors normally use the political authority of local government and form alliances with 'federals'. 'Old' oligarchs were V. Potanin, M. Fridman, A. Smolenskii and men associated with oil and finance; among the 'young', O. Deripaska, and R. Abramovich figure as the 'friends' of the 'old' group, while A. Mordashov (of Severstal) and Kaka Benukidze (of Uralmash) figure as the initiators of great holding companies, principally in the extractive industries. Other classifications deal with oligarchs in terms of their political association (members of the Yeltsin entourage or 'family' in the case of Deripaska, Aksenenko, Abramovich, and others); their local focus ('Petersburgers' in the case of Kogan, Reiman, Pugachev, Iashin, and others); or associative power (the main figures of the Russian Council of Industrialists and Entrepreneurs in the case of Potanin, Fridman, Veksel'berg, etc.). There are many who had their roots in one industry—Khodorkovskii of Iukos. Alekperov of Lukoil, and Bogdanov of Surgutneftegaz—in the case of the oil barons. Some broadened the scope of their business—Potanin's Interros has connections in the MIC and metals, Veksel'berg's Sual Holding in oil and aluminium, Fridman of Alfa Group in oil, telecom and iron and steel, Deripaska of Sibal and Rusal in aluminium, machine-building and aeroplane construction, Abramovich of Sibneft and Rusal in oil, aluminium and transport. Here some made major strides abroad—Lukoil came to have business in the US and Bulgaria and the Ukraine—whereas others kept close to home, venturing into the Ukraine or Kazakhstan if anywhere.

Intensification of the Banking Reform

Greater initiative for enterprises was linked both by 'reformers' and international advisors to the creation of a finance sector relatively independent of the state. Under perestroika banking was specialized, but dominated by the state. A number of banks, for instance, dealt with foreign banking under the aegis of the government: the Moskovskii Narodyi Bank, the Evrobank, the Danau-Bank, the East-West United Bank, the Mezhdunarodnyi Promyshlennyi Bank, the Rossiisko-

Latinoamerikanskii Bank, etc. Perestroika itself witnessed the rise of limited joint stock banking, but this took on a new dimension during the Yeltsin reforms, when the state was committed to dealing with private banks for a number of its arrangements.

Under the overall supervision of the Central Bank of Russia, a large banking network took shape. These included exchange banks (Vserossiiskii Birzhevoi Bank), insurance banks (Russian Insurance Bank, AKSO Bank), mortgage banks (Ipotechnyi Aktsionernyi Bank, Siberskii Ipotechnyi Bank, Vladimirskii Ipotechnyi Bank, etc.), land banks (Nizhegorodskii Zemelnyi Bank), 'innovation' banks (Alfabank), trade banks (Evropeiskii Torgovyi Bank), pledge banks (REM Bank), credit banks (Rossiiskii Kredit Bank), trust banks (Mostrastbank) and investment banks (Mezhdunarodnyi Investitsionnyi Bank). Personal savings continued to be dominated by the Russian Savings Bank (Sberbank), which in 1995 had 31,182 branches in the Federation, compared with about 5,500 for commercial banks (including the Agroprombank), but the network handled large funds in various quarters. In the regions, special regional banks not only dealt with their 'speciality' but branched out into other areas (as the now moribund Tveruniversalbank did in Tver province), but by and large, the banks kept to their own sphere, allowing some private transactions and deposits by the adventurous-minded. A crucial supplementary source of income was their activity as relays for Central Bank of Russia funds which were normally conveyed through them to regional authorities and production units.

Commercial banks appeared in large number during perestroika either as cooperative ventures or as units set up by impressive enterprises. After 1992 they mushroomed, growing on currency speculation. Among the main commercial banks were those associated with the petrol companies of the time, as in the case of the Alfabank, the NRB, the Imperial, and the MFK. The Mostbank was closely associated with the municipal government of Moscow. Menatep was based on the funds of the Komsomol. Mosbiznezbank was the offshoot of the old Zhilsotsbank. SBS-Agro was linked to the Agroprombank, and had a number of links to regional banks and agricultural enterprises. The great range of the banks is indicated both by the story of Oneximbank and Menatep. The Onexim was under the control of Vladimir Potanin, who led it and the Onexim group. It was backed by the MFK-Renaissance investment fund. The Bank was created (in 1993) by a group set up by the petrol companies Sidanco and Surgutneftgaz, and a public body, the State Committee for Customs, and was a depository of state funds. Onexim gained control of Norilsk Nikel and came to have a stake in Novolipetsk and Kuznetskmetal, as well as the telecommunications companies Sviazinvest and Rostelcom. It also controlled major newspapers, *Izvestiia* and *Russkii Telegraf*, and has some interest in *Segodniia*. Menatep established control over the Yukos Oil Company and various industrial interests through the holding company Rossprom.

As mentioned, a singular focus of commercial banking, until 1998, was currency speculation. Dislocation in industry discouraged investment in the private sector on an extensive scale. High interest rates meant that the demand for credit was always limited. Inevitably, bank participation in financial industrial groups, take-overs and boardroom battles was strictly one-off, and linked to their proprietors' activities. Otherwise, conversion of the funds that passed through their hands and speculation in short-term government bonds was the best way to operate in the climate of the early reforms. Speculation passed through even easier routes. Recognition as a commercial bank led to the issue of funds from the Central Bank—which could be converted into foreign exchange and used for currency speculation. The situation led to fraud in 1992–3, where commercial banks issued notes on each other for funds, obtained money from the Central Bank, and then closed shop. The Central Bank is calculated to have lost almost $500 million during the period in such cases of fraud.[47]

Compromise as a Motif of the Reforms, and the Role of the State in Economic Life

The reforms were implemented within a framework of compromise between the style of the old *nomenklatura* and that of Russia's new businessmen—a compromise whereby the authority of the state in the economy maintained a significant if imprecise role.

The Role of Red Directors

Central in this phenomenon was the presence in the ranks of the country's new entrepreneurial class of the so-called 'Red Directors', who were not proprietors but authoritative technocrats of the old order who controlled—more by negotiation than ownership—a large packet of shares in privatized industry. These figures maintained close liaisons with government and were often dependent on government, which itself possessed a large block of shares in the enterprises concerned. Their presence enabled government to make decisions for the privatized corporate entities, and they were pivotal in the energy sector, in extractive industries, and in the military industrial complex. Red directors often receive attention as almost indistinguishable from oligarchs—except in their competence, where they are judged to be comparable to Soviet bureaucrats. But what is clear is that more often than not they made a habit of asserting their loyalty to official structures—and their willingness to work with them. And through this, and through their lack of direct ownership of controlling shares in their enterprises, their position differed from that of the oligarchs. The fusion between this group and government is best indicated in the figure of Viktor Chernomyrdin, once chairman of Russia's most important natural gas corporation, Gazprom, and post-1991 Russia's longest serving prime minister (1992–98); but a number of other figures have also attracted attention in a survey by Joseph Blasi.[48]

Other Aspects of State Ascendancy

Overall, the compromise went far further than the preservation of networks. It preserved the authority of the state as property owner, regulator, and financier. The compromise was symbolized by the 'soft loan' policy followed by the Central Bank of Russia under Victor Gerashchenko; there were hefty budget allocations to regional authorities to help deal with dislocation with social services. Special tax rebates were available to firms that undertook 'social service' (maintenance of creches, schools, etc.); there were subsidies for companies remotely connected with the military industrial complex to assist them with the growing pains of 'conversion'. In the coal industry, subsidies of 20 per cent of costs were available in the Kemerovo region (albeit much less than the 80 per cent of the past). In law, the regulatory apparatus of the state was still in place—supervised by a Committee on Standardization and Metrology, and guided by licensing procedures for a variety of enterprises (which dealt with 500 activities, but also a number of lesser activities associated with the cardinal one).[49]

A number of organizations preserved a close relationship with the state as 'Federal State Unitary Enterprises', such as Technopromexport. Their defining feature was that they could not own property, but this did not prevent substantial control of the means at their disposal. FSUE Technopromexport showed the benefits that could be derived from the situation. The enterprise went well beyond its earlier status as an FTO, and, while working with the government, it came to control packets of shares in joint stock companies that worked in designing, power equipment manufacturing, and insuring export–import operations. It became a prominent share holder in the power plant at St. Petersburg. Working with its traditional partner, the Design Institute 'Zarubezhenergoproekt', Technopromexport went into the preparation of feasibility surveys of construction/rehabilitation of power projects. It worked with city and regional administration as well as financial bodies, provided back up information about the status of companies and personnel, and attested the veracity of documentation. It guaranteed the 'realization of the project undertaking the functions of the General Designer, General Contractor and General Supplier of constructed or rehabilitated project'. Using its contacts, it was able to negotiate tax and rate concessions as well as private finance, and to back up its authority, it provided access to warehouses and other buildings. Technopromexport's links with the federal government were always clear from the fact that it never ceased to see itself as a government agent. The company made its mixed concerns clear when it publicly stated that it specialized in operations related to the

> purchase of goods in other countries in repayment of the credits granted to such countries under international agreements, or within the framework of the obligations stipulated by the international agreements of the Russian Federation; arrangement of the construction and operation of enterprises and other projects abroad as well as construction of various projects in the Russian Federation, both on its own and with participation of Russian and/or foreign organizations and firms; acquisition and sale of technologies, licenses, 'know-how'.[50]

Here, and on other occasions, privatization was not mandatory, and enterprises did not opt for the path. As indicated in Table 2.2, there was a levelling off of privatization after the first spurt.

As late as 2002, 25 per cent of the Russian machine tools industry was classed as state owned. Major investments by government in the oil and natural gas sector as well as in electricity, gave the state a key role in the economy even after the first major wave of privatization was over.

TABLE 2.2: PRIVATIZED UNITS IN THE RUSSIAN FEDERATION 1992–9

(*in thousands*)

	Industry	Construction	Transport and Communications	Agriculture	Trade, Catering, Personal Services
1992	8.8	2.2	0.9	1.4	31.4
1994	24.7	8.6	3.5	2.8	67.2
1995	26.8	9.6	3.8	3.0	72.3
1996	27.7	10.1	3.9	3.1	74.3
1997	28.1	10.3	3.9	3.1	75.4
1998	28.3	10.4	3.9	3.1	76.1
1999	28.4	10.5	3.9	3.1	76.5

Source: *Statisticheskii Ezhegodnik 2000* (Moscow: Mezhdugosudarstvennyi Statisticheskii Komitet SNG, 2001)

In this, though, direct state control and intervention was helpful to a very limited extent. Revenues were poor, depending heavily on export duties on oil and natural gas. Possible earnings from export duties on manufactured goods, old machinery, and commodities were stymied by the lack of government control over the records of banks and companies. This was a natural result of the sudden abandonment of the system of planning, and the slow development of a proper system of tax inspection in the early years of the reforms. Earnings from privatization were low, enabling commentators of the process to describe it as 'piratization'. Poor management of loans and interest payments left the government in a sorry state by the mid-1990s. One commentator provides a sense of this new situation:

> At the end of the 80s, the process of degradation of state property set in. With the disintegration of centralized administrative controls, the meaning of state property was transformed almost into an abstraction: enterprises were considered "state", but many of them left the confines of state control and even paid taxes like other enterprises.[51]

With the onset of privatization, when legal status became more important, state enterprises that did not opt to change did come to find new masters within the bureaucracy. But in circumstances of poor state revenues and economic dislocation, this did not lead to tight controls and fixed rewards: it merely gave the enterprise that emerged from the uncertainties of 1989–92 a hollow hierarchy which it was required to acknowledge, and periodic handouts. Given problems of survival, the 'lifeline' that government provided was important; but the uncertain performance of government and irregularities of payment weakened its standing with enterprises.

Regional Variations in the Impact of the Reforms

In the background to these developments, local arrangements with regional financiers and regional authorities were useful to obtain funds, to survive, and to set up regional or inter-regional systems of cooperation and production. Various 'associations' of local authorities became central here: the 'Siberian Agreement',[52] the Far East and Trans-Baikal,[53] the Greater Ural Association, the Northern Caucasus Association,[54] the Greater Volga Association, the Black Earth Association, the Central Russia Association, and the North West Association.[55] Such bodies permitted some coordination in the style of the planned economy, and clearly appealed to managers who were used to that way of doing things. The associations of regional bodies offered the possibility of coordination of regional budgets that were under the direction of the economic interests which were crucial in a specific regional executive and 'legislative' body: and they performed this function to some extent. Individual local bodies often played a pivotal role in the arrangements that could lead to connections with foreign capital. In the case of Leningrad oblast, authorities brokered a series of transactions between Scandinavian firms and local firms to supply important public facilities concerned with telecommunications, shipping, food supply, etc. Trans-Caspian arrangements were brokered by the local government of Astrakhan, while many arrangements with China and Japan were brokered by Kamchatka and other Far Eastern governments.[56]

The arrangements were sometimes wholly independent of the regional associations and foreign capital. Hence, in Volgograd, Governor Nikolai Maksiuta (in 1997) took initiatives to shuffle funds to enable local industry to survive.[57] He explained the broad rubric of his programme and its assumptions:

> In fact, we constituted the council of directors anew. We came to agreements: to freeze prices of energy for industry. Besides this, we came to terms with factories, taking up their housing stock, and reducing their production costs by 15%. We began to work in fact with each enterprise individually, and, in accordance with their needs to take corresponding measures. We came to the conclusion that it was

necessary to provide many with specific benefits (essentially investments): especially to those who had a large rouble turnover. In the final analysis, we will get more funds for the budget as production picks up.

We began to work with agriculturists. The government had not found funds for them, but we arranged a reserve fund for them—at an interest of only 2%. We came to terms with Lukoil to provide agriculturists with 50,000 tonnes of fuel, against [profits] from the next harvest. Now we want to leave only the land tax in operation in the countryside. [In previous years] the entire system [of cultivation] had been destroyed. [Today] It is wholly unnecessary to decide what to sow and where. But it is possible to operate with the help of economic standards. Now we have constituted an oblast structure which guarantees 100% payment for the mortgaged wheat, sunflower and potato.

All round, such manoeuvres were crucial at a time when federal government limited itself to grand initiatives with long-term implications.[58] The manoeuvres often contradicted federal laws, but since the president had no right to override them, attempts to undo them were appealed to the Constitutional Court, where the cases were unattended for a long time. Certainly, the manoeuvres were severely restrictive. They included bans on export of various goods special levies on specific goods, directives to acquire goods, and more standard measures—such as charges on motorists from outside the area of Novosibirsk, Altai.[59]

But in some regions, rather than stimulate a failing economy, the authorities involved themselves in territorial disputes and fiscal disputes which destabilized what existed. This was true of the North Caucasus, where there was not only the Chechen–Moscow clash which led to confusion, but also tensions between Kabardina and Kalkaia sections of the Kabardino–Balkaria Republic, problems arising out of the creation of a united Karachaevsk–Balkaria Republic, and claims and counter-claims on each other's territory by various 'subjects' of the Federation—Kabardino–Balkaria, Chechnya, Adygei, etc. The formation of new autonomous units in Stavropol (new Turkmen and Nagai units) and Krasnodar (a new Greek 'autonomy') also complicated economic life.

The upshot of this situation was substantial regional variation in the terms on which reforms were implemented and accommodated: variation which could partly be explained by the resources of the region (as in the case of Siberia), partly by local initiative and partly by the area's history of ethnic and religious mobilization. General figures for industrial production merely indicate a flattening of the regional distribution curve with a slightly higher part of the pie coming from

Western Siberia (i.e. an overall reduction in production at all levels, maintaining the high points in the north-west region, Urals and Siberia, with an assertion of Siberian ascendancy to a slight degree). But these do not tell important regional stories, whose impact was substantially undermined by the crash of 1998. This is true of the influence of E. Rossell, the Governor of Sverdlovsk, for instance, and the importance of V. Platov, the Governor of Tver'. Both dominated their regions for the entire decade, and despite dislocation and depression, were responsible for important initiatives in their areas.

CORPORATE RESPONSE TO DISINTEGRATION AND THE YELTSIN REFORMS IN THE RUSSIAN FEDERATION

General Features

General surveys and individual case studies show a slow process of reorganization and recovery in many industries in these circumstances. Credits from banks were scanty, unless the manufacturing unit was associated with a bank group. The government in Moscow would only provide subsidies to those industries which had economic or political clout at this time, severely pressed as it was by the IMF, World Bank and EBRD to toe the line on monetarist policy,[60] and to encourage the growth of private commercial banking. In the early period of the reforms, officials were careful about loans and money supply—though they relaxed their stand somewhat after Gerashchenko took over the State Bank and Chernomyrdin became prime minister. By then, though, corporate reorganization added a further dimension to industrial confusion, further stimulating rouble-depreciation. Large-scale privatization and the new dispensation after 1992 were associated with low liquidity, confusion concerning where and how to sell, and contraction in manufacture. Possible solutions to the situation (other than bankruptcy) varied. They included strong links with new private banks[61] or financial organizations; submission to one of the major 'success' stories of the public sector (for example, Gazprom[62] or the reworked FTO Technopromexport); and inclusion in one of the 'oligarchic' empires created by the nature of 'transition'. Such a gambit was not always successful: for although the success stories were as gilt-edged as companies could be in Russian circumstances, their performance and their foundations often left a lot to be desired. Banks played with a highly volatile money market;[63] and since the stock exchange of these years took time to settle,[64] neither banks nor gilt-edged groups attracted confidence. In the circumstances, more limited initiatives took place. Integration of companies through associative financial industrial groups or FIGs and holding units was characteristic, either as a means of integrating with oligarchs and other hegemons of the economy, or as an independent manoeuvre. Here, associative FIGs were few in number (Uralskie Zavody, Sokol [Voronezh], Dragotsennosti Urala, Ruskhim, Sibir' and Interros) and were loose structures held together by common supplies of investment and limited state backing.[65] The 'holding' involved the formation of a separate company which held shares of various companies and featured representatives of those companies on its governing board. The step was tantamount to deep cartelization, where companies remained independent, but the 'holding' had a hold over production and sale quotas, and also had some foundation for working on investments.

Holdings and FIGs could be very powerful organizations, as is evident from the profile of the FIG Interros, which was one such. The organization has variedly been classified sometimes as an investment fund (following the general nomenclature of early privatization) and sometimes as a FIG (a special legal status). It was an investment company at the onset of privatization and amassed a fortune over the following decade. It came to have assets of $4 billion by 2002. Ninety-eight per cent of its investments were in Russia at this time. It was closely connected with the oligarch Vladimir Potanin, and the czar of Russian privatization, Anatolii Chubais. The enterprises under its control came to account for 2.5 per cent of the GDP of the RF. By the end of the 1990s, the holding controlled: Norilsk Nickel (which in turn controlled 20 per cent of global production of nickel, 10 per cent of cobalt; 3.1 per cent of copper and a substantial portion of world output of platinum and palladium at this time); Silovye Mashiny, a machine tools consortium, which controlled the former FTO Energomashexport marketing company, the Leningrad Metals Factory, the Electrosila factory, Turbine Blades Factory and the Kaluga Turbine Factory; the Agro-industrial Complex 'Agros' which dealt in cattle-breeding and plant-growing and which controlled Roskhleboproduct, a contracting agency; Rosbank, a joint-stock commercial bank that had 11 branches in Russia, had four affiliates (Primorye, Baykalunexim bank, Unexim-Volga, Monchebank), and a subsidiary in Switzerland—Rosbank (Switzerland); Interros-Dostoinstvo, a pension fund; OSG 'Soglasie', an insurance group, made up of 10 insurance companies; and Prof-media, a publishing house that supervised the group's interests in *Izvestiia*, *Komsomolskaya Pravda*, *Soviet Sports*, *Expert*, and the radio stations Autoradio, PM-radio, Novosti on-line, and TV and radio companies. Interros also had a real estate assets management company and major interests in Russia Petroleum. The organization had charitable and philanthropic concerns in Russia and elsewhere: it managed via the Vladimir Potanin Charity Fund and assisted St. John the Divine Russian Orthodox University, the Russian State Library, and the State Hermitage Museum. It gave scholarships in almost all fields.

Sectoral Variations in Industry

Owing to the widespread effects of dislocation, and the limited volume of regional budgets, however, neither holdings nor local associations were adequate safeguards for small enterprise, or for the small unit within the large enterprise. Managers and leading shareholders repeatedly resorted to limited initiatives after they had exhausted their raw material stock and the funds they received from the sale of what they produced. This amounted to a strategy of one-time associations with Western partners, who sought new opportunities in the Russian market; and to stripping assets, or 'tunnelling' (i.e. sale of plant and infrastructure without the approval of the smaller stockholders—a phenomenon which assumed great scale in the period 1992–6[66]) in order to make up capital as they went along. Such moves coincided with paid (and later unpaid) holidays for workers and barter to raise essential funds and equipment.

In such circumstances, dynamism in Russian industry and in the profiles of the enterprises varied from sector to sector. Seldom did manufactures move straight along the path that was promoted by American and European initiatives with the involvement of the leading commercial banks and Euro–American capital, streamlining technology and establishing a quick fix on specific areas of demand. Neither markets nor civil life (with complications of transport, property law, and storage) permitted this. Moreover, the involvement of organized crime in different ways ruled out a straight path in any field. Those who followed the path chalked out by the EBRD, IMF, World Bank, and USAID came down to about 500 enterprises, many of them registered on the Russian Trading Exchange and several linked with special extractive industries, import operations, and oil and natural gas. The rest worked within different arrangements cited above, and they 'made do'. These enterprises formed the greater part of the iceberg of the Russian economy.

In four areas that were important for Indo–Russian trade the situation took shape roughly as follows.

Pharmaceuticals[67]

The pharmaceutical industry took a sharp downturn following disintegration. By 1997, local production had fallen by 65 per cent, with a core of 140 manufacturing units and related centres working under-capacity to the level of 40–65 per cent. Thirty-five per cent of the country's needs were met by local producers, and 65 per cent was imported. In important areas such as vitamin production, over 80 per cent of requirements were imported.

The collapse in production must be attributed to disintegration and the collapse of planning; for the union and the command economy had linked chemical manufactures and R&D in various republics to arrive at a final product. Again, the pharmaceutical industry in the Russian Federation, as elsewhere in the USSR, was tied into the Soviet health care system: polyclinics and hospitals were the main buyers of the product. The reduction of government subsidies for the clinics, and the collapse of state health care thereby, meant a crisis for the industry. Although by the early 2000s 'reimbursed drugs' made up 20 per cent of the market for pharmaceuticals (17 million get drugs free and 11 million pay 50 per cent), official agencies did not pay their bills, making production difficult in a capital-strafed situation.

In the burgeoning world of private drug shops, foreign competition from Euro-American companies was strong, since there was a range of drugs produced abroad which had no equivalent in Russia. Also, at the lower end of the market, where cheap products were called for, Russian products were tagged with high prices and became prohibitively expensive. Local drug manufacturers were forced to go to China and India (even to Europe) for cheaper substances. Most of the major Western MNCs (Glaxo, Pfizer, etc.), as well as prominent Eastern European producers who had supplied the USSR (from Latvia, the Czech Republic, and

Slovenia), came into Russia; and production centred on coming to terms with them in the commercial market for drugs. By 1998 Germany, Italy the US, the Czech Republic, Latvia, Hungary and Switzerland came to provide about 70 per cent of imports, and China, India *c.* 30 per cent.

Old producers made a slow comeback, and once established, proved resilient and survived the crash of 1998. Their position was due to links with old suppliers in the CIS and in Eastern Europe. They drew in investment from abroad and changed product. The comeback depended on networks that were set up between suppliers and distributors by a number of private companies that acted as traders, consultants, and go-betweens. Most of these operated on the pharmaceutical 'exchange',[68] and through the Internet, which became an important means of order and advertisement. In the overall hierarchy of the principal national distributors that covered a large list of drugs in their order list, the network took precedence over the *Pharmatsias* or government controlled distributors that supplied state hospitals and state clinics. The most important distributors here were the Protek, SIA, and Shreya corporations; they operated in association with a number of small companies that had a regional or local spread. The companies worked closely with the main source of advertisement and promotion of pharmaceuticals in the Federation—the lists of acceptable drugs that were issued by federal and local government. These lists acted as the reference point not only for the drugs bought by government for its own clinics, but were also used by local drug-retailers (such as the partly privatized Apteka chain).

Seventy per cent of Russian producers were privatized by the end of the 1990s, and three companies stood out as the most successful. Bryntsalov, founded in 1990 as Ferein (renamed in 1996)[69] was reputed to control 9 per cent of local pharmaceuticals production by the end of the 1990s. It set up new production units and operated with equipment from Italy and North Korea. AKRIKHIN Khimfarmkombinat (Staraia Kupavna, Moscow Oblast), had been the largest Russian producer of active ingredients since 1936. It had major investments from the Alfa group. The company reputedly controlled 3 per cent of Russian production and had collaboration from the French Servier group and the Slovenian KRKA by the beginning of the 2000s. Vremya was set up in 1991 and was initially a distributor of foreign and local products. It came to be among the top ten distributors, a producer of repute, controlling shares in Belgorodvitaminy, which produced raw chemicals as well as vitamins and pain killers in tablet form; and Voronezhkhimpharm, which used to make sterile ampules and the bulk of the country's adhesive bandages. The company's sales from its Voronezh and Belgorod factories came to US $155 million in 1997. In addition to these leaders, there were a number of major actors that emerged, among them the range of companies which made up the Volga-Natur Produkt network ('filials' in Ekaterinburg, Kazan, Nizhniy, Penza, Perm, Samara, Saratov, Ulianovsk, Cheliabinsk), the companies which made up the Moron OOO network (headquarters in Moscow, filials in Nizhnii, Smolensk, Saratov, Tomsk, Cheliabinsk, Voronezh, Irkutsk), Imploziia OOO (Samara), Imskmed ZAO (St. Petersburg), Interkor (Moscow), Interleazing TKZAO (Moscow), Konstruktor NTFOOO (Ivanovo) and a host of others.

Production by foreign companies that took over Russian plants accounted for some of the Russian comeback. By 2001, some 150 products came to be manufactured under joint ventures. The companies from Europe and Britain that were involved here were: AB Astra, Ciba Geigy, Hoechst, Roche, Glaxo Holdings PLC, ICI Pharmaceuticals Ltd., the Welcome PLC; a limited interest was taken by the Japanese Takeda Chemical Industries, Fujisawa Pharmaceutical Industries Ltd. and Yamanouchi Pharmaceutical Industries Ltd. U.S. exports to Russia stood low at about 4 per cent of imports but a number of firms were set up in the country. These included Baxter, Bristol-Myers Squibb, Eli Lilly, Johnson & Johnson, Procter & Gamble, Lederle, Merck, Sharp & Dohme Idea Inc., and Pfizer International. They had representative offices and distribution networks. More important, U.S. companies worked under the Medical Technology Transfer Activity Program run by USAID[70] and Gore-Chernomyrdin Commission (set up in 1993) that promoted US–Russian business contacts. Grants were given to a number of companies, including Bristol-Myers Squibb and Searle, to help start in Russia. Bristol-Myers Squibb used this to build the country's the first GMP standard, foreign-owned, pharmaceutical production unit.[71] Searle Pharma, a Russian subsidiary of Searle, set up pharmaceutical plant at Izvarino, about 15 kilometres from Moscow in collaboration with the All Russian Institute for Molecular Diagnostics and Therapy, which was part of the Russian firm Biopreparat.[72] Independent of the state-aided programmes, the major entrant from the US into the Russian market was ICN-pharmaceuticals which, in the turbulent period of the mid-1990s, bought five Russian pharmaceutical plants in St. Petersburg, Kursk, Chelyabinsk, Tomsk, and Yoshkar-Ola. Substantial investments were made in plant modernization. The company moved its European corporate headquarters to Moscow and was probably the leading pharmaceutical production, sales and marketing company in Russia.

Twenty-five per cent of production plants still remained in government control in the country, and there were major impediments that prevented share-acquisition in the Russian pharmaceuticals' manufacturing sector. Shares were primarily traded locally. Government had all through encouraged foreign participation in this sector through direct investment in modernization.

Textiles

The textile industry suffered considerably following disintegration, with the collapse of supplies from Kazakhstan and Uzbekistan. Production fell annually until 1997, when there was some improvement, after arrangements with former suppliers of cotton began to work, and imports of machinery came to have their effect on local production. A number of companies associated with textile machinery were badly hit and took to selling abroad and radical restructuring. These included the Moscow machinery producers Vympel (machine-building plant) Mostrikotazhmash (knitting machinery plant) Tekhosnastka (textile equipment plant). Units at Ivanovo such as Impuls (textile equipment experimental plant), and a number of manufacturers elsewhere (in Kostroma, the KZTM (textile machine-building plant) followed the same course. The strategy revived this section of the trade. Flax did not suffer so considerably (since much raw material production is local) and a number of mills took easily to a search for foreign tie-ups.

Associative action was a standard resort of textiles producers to find funds (sometimes within the framework of regional cooperation associations) and to organize their survival. The formation of the 'holdings' Rostekstil and Konteks was crucial here, with the former a clear strategy of textile manufactories to handle new times. These gradually decided the fate of the industry, acting closely in conjunction with networks among the manufactories. In the case of Rostekstil, the 'holding' was created before corporatization (1992), and, following the event, held shares in a vast number of units. Rostekstil thereafter acted as a lobbying device and an organizer, eventually putting together 'tolling' for the manufactories, i.e. distribution of raw material with an eye to the market, yet leaving market strategy to the companies themselves.[73] Here, the mark of foreign capital or the oligarachs was hardly evident. Rostekstil conducted the negotiations which produced special arrangements with the European Union (under the TACIS programme) and the minor trade war (denying Belgian textile manufactories access to Russia) when the EU imposed rigid quotas on Russian textiles. The holding was a crucial player in official negotiations with Tadjikistan and Uzbekistan for the import of cotton, arrangements with Egypt for tolling raw material from that country, as well as the US programme GSMIOZ for special imports. It was crucial to the ultimate removal of export duties on the textile industry and the reduction of VAT on textile goods. Such strategies led to the gradual exclusion of Euro-American textiles from the Russian market by the end of the 1990s, with a few exceptions (the German companies Hochst, Lenzig, and Bayer, the Swiss company Du Pont and the Czech polypropelene producer Hemoswit).[74]

Iron and Steel

The great kombinaty in steel suffered considerably from disintegration, registering a sharp fall in production. This applied uniformly to the main giants, Magnitogorsk Metal Kombinat (MMK), the Novolipetsk Metal Kombinat (NLMK), and the Severstal' Joint Stock Concern (at Cherpovets). In all cases, the bulk of shares passed on to existing management during privatization.[75] The cohort of Soviet-style managers found their positions often challenged by the oligarchs (especially Potanin), and worked a major tie-up with US interests in 1999. The subsequent revival of the industry, however, was not without problems.[76]

Machine Tools

Machine-building was badly hit by disintegration, except in cases where machinery for the oil and natural gas industries were concerned. The sector was varied, ranging from machine-building for the MIC to building for various branches of the energy complex to machine-building for transport, mining, textiles and manufacture. And, as often occurred in the Federation, there was an overlap among these, following the pattern of the planned economy. Steps were taken by individual concerns, in association with local authorities, to make structural adjustments and to deal with the crisis quickly: The rapid onset of the crisis, though, undermined such plans. This was the case in the Britosiko joint venture, set up on 1 February 1991 by the Polosukhin mine, Kuznetsugol, the Novokuznetsk division of the Kemerovo railroad, the Kemerovo regional executive committee, and British company Mons Cartwright & Co. These units worked to reorganize plants in Prokopyevsk and Kiselyovsk to build Russia's first mining machine-building holding. But the plans collapsed because of the crisis of the coal industry.

It was only in 1993 that a comparable holding plan fructified in another section of the industry. The Energy Machine-Building Corporation (EMK) was founded by the Leningrad Metals Plant, Elektrosila, Belgorodenergomash, Podolsk Machine-Building Plant, Chekhovenergomash and Petrozavodskmash. By then, structural re-adjustments were underway under the aegis of the government privatization programme, and affected various sectors, some units being controlled by the majority stakes of workers.

Depression and steep competition from foreign manufacturers led to a rapid slow-down. In some cases the state continued to control units, occasionally allowed their partial reorganization, but battled out the form of organization. In the case of machine tools linked to the aircraft industry, Rybinskye Motory and Permskye Motory (details below) provide excellent illustrations of the complexities of the time where direct government interests were involved. These were holdings designed to save a number of smaller units but whose activities generated a series of conflicts over control where the government thought it should periodically intervene. Whereas in the first instance, the holdings worked out some common business, the course they took thereafter (forced on them by the government) wrecked such initial intentions and involved the two concerns in orgies of reorganization[77] which had more to do with their potential than with getting out of the prevailing crisis or with improvements in productivity.

In other cases of government control, there was hardly any reorganization, and squabbles were rare. Depression and lay-offs continued to be the feature of the day, as grants and orders dribbled in, adequate to prevent wholesale closure. This was true of metallurgical, chemical, oil, and electricity machine-building units where either the state or red directors are still in charge. Many units in different sectors were labelled as having no serious direction.[78]

The first attempt at reorganization (the EMK) was a site of contest and initiative over the greater part of the 1990s. Given the sensitivity of the atomic energy which the organization controlled, a battle developed between Vladimir Potanin's Interros group—which worked a breakaway from EMK that led to the formation of Silovye Mashiny—and the mother company. Conflicts of small scale took place elsewhere, in the case of prestige institutions or crucial areas where the state had let go (e.g. engine building, which can affect the motor car and lorry production industry). Hence the interest of Kaka Benukidze in making United Machine-Building Plants (OMZ), which made up a private group of Izhorskiye Zavody and the old Uralmash heavy machine-building plant and provided Benukidze with a pivotal position in the machine tools industry as a whole. This involved minor scuffles with established interests in these companies. Elsewhere, the owners of the Ulyanovsk and Gorky automobile plants, Severstal and Sibal, deliberately set out to control engine producers. For its diesel engines, Sibal made sure of the Yaroslavl engine plant and diesel apparatus plant and Barnaultransmash. And it set out to acquire the ZIL plant in Moscow and the Minsk automobile plant in Belarus.

Rumours of great possibilities led to frenetic buying, but this merely led to regrouping with an eye to the future. This happened when reform of the railways began (2001). Metal producers, who thought to organize the freight in the new set up, quickly went to work. Severstal's transport subsidiary, Severstaltrans, bought into the Kolomensky Zavod holding company. Associates of Urals Mining and Metals Company (UGMK) took over the Bryansk machine-building plant (and there was a dog fight with the GALS group), companies linked to Taganrog steelworks came to run the Novocherkassk electric locomotive-building plant, while Sibal took control of Abakanvagonmash, which had a monopoly in producing transport containers.

Otherwise, this sector remained lacklustre. Agricultural machinery production was marked by low output because of the prevailing depression in agriculture. Private capital did not come in beyond the points mentioned. Some foreign investment did come in, but it was limited to cases like the St. Petersburg machine-tool plant Sverdlov and the Sedin machine-tool plant (Krasnodar), which was linked with Schisse. There was some export, but it was limited to the energy sector. By and large, machine tools units confined themselves to slim orders and state grants—passing them around through cooperative arrangements under the old hetman of the industry Rosstankoinstrument—an association which had a complex share structure which, along with a similar body, Stankoinstrument, had been looking after the welfare of more than half of Russia's machine tools units.

The Producer Unit

In a scenario where holdings and 'groups' possessed a limited significance for individual enterprise, an important sociological literature on such smaller units reinforces the perspective provided by sectoral studies. The point holds good also for the value of assistance from regional authorities. Aid was useful, but it did not provide a rigorous or stable producer–supplier–distributor network to replace the state in the case of units that did not mesh with oligarchic empires. The new structures may have shored up enterprises, helping out stragglers, but ultimately, many producer units had to make their own way in the world with some independence and great difficulty. Evidence of this occurs in case studies of 1989–95, that V.I. Kabalina has brought together to draw attention to the way in which the producer unit, faced with loss of subsidies and orders, resorted to strategies of balancing conservatism, radical economism, organizational avantgardism, and market administrative drift. The picture substantiates and advances fieldwork that has not adhered to the same categorization.[79] Drawing up their studies, Kablanina and her associates worked out of a representation of the post-Soviet enterprise as something more than a producer unit: a conglomerate of manufacturing units, with residential buildings, food-finishing, schools, clinics, etc. In the early stages of the 'reforms', such units resorted to continuous production and arrangements both in barter and in money with a limited set of customers whom they knew. With the disappearance of raw material or semi-finished product, they pruned their responsibilities (demanding payment for some services) and resorted to 'compulsory leave' for workers and delays in paying salaries. They then focused on fixed customers and limited their product list, continuously lobbying with government (local and central) for assistance under one scheme or another and living in the hope that the old system would reemerge in one form or another (balancing conservatism). Where the opportunity arose, they 'dovetailed' with state enterprise (market administrative drift). In other cases, they developed some market savvy, through association with commercial structures of the new Russia, established marketing departments, obtained a list of old customers from Gosplan, and worked with agencies (radical economism). In the case of some orders, foreign capital was involved. Also involved was a dedication to specific strategies of a new organizational orientation (e.g. a specific fix on Hubbardism in one case).[80] The picture has been substantiated with reference to extensive information from various unit: the ball-bearing company Kol'tso, of the Samara region, which showed signs of 'balancing conservatism' initially, but, from autumn 1993, threw up new structures and approaches under a young consultant who had worked for a commercial bank; an anonymous 'Passenger Autotransport Enterprise', which was responsible for a variety of urban and rural facilities (taxis, buses, etc.), which showed features of administrative-market drift; a Siberian Chemical unit, Plastmass, which moved to radical reform early on (before disintegration); and the most radical Moscow machine-building unit, Lenkon.

This range of options and strategies in a world apparently dominated by oligarchs and holdings indicates a state of continuing instability. Such instability had an important social dimension whose implications are difficult to gauge. At issue here is not institutionalized labour activity (through the standard labour representatives in the Federation of Independent Trades Unions and the much smaller Sotsprof). For these were emasculated either by their previous record of inactivity (as in the case of the Federation) and/or by their direct involvement in the official bargaining system that was set up by the Yeltsin government. Wild cat organizations such as Alexei Belov's 'Edinstvo' union in Samara, again, despite their popularity, did not produce serious threats to the prevailing dispensation. More significant was an anomie which is difficult to identify and whose implications are not easy to quantify.

UNSTABLE CONTEXT

The Problem of Social Decay

The phenomenon that posed a major problem for the reorientation of industry in the 'new Russia' was the result of 'drift' and lack of clear and workable models for survival and living in working-class society in the country. This was directly linked to the state of employment and entitlements. As a World Bank report indicated, through the decade labour was seldom laid off: and, as individual studies show, the social accoutrements around a producer unit rarely separated from it; nor did the unit itself disavow its responsibilities to clinics, quarters, crèches, etc., even if it could only pay for their maintenance sporadically. So, whether there was employment or not, workers continued to live in the vicinity of their former factory, since it provided them an affiliation, some minor benefits, a claim to work in the future, and odd payments of arrears of salary. Consequently, corporate units came to work against the background of a decaying social environment—poor welfare infrastructure, families in a state of degradation, local gangsterism, etc. Long periods without salary and employment in such circumstances rendered the workers discontented—creating a dour environment for restructuring. Utter desperation was the consequence of poor nourishment and the collapse of the state health care system, which, even if it existed in name, threw up so many problems that it drove the sick to penury or hopelessness.[81]

The privatization itself left many untrusting, disinterested and excluded, despite the standard option for most enterprises for the corporatization with shares passed on to workers. An interview with workers at one of the branches of the enterprise Prokat indicates why. In an exchange that was organized at the time of privatization, the response of the worker representative indicates a general sense of futility which, even if it was not always present, finally came to characterize worker response to the world around.[82]

In the unit, a preliminary subscription for shares has begun; how do you react to the privatization?

- People have filled out the forms, but only a few will buy the number of shares on offer, since additional vouchers are required. People don't want to buy these and invest them in the enterprise. It's not certain what will be gained from it and whether anything will be gained from it at all. If something does come of it, it won't be quickly, so why stretch oneself, deprive the family or go into debt ? So they buy the minimum number of shares—that comes to 11—for which only one voucher is needed.
- And, perhaps, generally, it was wholly worthless to buy shares?
- Some, perhaps did not bother to buy, but then, there will be layoffs, and then those who did not buy will be the first to be laid off.

- Did anyone speak to you about this ?
- No, nobody spoke about it and it's not necessary to speak about it – it's all clear. Once you do not invest resources, it's the end of the road. And certainly, there will be more layoffs. There is superfluous workforce almost everywhere, and 50% are on leave, and there are many who are working in the construction group....

The situation, as Roy Medvedev points out, did not lead to a resurgence of Russian Communism; and the 'wonder of the century' has been that labour accepted its lot without an organizational backlash. But limited sabotage, and a poor work environment was certainly the result, and it was wholly uncertain whether this would not have broader ramifications on the work environment than had hitherto been anticipated—a major problem for investment and sustained trade.

Russian Entrepreneurship in Question

The situation was not mitigated by the evolution of a firm corporate ethic or a reasonably steady entrepreneurial class. World Bank commentators pointed out that Russian industry and commerce did not witness the evolution of clear rules of behaviour, and, in Russian analytical literature, doubts have been raised about the entrepreneurial spirit in the country.[83] Oligarchs are said to have adhered to a code of practice, but the rules of this code regulated spheres of influence, not entrepreneurial and commercial activity. Certainly, the corporate community was fractured. The social analysts Kukolev[84] and Gimpelson[85] distinguish various groups at this time: 'Komsomolers', 'physicists', 'managers', 'bankers', 'directors', 'elite families', 'free artists' and 'economic dissidents'. Their social background often led to acrimonious relations that emerging corporate bodies could seldom overcome. Industrial and commercial dislocation, moreover, often undermined the significance of the social or cultural capital that can bind managers together. How far this led to a debilitating and sluggish business environment is uncertain: but it did lead to uncertainty, which became the rule of the land.

Boardroom Wars: The Case of Rybinskie Motory and Permskie Motory

Unproductive boardroom battles in the circumstances characterized industrial and commercial reorganization. The fate of two companies of the machine tool industry (Permskie Motory and Rybinskie Motory) provides an instance well described in the Russian press[86] of Russian capitalism (including the use of strong arm). The persistent role of the state is also evident, as are its powers (using areas of strength such as unpaid taxes).

In October, 1992, Permskie Motory, the country's largest producer of aircraft engines, was founded during the privatization of the state-owned company Motorostroitel. The latter was almost bankrupt, as the domestic aircraft industry produced fewer and fewer planes. In November, Permskie's main rival, the Rybinsk engine plant (producers of D-30 engines for the Il-76 cargo plane) followed suit and was privatized as Rybinskie Motory. Struggles over the direction of the companies began almost immediately, between the government, which had authorized the privatization, and independent managers. In June 1994, Rybinskie Motory held its first shareholders' meeting, which refused to register with the State Defence Industry Committee, which held 37 per cent of the company's shares. Valerii Anikin was elected general director and quickly came into conflict with the state committee over his refusal to cooperate with Permskie to produce PS-90 engines for a new generation of aircraft. In November, Prime Minister Viktor Chernomyrdin ordered Permskie's contract with Rybinskie Motory dissolved. The State Defence Industry Committee had Anikin replaced at a shareholders' meeting, and the company's chief engineer Valerii Shelgunov became the new general director (April 1995).

Official intentions moved now to revitalization, reorganization, and involvement of foreign investment in Rybinskie—steps that apparently the old management had resisted. In August 1995, Chernomyrdin signed a decree selling the 37 per cent federal stake in the company. Gazprom, the Tupolev aviation holding and General Motors bought the shares. In July 1996, a shareholders' assembly went ahead with restructuring of the organization. Integration with the Rybinsk Engine-building Design Bureau took place, as Alexander Novikov, general director of the Bureau became chairman of the board of directors of Rybinskie. Valerii Shelgunov, the director of Rybinskie, in turn, was elected chairman of the board of directors of the Bureau by a shareholder's assembly a little earlier.

At Permskie, meanwhile, in July 1994, the Mikrodin company (Moscow) in which the government had a substantial share acquired a 25 per cent stake in the company at auctions and established a dominant position in the management. In December 1995, Mikhail Makarov, the chairman of the Permskie Motory board of directors and representative of the Dinamika company (part of the Mikrodin group) demanded the resignation of Permskie head Vladimir Kinderknecht. Kinderknecht in turn proposed that Makarov himself step down. A vote on the issue brought no result; the members of the board of directors were divided evenly on the question, and a conflict began to take shape between shareholders and managers.

To break the deadlock, the government issued an order requiring Permskie Motory and Vladimir Potanin's Interros—which had become interested in the company—to transfer 49 and 1.4 per cent, respectively of shares in the Perm Engine Plant to the Federal Property Fund as collateral for Permskie Motory's budget debts. In November 1996, the Perm administration attempted to remove the management of Permskie Motory by force. Several armed men surrounded the plant's administration building. General Director Viktor Kobelev was ordered to write a letter of resignation, but refused to do so. Negotiations persisted, and an uncertain situation continued.

Little was achieved through this dogfight by way of actual improvement of production. A series of interests were fixed on Permskie and were using political clout to get their way. Interros was one player. In February 2000, for example, Gazprom announced plans to increase its stake in the charter capital of Permskie Motory from 2.9 to 25 per cent, and in the Aviadvigateli company from 16.3 to 25 per cent. It also announced plans to acquire a 25 per cent stake in the Perm Engine Plant. As a result of these deals, Gazprom would have gained control over the gas-pumping equipment sector. Gazprom intended to increase its share in Permskie Motory's charter capital through an additional share issue, but the project never went through. Clearly, Chernomyrdin's actions as prime minister were the upshot of his loyalties to Gazprom as much as to his sense of what was best for government. Ultimately, continuous instability was the result, and demands on the budget for subsidies to help two factories that were linked to the Military Industrial Complex to survive.

The Mafia

In this background the rise of organized crime was an additional destabilizing factor and lent its own colouring to Russian entrepreneurship. This is exemplified in the connections of Boris Berezovskii, reputed to

TABLE 2.4: INDICATORS OF DEMAND IN THE RUSSIAN ECONOMY

	1992	1993	1994	1995	1996	1997	1998	1999	2000	2001
GDP	85.5	78.1	68.1	65.3	60.9	61.5	58.9	61.3	67.0	70.1
	-14.5	-8.7	-12.7	-4.1	-6.7	+0.9	-4.3	+4.7	+8.7	+4.9
Household	69.6	70.4	71.3	69.3	66.0	69.6	67.9	65.6	71.4	77.7
Demand	-30.4	+1.2	+1.2	-2.8	-2.8	+5.4	-2.4	-3.4	+8.9	+8.7

Source: Stanislav Men'shikov, *Anatomiia Rossiiskogo kapitalizma* (Moscow: Mezhdunarodye Otnosheniia), p. 286.

some optimism. Such optimism was undermined by the depreciation that followed the financial crisis. Important banks found themselves in serious difficulties, and their operations in trade, based on a weak capital base, collapsed. Demand was severely affected. These features of what transpired are clear from the Table 2.4 which provides indicators of GDP and demand and uses 1991 as the base year and shows fluctuations over the previous year.

However, as the figures indicate, the severe slump was followed by good years in 2000 and 2001—the result in part of import substitution and a greater competitiveness of Russian domestic industry on the international market. Increasing international energy prices improved the profitability of Russia's energy industry and there were major benefits to domestic industry of a sharp differential in prices (international and domestic) for such products that the state ensured. However unstable Russian society was as a consequence of the reforms, it seemed that the 'transition' might have achieved a degree of equilibrium by the early 2000s. As the political establishment acquired a new hue under President Vladimir Putin, it appeared that the economy was also developing a more robust quality.

NOTES

1. The standard reference for Russian trade policy of this period is Vladimir Konovalov, 'Russian Trade Policy', in Constantine Michailopolous and David G. Tarr (eds), *Trade in the New Independent States* (Washington: The World Bank, 1994). The argument is summed up in Barry P. Bosworth and Gur Ofer, *Reforming Planned Economies in an Integrating World Economy* (Washington: The Brookings Institution, 1995), pp. 91 ff. and 106 ff.
2. The terminology and rhetoric which formed the background to the formation of the CIS was sparse. Although the Minsk Agreement of 8 December 1991 (to which all the CIS leaders were ultimately signatories) made no statement

concerning what the Commonwealth was to be, it implicitly assumed a link between Soviet states and it primarily addressed the failure of M.S. Gorbachev's negotiations at Novo-Ogarevo between September and November and specifically his failure to find adequate institutional expression for this 'link'. The CIS leaders agreed firmly, in the Alma Ata declaration of 22 December 1991 that they 'considered that the strengthening of relations of friendship, good-neighbourliness and cooperation among their nations—which had profound historical roots—essential for the fundamental interests of our peoples'. See *Izvestiia*, 23 December 1991. In the Minsk Agreement leaders were categorical that their main quarrel was with the instrument of unity among Soviet states, viz. an overweening and incompetent 'centre' (*Izvestiia*, 9 December 1991). And it was to avoid a 'Yugoslav variant', Andrei Kozyrev argued, that the CIS had been formed: to prevent an uncontrolled disintegration of the Union and a conflict of peoples (*Izvestiia*, 12 December 1991). In doing this, according to the Russian Foreign Minister, historical legality had been followed, since the original founders of the Union were now agreed on its dissolution. In all this talk of unity, however, no major reference to institutions of any substance was made; and the only serious arrangements of the time dealt with a provisional leadership for the CIS armed forces (paradoxically even while showing how each of the republics could form their own national force from these military units).

3. These covered a broad band of territory: in north Kazakhstan, Kokcheta, Tselinograd, Kustana; in east Kazakhstan, sections of Pavlodar and Semipalatinsk; and northern sections of Ural and Aktiubinsk oblasts.
4. The Karakalpak region aspired to link with Kazakhstan and leave Uzbekistan.
5. Kyrgyz claimed the southern sections of Alma Ata and Taldy-Kurgan oblasts, while the Kazakhs claimed sections of Issyk Kul oblast.
6. Turkmens claimed sections of Mangystauk oblast.
7. Turkmens claimed parts of Bukhara oblast, while Uzbeks claimed territory near the Amu Dar'ya in Tashauzsk and Chardzhoy oblasts.
8. Tajiks claimed sections of the Osh region and Kyrgyz claimed sections of Gorno-Badakshan.
9. Uzbeks claimed sections of the Osh region.
10. Tajiks claimed sections of Uzbekistan's Sukhandar oblast and parts of Bukhara and Samarkand oblasts.
11. Azerbaijan claimed the south-western region of Georgia and Georgia claimed the north-western region of Azerbaijan.
12. Azerbaijan claimed the southern region of Armenia.
13. Armenia claimed the south-western region of Georgia.
14. World Bank Policy Research Working Paper 2378. Simeon Djankov and Caroline Freund, *Disintegration and Trade: A Study of Trade Flows Among and Between Nine Regions and Fourteen Republics of the Former Soviet Union* (The World Bank Financial Sector Strategy and Policy Department, June 2000).

15. The initial complications of the rouble zone are dealt with in Juliet Ellen Johnson, 'The Russian Banking System: Institutional Responses to the Market Transition', *Europe Asia Studies*, vol. 46, no. 6, 1994.
16. For the broad structure of the 'Oil-energy complex', see Evgenii Sokolov, 'Energeticheskaia Bezopasnost' Rossii', *Nezavisimaia Gazeta, Stsenarii*, no. 3, 1998.
17. The best account of the consequences and character of the transformation is Stanislav Men'shikov, *Anatomiia Rossiiskogo Kapitalizma* (Moscow: Mezhdunarodnye Otnosheniia, 2004).
18. V. Kudrov, 'Soviet Union: Programmes of Economic reform', in C. T. Saunders (ed.), *Economics and Politics of Transition* (London: Macmillan, 1992).
19. The main details of the reforms are to be found in Jaques Sapir, *Le Krach Russe* (Paris: La Decouverte, 1998); Myriam Desert and Gilles Favarel-Garrigues, *Les Capitalistes Russes* (Documentation Francaise, Problemes Politiques et Sociaux, no. 789, Paris, 1997), Rose Brady, *Kapitalizm* (New Haven: Yale University Press, 2000); Anders Aslund, *How Russia Became a Market Economy* (Washington: Brookings Institution, 1995) and Frydman, Rapaczynski and Earle, op. cit. In India, a range of writing delineated these developments and their consequences—mainly in terms of degeneration and decline, with little to be said for the future. All the writing of R. Gidhadhubli was in this vein, while Nirmal Chandra, though more refined in his arguments, is as jaundiced, in 'Russia's Sinking Economy: External Dimensions', *EPW*, 15 May 1993, and 'Dimensions of Social and Economic Crisis in Russia Today', *EPW*, 1 May 1996, although he did admit that he would not guess at the future. The tenor of a range of Euro–American literature was not quite as harsh, as in the work of Brady, and in the case of most World Bank literature, which was more concerned with stress on attempts at reform whatever the limitations. The work was oriented to an extraordinary degree to evaluations of 'success' or 'failure', and like Chandra and Gidhadubli was silent on the social formations that were taking shape, except to refer to them as 'mafia' style. A noble attempt was made to go beyond this in the work of Jaques Sapir, but it was restricted to surveys, and did not have the imaginative content of his earlier work (cited above).
20. The initial 'exceptions' were: 'the Pension Fund of the Russian Federation, radio and television centres, pipelines, enterprises involved in monitoring and protecting the environment, highway maintenance organizations, enterprises producing narcotic and toxic substances, ports, waste disposal enerprises and equipment, gold and diamond reserves, public utilities, most of the nuclear industry, specialized hospitals, nurseries and sanatoria, water resources, resources of the continental shelf, minerals, objects of historical and cultural heritage.' But almost all these could be privatized by special statutes of the government. Frydman, Rapaczynski and Earle, op. cit., p. 47.
21. Ibid., p. 71.
22. Its personnel were transferred to the Economics Ministry. 'Deregulation'. Web

article by Konstantin Yanovsky, Sergei Zhavoronkov and Olga Makarova at www.ictru/files/personal/yanovsky/msps.pdf.

23. Rose Brady, op. cit., pp. 29–30. Brady points out that goods continued to be produced and shipped as usual for some time. She argues that raw materials were available in stock in many cases, so production was not impossible. However, with an eye to rising prices, finished products were priced exorbitantly, irrespective of actual awareness of distribution networks and demand. This led to an accumulation of products in warehouses, and large inter-enterprise debts. Brady puts the debt in March 1992 at 800 billion roubles ($4 billion at current rates of exchange); by June, the figure stood at 3.2 trillion roubles. Prevailing banking practices, which were linked to the planning mechanisms of the past, permitted this accumulation of debt.
24. *Ekonomika i Zhizn*, no. 8, February 1994, p. 9.
25. See N.P. Zimarina (ed.), *Russkii Rubl* (Moscow: Progress Akademia, 1994), Chapter IX for a discussion of the changing fortunes of the rouble during the early post-disintegration period.
26. Discussions and programmes were arranged by the Royal Institute for International Relations (Chatham House) for the states of the CIS. A rash of programmes were organized by US universities and research institutes—among them regular courses in the University of Illinois, Indiana State University, Columbia University, Stanford University, etc. The European Union, along with individual European governments, disbursed special funds for similar ventures as did various British institutions. For the Rand Corporation's Forum see C. Richard Neu, *Rand, Russian-American Business Leaders' Forum: Report on Inaugural Meeting* (Santa Monica: Rand, 1997); *Rand, Russian-American Business Leaders' Forum: Report on the May 16-17 1998 Plenary Meeting* (Santa Monica: Rand 1998); *Rand, Russian-American Business Leaders' Forum: Report on the October 31-November 1 1998 Plenary Meeting* (Santa Monica: Rand, 1998); *Rand, Russian-American Business Leaders' Forum: Report on the May 15-16 1999 Plenary Meeting* (Santa Monica: Rand, 1999).
27. A number of books have raised serious moral questions about the US role in the transformation of the Russian economy. See Janine R. Wedel, *Collision and Collusion* (London: St. Martins, 1998) and the writing of Anne Williamson, as yet only in a number of articles. This does not wholly differ from the 'positive' accounts of the process by those who participated—as in A. Shleifer and A. Boycko, *Privatizing Russia* (Cambridge: The MIT Press, 1995). The European side of the story is hinted in Brady, op.cit. But there is little currently available beyond newspaper literature.

    Wedel gives a good account of the influence of the Harvard group, and also tells how it used its position for personal and institutional profit. This was the consequence of a close tie-up with USAID, which gave responsibility for reshaping the Russian economy to HIID (founded in 1974 to assist countries with social and economic reform). This 'favour' presumably came from HIID's close links with Jeffrey Sachs, who was seen as the architect-to-be of most of the Eastern European economies, and the unusual connections that HIID had with various members of the US government. Here, HIID had supporters in Lawrence Summers, former Harvard economics professor and Under Secretary (later Deputy Secretary) of the Treasury for International Affairs under the Clinton administration, and his assistant David Lipton (ex-Harvard, a close associate of Jeffrey Sachs and Under-Secretary at the Treasury after Summers).

Wedel tells a sordid story of old-boy networks, skullduggery, and the rape of the Russian economy, as well as scandalous goings-on at USAID. The director of the HIID project was Andrei Shleifer, professor of economics at Harvard. The director of the Moscow office of the HIID project was Jonathan Hay, a Rhodes scholar and a consultant with the World Bank. HIID received substantial funds from USAID—about $57.7 million (for a Russian legal reform programme and other work)—contravening all norms. It also coordinated the spending of $300 million in USAID funds for Russia. As a result of this affluent position, and their close links to government, the HIID group (not just Sachs) drafted many of Chubais' decrees and assisted his associate Maxim Boiko to supervise the spending of substantial aid grants (over $300 million). Who worked for whom, according to Wedel, was never very clear. Boiko was CEO of the Russian Privatization Centre, and Schliefer was on the Board. The reputation of the 'group' enabled it to push the range of this organization well beyond USAID. Hence, by itself the body received $45 million from USAID. Grants from the European Union, various European governments, and Japan, as well as loans from the World Bank and the EBRD amounted to $100 million, all of which were repayable by the Russian government. HIID, meanwhile, gave grants to another associate of Chubais: Dmitri Vasiliev and the Federal Commission on Securities that he ran. And USAID gave $20 million to the Institute for Law-Based Economy (ILBE), which was close to the Chubais team.

Against this background, Jonathan Hay got USAID money for his girlfriend, Elizabeth Hebert, to establish a mutual fund, Pallada Asset Management, in Russia. ILBE funds were used to set up a private consulting firm that worked with Shleifer's wife, Nancy Zimmerman, who dealt in Russian bonds. According to Russian registration documents, Zimmerman's company set up a Russian firm with Sergei Shishkin, the head of the ILBE.

Wedel argues that as a result of such arrangements, the Harvard Management Company (HMC), which invests the university's funds, participated in loans-for-shares. HMC became a shareholder in Novolipetsk Steel mill, and Sidanko Oil. A close relationship was established between HMC and George Soros, which helped both. Meanwhile, Andrei Shleifer was influential in the work of the Gore-Chernomyrdin Commission and its various arrangements (monetary and non-monetary) for business development.

Much of this story came to light when USAID brought Jonathan Hay and Andrei Shleifer to book for using their official positions to make private fortunes at the end of 1997. But both seem to have been relatively unscathed, and

Hay later became an associate of Kenneth Dart (Head of Dart Capital) and had substantial interests in the Lukos Oil Company. Janine R. Wedel, 'The Harvard Boys do Russia', *The Nation,* 1 June 1998 and A.A. Mukhin, *Novye Pravila Igry dliia bol'shogo biznesa* (Moscow: Gnom I D, 2002), pp. 110–11.

28. See discussion of trade in A. Hewett and Victor L. Winston, *Glasnost' and Perestroika* (Washington: Brookings Institution, 1991).
29. See Bosworth and Ofer, op. cit., and 'Instructions on the application of import tariffs' (20/3/93), in *Ekonomika I Zhizn*, no.14, April 1994, p. 14.
30. Ludmilla Maksimova, *Pharmaceutical Market in Russia* (Washington: US Department of Trade, 1997).
31. Brady, op. cit., pp. 68, 69.
32. Ibid., pp. 67, 68. Also Frydman, Rapaczynski and Earle, op. cit.
33. See n. 20 above, Frydman, Rapaczynski and Earle, p. 47.
34. Ibid., p. 71.
35. Frydman, Rapaczynski and Earle point out that there were many confusions in the Commercialization Statute which dealt with privatization. The Statute allowed for privatization of these large concerns as well as most with assets of *c.* 10 million roubles and employing *c.* 200 persons, leaving questions about the status of those that fell in between. In general it seems safe to assume that almost all producer units except those excluded from privatization were required to move out of the state sector. The law could, however, be used to prevent privatization or delay it in various cases. See note 16 in Frydman, Rapaczynski and Earle, p. 49.
36. Applicable to enterprises with more than 200 employees and fixed assets between one million and fifty million roubles. Frydman, Rapaczynski and Earle, p. 56.
37. The auction process is best described by those who ran it. See Maxim Boycko, Andrei Schliefer, Robert Vishny, *Privatizing Russia* (Cambridge Mass.: The MIT Press, 1995).
38. The variety of such *nomenklatura* privatization is handled by Chrystia Freeland's excellent *Sale of the Century: Russia's Wild Ride from Communism to Capitalism* (New York: Crown Business, 2000).
39. Vladmir Potanin. Potanin was a graduate of MGIMO (the Moscow State Institute of International Relations) and had worked in Soiuzpromekport, a unit of the Soviet Ministry of Foreign Trade. He had an extensive network of contacts among diplomats, FTOs, etc., when he set up Onexim Bank and to Onexim Group (with Anatolii Chubais) in 1993, after establishing and extending the hub of the future offshore company, Interross, with Mikhail Prokhorov. In 1991, Interros was a trade company associated with the former Comecon Bank (International Bank for Economic Cooperation), the Sberbank, and the Vneshtorgbank in the formation of the International Company for Finance and Investments. Its later history, when its financial interests increased and it was involved in share purchases, company buying, dismantling, and building, is indicated below in discussions of Financial Industrial Groups and

Holdings. See also notes on the Iron and Steel industry below. Sapir, op. cit., pp. 81–2. Sapir does not indicate the complications of the metal industry and overstates Onexim's control over the Novolipetsk company.

40. Vladimir Gusinsky was the brain behind the Mostbank. Under perestroika, Gusinsky put together cooperatives which bid for government construction contracts in Moscow. He became involved in many Moscow deals as a result of his proximity to future Mayor Luzhkov, and set up the NTV TV station. Gusinsky was the main figure in the management of the newspaper *Segodniia*. Owning to clashes with the government, Gusinsky was forced to quit the Federation, though his financial influence in the country persisted after his self-exile. See Brady, op. cit., pp. 100, 101 and passim.
41. B.A. Berezovskii's empire is based on the Lada producing unit Logovaz, but has expanded into petrol and petrol distribution (through control of Sibneft), Aeroflot, TV (the station ORT), and the Press (*Nezavisimaia Gazeta* and *Moskovskii Komsomolets*). Like Gusinsky, he was forced to quit Russia to avoid prosecution under various scams, but remained a force to be contended with after he left the country.
42. Roman Abramovich, close to Boris Yeltsin and his daughter. A prominent investment company figure.
43. Peter Aven's Alfabank had a number of interests, making money by taking charge of placing Eurobonds for the government. Its position *vis-a-vis* the Potanin–Chubais coterie in government was weak, however, and it did not expand very extensively.
44. The Onexim Bank got 38 per cent of the wealthy Norilsk Nikel, 25.5 per cent of North-West Shipping, 51 per cent of Sidanko Oil Holding and, indirectly, through International Financial Company, 14.8 per cent of the Novolipetsk steel company. Menatep won 45 per cent of the Yukos Oil Holding. All purchases were made at slightly over the minimum set by the government and despite higher bids by other parties. See Brady, op. cit., pp.137 ff. for details.
45. Mikhail Minkevich, *Drugs and Pharmaceuticals in Northwest Russia* (US Department of Commerce Report, 1998).
46. Mukhin, op. cit., pp. 16–17.
47. For a good account in English of the banking system, see Iurii A. Sokolov et al., 'Commercial Banking in Russia', *Russian and East European Finance and Trade*, March–April 1996. Finance speculation is dealt with in Pavel Khlebnikov, *Krestnyi otets kremlia: Boris Berezovskii* (Moscow: Detektiv Press, 2001), p. 31.
48. For a note on the Red Directors and Joseph Blasi's work (Joseph Blasi, Maya Kroumova and Douglas Kruse, *Kremlin Capitalism: The Privatization of the Russian Economy* [Ithaca, New York: ILR Press, 1997]) see Freeland, op. cit., pp. 72 ff.
49. 'Deregulation'. Web article by Konstantin Yanovsky, Sergei Zhavoronkov, and Olga Makarova. This contains details that are absent in the broad treatment of the subject, S. Zhavoronkov, V. Mau, D. Chernyi, and K. Ianovskii, 'The

Deregulation of the Russian Economy', *Problems of Economic Transition*, September 2002.

50. See the Technopromexport website www.tpe.ru
51. V.I. Kabalina (ed.), *Predpriatie I Rynok: dinamika upravleniia I trudovykh otnoshenii v perekhodnyi period (Opyt monograficheskikh issledovanii, 1989-1995 gg.* (Moscow: Rosspen, 1997).
52. Republics of Altai, Buriatia, Tuva, Khakasiia; the administrative areas (krai) of Altai, Krasnoiarsk; the regions of Kemerovo, Irkutsk, Novosibirsk, and Omsk. See Vladimir Klimanov, 'Mezhregional'noe sotrudnichestvo', *Russkie Regiony* 1998 (Moscow: Carnegie Centre, 1999).
53. Republics of Buriatiia, Sakha; the administrative territories of Primorie, Khabarovsk; the regions of Amur, Kamchatka, Magadan, Sakhalin, Chita, Birobidzhan, Aginsk Buriat, Koriak and Chukota. See Ibid.
54. Republics of Adygei, Dagestan, Ingushetiia, Kabardino-Balkariia, Kalmykiia, Karachaevo-Cherkassk, Northern Ossetiia-Alaniia; administrative territories of Krasnodar, Stavropol, Rostov. See Klimanov, op. cit.
55. Republics of Kareliia, Komi; regions of Arkhangel, Kaliningrad, Vologda, Kirov, Leningrad, Murmansk, Novgorod, Pskov; the city of St. Petersburg and the Nenets autonomous region. See Klimanov, op. cit.
56. *Rossiia*, October–November 1996 for a discussion of Kamchatka, May 1997 for a discussion of the Leningrad oblast and July 1997 for a discussion of Astrakhan
57. *Rossiia*, 1998, p. 47.
58. A good case was the Tumenjiang Project. It was a project backed by UNDP, involving a gestation period of twenty years and investments of over $30 billion. It aimed at the creation of a crucial centre of growth, similar to Hong Kong, in North-East Asia, and focused on the north-eastTumenjiang Economic Development Area, comprising territory between the ports of Vladivostok, Nakhodka, and Vostochny in Russia, the city of Yanji in the PRC province of Jilin, and the town of Ch'honjin in North Korea. Necessary legal work has been done by the government and a series of investment inputs have been made by the local administration of the Primorie Administrative Territory to assist the Project. Vladimir Portyakov, *The People's Republic of China: Economic Policy of the 1990s* (Moscow: Institute of Far Eastern Studies, RAN). 'The Tumenjiang Project and Russia's Interests 1995-98)', 1999.
59. Konstantin Yanovsky, Sergei Zhavoronkov and Olga Makarova, op. cit
60. The authority of the agencies was partly a consequence of Russian acceptance of their advice and partly a consequence of rising indebtedness. The Russian debt in 1996 stood at $117 billion (including $100 billion of the old Soviet debt). Of this, Germany held $23 billion and the US $ 4 billion. In 1997, about $9.2 billion were being set aside for debt servicing. See Alexander Elder, *Roubles to Dollars* (New York: Institute of Finance, 1998), p. 119.
61. Assessments of corporate response to the banking system indicate that few

major producer units took credit from these banks, or from the new financial organizations. Hence, it can be argued that India relations were hardly affected by adaptation to this form of finance.

'Links' with the new credit sector, however, and actual financial dependence are not the same. The banks constituted a crucial component of the 'oligarchy' that was prominent in the Federation into 1998: and adaptation to new times required some form of link with this oligarchy and its place in various levels of the Russian establishment. Good books on the banks include: M. Dmitriev and S. Vasiliev (eds.), *1998: Russia's Banking Crisis and the Stabilization Phase* (Moscow: Carnegie Centre, 2001) and M. Iu Matovnikov, L.V. Mikhailov, L.I. Sycheva and E.V. Timofeev, *Rossiiskie banki: 10 let spustia* (Moscow: Mak Tsentr, 1998). Major financial organizations other than these banks included insurance companies which were tied to fixed companies—Lukoil, Gazprom, etc.—or which were independent, such as Interros-Soglassie; investment funds such as MFK Renaissance or Alfa-Capital; or pension funds such as Surgutneftgaz, Lukoil-Garant and Gazfond. See Jaques Sapir, *Le Krach Russe.*

62. Formed as a restricted Joint Stock Company in November 1992, Gazprom was the largest gas-producing and supply agency in the Russian Federation during the early reforms. It took over the bulk of contracts dealing with western Europe. It was closely connected with former Prime Minister Viktor Chernomyrdin, who was its Chairman.

63. Banks derived a good deal of their substance from closeness to municipal, regional, and Federation government. Here, they dealt in assets that seldom placed them in difficulties: GKOs (Russian Government Treasury Bills), which were for 3, 6, or 12 month periods, Federal Loans, Bonds (OFZs), Federal Savings Bonds (OGSZs), and MinFin Bonds. Almost all banks, however, were involved in great speculation on the exchanges, and certainly made money out of speculation in currency futures and currency exchange at the height of Russia's inflationary period (1992–5). Such speculation, and the problems of being dependent on government, led to a degree of instability in the credit they offered. Dependence on GKOs as a foundation for operations and excessive speculation brought most banks near bankruptcy when the Russian government failed to meet its obligations in August 1998. See Sapir, op. cit., and Elder, op. cit., Chapter 7.

64. There was a proliferation of stock exchanges in the Federation in the early 1990s. As many as 60 existed as late as 1995. Quoting was used as a means of testing the water rather than real trading. Planning, sale, and purchase of stocks was highly erratic, and reneging on deals was common. It was in 1994 that ten major brokers formed an association (The Professional [later National] Association of Market Participants) to establish a code of conduct. Their approval became essential for possession of a terminal on the Russian Trading System. Even as time wore on, settlement and clearing of trades continued to be a lengthy process, with irregularities to boot as a result. Registration of shares was

also fraught with difficulties, and many shares were registered in private firm registers where local management often dealt in fraudulent practices. Proper auditing was rare in many companies, and it took some time to evolve respect for the normal Generally Acccepted Accounting Principles (GAAP) that are accepted in the West, or the International Accounting Standards accepted in Europe, the US, and India. The popularity of the system only came when its value in attracting foreign investment became clear. This occurred after Mosenergo (1995) issued American Depository Receipts (certificates traded outside the country of origin, which represent ownership of shares), with huge success, after following GAAP. It is comparatively recently that various forms of market activity (such as trading in futures and trading in options), have come to be established on Russian exchanges. Even today, they are only popular in the case of futures trading in shares of popular and lucrative companies such as Rostelcom and Lukoil. The Russian Exchange first listed futures in shares of Mosenergo in 1996 September. The Moscow Central Securitites Exchange began trading in options in 1995. See Elder, op. cit., Chapters 8 and 9.

65. S. Batchikov and Iu. Petrov, 'The Formation of Financial Industrial Groups and the State', *Russian and East European Finance and Trade*, vol. 33, no. 1, 1997, pp. 79–91; O. Botkin and M. Kozlov, 'The Ural Plants Financial Industrial Group', *Russian and East European Finance and Trade*, vol. 33, no. 2, 1997, pp. 59–71. For Interros, see www.interros.ru
66. World Bank Policy Research Working Paper 2150. Martin Ravallhon and Michael Lokshin, *Who Wants to Redistribute?* (The World Bank Development Research Group, Poverty and Human Resources, July 1999).
67. Unless otherwise stated, the main reference for data here is Ludmilla Maksimova, *Pharmaceutical Market in Russia* (Washington: US Department of Trade, 1997). See also Minkevich, op. cit.
68. See www.webapteka.ru for the members of the exchange.
69. President, Vladimir Bryntsalov. Based in Moscow, the company had eight subsidiaries by 2002 and had a strong network in Chita, Primorskii Krai, and elsewhere.
70. The programme was designed to help investment in the production of US GMP-quality essential drugs.
71. The investment ran to about US $5 million in 2002 and the plant focused on cardiovascular drugs.
72. The investment was about US $34 million and focused on cardiovascular, gastrointestinal, and anti-infection drugs. 75 per cent of the capital was US, 25 per cent Russian.
73. Information on the corporate structure of Russian textile companies shows the strength of these organizations. Rostekstil controlled 415 textile companies by 2002, and sharpened its hold through acquisition of shares (in companies such as Reutvo Manufactura). Konteks (a major Russian cotton importer) took over controlling shares in the Kamyshin Gin Mill in the Volgograd region and the

Vogzhanov Gin Mill in Tver during 1998–9, to form a 'holding'. Both Rostekstil and Konteks were acting as investors in these cases (in Konteks' case an investment of $10 million for renovation was predicted).

Consortiums emerged in the flax industry, uniting flax producing enterprises, flax deep processing plants, machine-building plants, and companies focused on research and development and sales. Linking enterprises varied: in the Volga region, a Flax Growers Association; in Perm, the consortium Uralsky Lyen; in Kurgan the financial and industrial group Zauralsky Lyen; and in Omsk the consortium Sibirskty Lyen. In Altai, the Biysk Flax Plant set up a raw material producer unit, buying up the land of various bankrupt agencies. 30 spinning mills in St. Petersburg and the north-western region formed the Linum complex, and 16 textile enterprises formed the financial and industrial group Vladimirskiy Lyen.

74. Oleg Miliukov, '*Trudnoe vyzdrovlenie*', in *Rossiiskii Eksporter*, no. 8, 2000, pp. 10–12.
75. Basic updated details of the history of the 'metkombinaty' are to be found in Denis Prokonenko, '*Bol'shaia Troika I Drugie*', *Nezavisimaia Gazeta*, no. 18, 26 December 2000 (*Politekonomika* supplement). Earlier articles in the newspaper's supplements and in *Finansovye Izvestiia* provide snapshots of the history. Among the metal giants, after privatization, management control was either through direct acquisition of shares, or through acquisition by companies formed for the purpose. Hence, in the Magnitogorsk case, command was maintained through Magnitogorskaia Stal'; in the case of Novoliptetsk, it was managed through the Rumel'ko company; and in the case of the Cherpovets kombinat, a series of enterprises bought up the majority shares. See D. Prokonenko, '*Po Puti kontsentratsii*', in the same issue of the paper, which shows the comparative authority existing management was able to maintain.

    Prokonenko points out that a series of 'holding companies' had an eye on the steel and light metal industry and bought into the metakombinaty. The lead activists here included Vladimir Potanin and the main figures who ensured concentration in the smaller units in steel production in the Urals were Alexander Abramov and Oleg Boiko through their company, Evrazmetal, and Iskander Makhmudov. The latter worked closely with regional governors to effect major changes of management in various units: the Kachkanarsk Kombinat 'Vanadii', the Western Siberian Metallurgical Kombinat, the Kuznetsk Metallurgical Kombinat and the Nizhnetagil'sk metkombinat.
76. *Steel-Makers Come to Their Senses* (Zoya Kaika, *Vedomosti* 24/5/02). At issue is the Comprehensive Steel Agreement signed with the USA in 1999, which involved, among others, the four biggest steel companies already mentioned: OAO Severstal, Novolipetsk iron-and-steel works, Magnitogorsk iron-and-steel. The Comprehensive was linked to a further Agreement on Hot-Rolled Coils. Here, the Americans stopped anti-dumping proceedings against Russian hot rolled stock, while restricting its supplies by annual quotas. And in

exchange, Russians agreed to limit export of various steel products under the Comprehensive Agreement. The various treaties did not, however, prevent sanctions in March 2002 on Russia as much as Europe. This led to threats to withdraw from the agreement.

It became clear thereafter, that Russia was incapable of making such threats count, since her units were still dealing with limited margins, and could not afford to make losses as would be incurred if the hot-rolled coils treaty was scrapped. Hence, although Russian Economic Ministry personnel waved the flag, Novolipetsk ISW deputy general director Andrei Petrosyan went on record saying that the US domestic steel prices had started to grow in the second quarter of 2002, and that Russia had a renewed opportunity to supply hot rolled stock to the United States which should not be lost. According to Petrosyan, if price increases continued, Russians would deliver to the USA 600,000 tons of steel during 2002, and earn around $120 million. Petrosyan, hence, was against quitting the Comprehensive Agreement, since it would mean anti-dumping steps against hot coils would lead to an immediate start of anti-dumping proceedings.

77. The companies provide a good example of a tussle among entrepreneurs, the government, local managers, and shareholders of different sorts. The example is illustrative of the chaos into which the machine tools industry could lapse at this time, and a thorough account was provided by Dimitri Butrin in *The Russian Journal*, 12 April 2002. Each unit had lateral links with various companies, creating a basic picture of complexity. This could be used by competing factions in the struggle for authority. In the case of this aviation sector, the government was determined to keep a firm hold while operating through financial industrial groups (such as Gazprom), and the full panoply of shareholders' meetings.
78. The Moscow Oblast group, made up of the Elektrostal Heavy Machine-Building Plant (EZTM), Elemash and the Podolsk Machine-Building Plant was one such group.
79. Simon Clarke, Peter Fairbrother, Vadim Borisov and Peter Bizyukov, 'The Privatization of Industrial Enterprises in Russia: Four Case Studies', *Europe Asia Studies*, vol. 46, no. 4, 1994. See also Oleg Khakhordin and Theodore P. Gerber, 'Russian Directors' Business Ethic: A Study of Industrial Enterprises in St. Petersburg, 1993', in *Europe Asia Studies*, vol. 46, no. 7, 1994. Andrei Kuznetsov, 'Economic Reforms in Russia: Enterprise Behaviour as an Impediment to Change', *Europe Asia Studies*, vol. 46. no. 6, 1994.
80. Kabalina (ed.), op. cit. Supportive literature on the Russian side is the work of I. Boeva, T. Dolgopiatova and V. Shironin, *Gosudarsvennye predpriiatiia v 1991-92 gg.: ekonomicheskie problemy I povedeniie* (Moscow: Institut Ekonomicheskoi Politiki, 1992), T. Dolgopiatova and I. Evseeva, 'Ekonomicheskoe povedenie promyshennykh predpriiatii v perekhodnoi ekonomike' in *Voprosy ekonomiki*, no. 8, 1994, T.G. Dolgopiatova, *Rossiiske predpriiatiia v perekhodnoi ekonomike:*

ekonomicheskoie problemy I povedenie (Moscow: Delo Ltd., 1995). See also other interesting perspectives in I. Gurkov, 'Strategiia vyzhivaniia promyshlennykh predpriiatii v novykh uslovkiiakh', *Voprosy Ekonomiki*, no. 6, 1995, and E. Belianova, 'Motivatsiia I povedenie rossiiskikh predpriatii', in *Voprosy Ekonomiki*, no. 6, 1995.

81. At the beginning of the 2000s, 46 per cent of Russians were chronically ill or disabled—which included some section of the population that was retired (19 per cent) though the two groups did not wholly overlap. So half of the population had health problems of a regular nature, and this meant a large number of families ran with this burden as well as the burden of adaptation to a fast-changing economy. Significantly, 65 per cent of the population lived in areas where the air was bound to cause problems in the long run (according to Ministry of Health data).

    Some help was given to deal with all this by the federal government and by local governments. Various sections of the population received free drugs and health care: war and Chernobyl veterans, and a number of groups of disabled people. Some got drugs free for specific ailments –those with cancer, post-heart attack problems, diabetes, AIDs. However, when the cost of treatment (and medicine) went beyond a point where the hospital and the drug provider knew that the state would not pay, treatment was not provided, and the patient had to fall back on his/her own resources.

    Inevitably, the country witnessed mortality rates getting worse. Between 1991 and 1995, the rate rose by 31.6 per cent and life expectancy fell by four years (to 65 in 1995), while mortality in the more active section of the population rose by 60 per cent in the same period. Mortality rate stood at 14.4 per cent in 1996 compared with 10.5 in the EU. The basic information here is provided by the sources that deal with pharmaceutical products.

82. Kablanina, op. cit., p. 56.
83. V. Mar'ianovskii, 'The Russian Economic Mentality', in *Russian Social Science Review*, vol. 38, no. 4, 1997, pp. 34–7. For a broader perspective, see E. Maiminas, 'The Russian Socioeconomic Genotype', in ibid., pp. 18–33.
84. Igor V. Kukolev, 'The Formation of the Business Elite', in *Russian Social Science Review*, vol. 38, no. 4, 1997, pp. 62–82.
85. V. Gimpel'son, 'Novoe rossiiskoe predprinimatel'stvo: istochniki formirovanie I strategii sotsial'nogo razvitiia', in *MEIMO*, no. 6, 1993.
86. See Alexei Byelov, 'Who Owns Russia: Russia's Machine Building Industry', *The Russian Journal*, 15 March 2002.
87. A. Gurov, *Krasnaia Mafiia* (Samotsvet, MIKO, 1998) deals with the early history of the mafia in the USSR. Information on the mafia is available in a special information sheet of *BBC News 1998*, though the best accounts are by the late Pavel Khlebnikov, who provided a good resume of his research in *Krestnyi otets kremlisa: Boris Berezovskii* (Moscow: Detektiv Press, 2001).
88. The Chechens were linked by their 'Obshchina'—or Community—where

there are several 'clans', based on regional and personal divisions within the Community. The Central was the most powerful under Lechi the Bearded (Borodatyi). Together, before they moved into business, the bands had great influence in the use of Russia as a transmission point for the movement of contraband in hard drugs from the Golden Triangle to Europe and the US.

89. Khlebnikov, op. cit.

CHAPTER 3

Indo–Russian Relations After 1991: Trade and Business

India's economic relations with the Russian Federation, which came into existence as a sovereign state in December 1991, cannot be easily compared with the Indo–Soviet relationship of previous decades. But given that the Federation declared itself the successor that would inherit the USSR's international responsibilities, and since Russia occupied the bulk of the territory of the USSR, it was natural to talk in terms of comparisons and argue that trade declined sharply when statistics were evaluated.

Undoubtedly, economic relations between the two countries became uncertain in the extreme. This was due to the chaos in Russia, but it was also linked to poor relations between New Delhi and Moscow. In January 1992, the Government of India and Indo–Soviet friendship were firmly linked in Russian public circles with the USSR and its foreign and economic policies. No attempt had been made by officials (or anyone, for that matter[1]) in India to deal with the democratic resistance to the CPSU. The Ambassador in Moscow, Alfred Gonzalves, erred in August 1991 in his advice to New Delhi that the Yanaev putsch would succeed; the Narasimha Rao government built on the mistake when it equivocated concerning whom to support during the attempted coup.[2] Inevitably, in the first six months of 1992, the Embassy was in a state of semi-ostracism in Moscow, although personal contacts between individual members of staff and highly placed officials in Russian government continued to be of some importance. The interest in Moscow in the West, as well as the preoccupation with the 'new abroad' (the republics of the CIS) made the lack of interest in India even greater: a point well shown by Andrei Kozyrev's overall disinterest in the country.

Vladimir Lukin and other leaders among 'democratic' politicians, though, advised some demarche towards India—not least because of the gains Russia stood to make from favourable arrangements regarding India's debts to the former Soviet Union. J.N. Dixit, India's Foreign Secretary at the time, remembers a discussion with Yegor Gaidar, Russia's Finance Minister, and 'prime mover' in the first Yeltsin Cabinet post-disintegration, where Gaidar pointed out that if India remembered that the Russian Federation was not the Soviet Union, a useful and profitable relationship would emerge. Pro-India lobbies existed among the old Soviet intelligentsia, the FTOs, important enterprises and the banned Russian Communist Party (which had authority in the regions despite its weakness in central government).

With time, interactions between functionaries and statesmen of the two sides drew sections of the Yeltsin administration into an interest in Indian trade; and scientific institutions in Russia took advantage of the interactions to develop plans for cooperation with bodies in India. The tendency persisted under the Putin administration after January 2000. Trade relations stabilized owing to the efforts of agencies of the Government of India to establish a clear financial and economic relationship with the Russian Federation. Entrepreneurial initiative from non-resident Indians in Russia—associated with the names of Shiv Khemka, Sujit Singh, and Sudhir Gupta—supported the trend; as did a major strike into the Russian market by Indian pharmaceutical companies.

Officials and statesmen saw the relationship independently of Indo–Soviet friendship. Spokepersons for the relationship referred to the achievements of the past, but they were more inclined to follow the description given during A.B. Vajpayee's visit to Moscow (2001) by A.P. Losyukov, Deputy Foreign Minister of the RF. This description spoke of mutual commitments to 'democracy', 'reform', and 'common interests'.

> Our relations with India have traditionally evolved in an upward-moving direction. We have never had any serious conflict and controversy. Moreover, it would be justified to note the coincidence of the geopolitical interests and in principle, the mutually reinforcing national interests of our states when they come into contact. In this specific sense, the Russian-Indian relationship may be called unique. Its stability and steadfastness as regards conjunctural fluctuations have stood the test of time in very many turns in the political life in both countries and in the course of complicated changes in the international arena. Both countries adhere to democratic principles of development and they are mutually interested in ensuring a favorable external environment and internal stability for the sake of social and economic reform undertaken in their countries.[3]

As had occurred in the late Soviet era, different assumptions often guided the two sides as they came to an understanding of each other. In India, perspectives were guided by a self-perception that took its bearings in notions of the country's status as a 'developing' economy with firm foundations in market practices and the legal awareness that went with such practices—as well as the possibility of graduation to a status as a 'developed' economy with the levels of per capita GDP normal in other countries of the group. In Russia, priorities were set by self-perception that dealt with the compulsions of an economy in transition from socialism to capitalism—with references to changes in Eastern Europe and the PRC for comparison.[4] Deliberations concerning the future led, in India's case, to direct membership of the World Trade Organization and in the Russian case to protracted negotiations that have still not been completed. However, despite these differences, sympathies of the past and a mutual sense of being peripheries in global growth—as well as awareness of economic strengths—led to regular investigations of how best to work for mutual benefit.

The economic relationship developed distinct contours. Indian PSUs provided Russian public corporations and new enterprises with business opportunities. Indian businessmen established formidable networks in the RF, and Indo–Russian relations enjoyed a degree of social acclaim and status. Trade figures, though, were unchanging (and unimpressive when compared with Russia–US/India–US and Russia–China/India–China trade). Indian entrepreneurs in the Federation kept a close eye on international opportunities as much as on Russia, an important act of caution given the state of the Russian economy. Uncertainty regarding where trade would go was compounded by the self-effacing attitude of the state in Russia and India where economic policy was concerned. Functionaries were unhappy to play a role in the promotion of the Indo-Russian relationship that went beyond the formation of ground rules and the organization of committee meetings. Regular work by Indian bureaucrats to sustain and develop trade and an economic relationship was not the upshot of any agenda set up in New Delhi for sustained governmental activity in this sphere.

OFFICIAL POLICY

In fact, in what happened, governmental initiatives to set a new dispensation in place after 1991 were prompted by a factor outside standard commerce: the insistent demand from the Indian armed forces for a framework that allowed the purchase and import of spare parts for India's stock of Soviet-era hardware. Later, N.N. Vohra, Defence Secretary in January 1992, was to describe a desperate time when the GOI had to form a careful network to find spares for the Indian armed forces because of the lack of a relationship with Russia.[5] True, economic policy was also driven by the abysmal state of India's foreign exchange reserves, a situation that required the promotion of exports wherever possible. But Russia was hardly the best market at this time to generate steady foreign exchange earnings.

To achieve these limited official goals, a new basis for financial transactions was essential, given the lack of interest on both sides in the old rupee–rouble arrangement that came down to barter in goods and services. Such arrangements, anyway, were not in accord with IMF advice that claimed ascendancy in both Russia and India; and the arrangements became impossible with the growing crisis of the Russian currency.

Arrangement of the Rupee–Rouble Exchange Rate

Official policy in Delhi and Moscow initially focused on how payments were to be made for imports and exports. In the case of arms spare parts purchases or sales and direct enterprise-to-enterprise links between India and Russia, the crisis in the rupee–rouble arrangement made business difficult[6] in the months immediately after Soviet disintegration. Hitherto all trade had been handled in terms of rates fixed under inter-governmental protocols where the rate was decided by mutual agreement. Such a rate was not strictly in accord with the rates the rouble and the rupee commanded against convertible currencies, but it was not wholly unconnected. The collapse of the rouble's value on international markets made respect for protocols impossible. The monetarist preferences of the Gaidar government in the post-1991 state of affairs in Russia did not indicate the possibility of a return to old rates or a desire in Moscow to come to equivalent arrangements.

The problem might have been resolved by the summary use of dollar-equivalents of rouble and rupee for commerce, if the issue of India's Soviet era debts, which the Russian government took over, was not linked to a decision on the exchange rate. Here there was an impasse. The prevailing value of the rouble, Indian commentators argued, necessarily affected repayments of the pre-1992 debt. In the past, the USSR had adjusted the debt when the Indian rupee devalued: and Russians were required to follow the principles they themselves had established. Russians contended that value for value must be borne in mind—and that too past value; for this had been the basis of the old rate, not merely international equivalence. The Russian Finance Minister, Yegor Gaidar, who did not anticipate a steep decline in the rouble's international position, hoped to use Russia's takeover of the Soviet debt in a meaningful manner; and he was not willing to treat this as a mere political gesture. With time, as privatization became drawn out in Russia, government agencies in Moscow became insolvent and the value of the rouble deteriorated further, sound use of the debt became more important—even if it meant nothing in the case of Iraq, Ethiopia, and Cuba, who could pay little. On the Indian side, on the other hand, given the financial crisis of 1991, officials were keen to remove all possible pressures on the rupee; and reduction of the amounts involved in the Indo–Soviet debt was one means.

Whatever the compulsions in each case, clear agreement was necessary for future commerce: for without it, difficulties with the Russian bureaucracy were bound to occur whenever Indian commerce attracted official attention—a major likelihood given the prevailing reorganization of the Russian economy. Purchases of spare parts for armaments could be affected, since such purchases required Russian government clearance. On both counts, businessmen were worried about a possible intensification of the impasse; or a resolution which would make unprofitable any deal they may get into. They were reluctant to undertake business with any degree of vigour; and public sector collaboration was even more difficult. Aware that dealing with the debt was work that would come to them easily, Indian entrepreneurs fixed their attention on the repayments issue even though they faced everyday compulsions to get back to trade in some other form.[7]

Various agreements that followed the visit of State Secretary Gennadiy Burbulis (in February 1992) did not clarify the picture. They merely allowed for both trade in convertible currencies and 'bilateral trade', based on India's debt to the former Soviet Union, without a solution to quarrels over the exchange rate to be applied to debt. Both countries agreed on new principles for a working exchange rate for the rouble in existing conditions on 1 April 1992; and, in accordance with the Agreement on Trade and Economic Cooperation that followed (signed on 4 May 1992), allowance was made for 'payments and settlements . . . in freely convertible currencies'. The Agreement was followed by a MOU that set out the banking procedures, including the designation of the Vneshtorgbank (BFTR) as the sole agency with which LCs could be opened in the case of exports from India. These arrangements became the basis of a temporary regime of trade, until further clarifications followed concerning the exchange rate to be applied to the debt. The regime was of limited value for furthering anything more than speculative business given the wild fluctuations in dollar rates; and confusion pervaded the interpretations of even this limited agreement. LCs of this time, for example, were often taken on banks other than the Vneshtorgbank[8] (BFTR), since the latter divided its responsibilities among 'banks maintaining the accounts of the BFTR'. This took place despite the fact that the prevailing agreements made it clear that 'no other bank in the Russian Federation shall open a Letter of Credit covering exports from India' and that 'issue of any other documents of payment will not be eligible for the settlement'.[9]

The lack of vitality in trade during this period is indicated by interim attempts by both governments to inject life into it. On the Indian side, as a result of the Agreement of 4 May 1992, the government extended technical credit to Russia of US $285 million, with the right to use US $85 million for the purchase of tea, coffee, tobacco, and spices.[10] On the Russian side, on 17 September 1992, an agreement was signed that the RF would provide India with credit in Special Drawing Rights to help long-term projects in technical cooperation and for the purchase of equipment. Ten per cent down payment (in US $) in each case was to be followed by a seven-year pay-off (again in US currency). The funds received in instalments by Moscow would be used to settle payment for goods and services in India and would not be repatriated.[11]

Such measures did not diminish the importance of the main issue. But it took until the end of 1992 before there was an adjustment of the rupee–rouble exchange rate to be applied to the Indian debt, paving the way for a fundamental resumption of amicable commercial relations. This occurred after an exchange of letters between the Minister of Commerce (India) and the Minister for Foreign Economic Relations (Russia) on 28 November 1992, and a final agreement between the Prime Minister of India and the President of Russia in New Delhi on 28 January 1993.[12] By these arrangements (and by negotiations that followed), a sum of about Rs. 3,000 crore was made available to the RF annually until 2005 as payment for debts accumulated before 1991, and India and Russia agreed that fresh trade would be handled in accordance with the exchange rate commanded by rupee and rouble in freely fluctuating currencies. The annual repayment would be deposited in a special account with the RBI, and the Russian government could call upon it to pay for imports of selected goods by FTOs acting on behalf of government agencies or independently by government itself.[13] Traders and manufacturers in India were expected to lobby agencies/government in Russia to 'push' their products; and it was also understood that the Russian government could do with the products as it wished within the Federation, should it not wish to pass such products on to its own departments (e.g. hospitals under the Ministry of Health).

The arrangement, which established a rate for the debt-rouble that was vastly higher than its prevailing international value, essentially provided a subsidy for Indian exports to the Russian Federation, although the thinking of the time represented it as a legal necessity or a means of ensuring bilateral goodwill to assure regular supplies of military hardware and spare parts. Accounts of the arrangements of 1993 normally neglect this aspect of the way the exchange rate for the debt was fixed at this time, although this was probably what prompted Montek Singh Ahluwalia to oppose the way the matter was handled.[14] Any public statement to this effect would, of course, have attracted uproar, and there was skepticism thereafter about the value of the move. Officials and businessmen who are interested in the improvement of Indo–Russian relations were to argue that the debt was a disservice to trade:[15] that debt-trade prevented Indian firms coming to terms with the realities of business in Russia. They ignored that the debt-trade was to provide the cushion on which stable Indian ventures (especially in pharmaceuticals) were to take shape at a time when few Russian companies were corporatized, Russian banks were in a shoddy state, and fluctuations in currency rates made LC business unstable. Other countries provided subsidies to their businessmen in Russia. US and European businessmen in Russia, for all their wherewithal, received assistance through USAID schemes, arrangements backed by the Freedom Support Act and strategies of the EBRD.

After the initial agreement, officials refined and reworked strategies about how the debt was to be used, and the agreement over the debt itself was streamlined. Civil servants ironed out anomalies. For example, a number of payments of the 'transition' period (before the agreement of 1993) were outstanding for some time, and had to be addressed within the framework of debt transactions.[16] This problem was settled by 1996. Again, the Russian side had to press repeatedly for attention to an important anomaly of the system of purchases under the debt until 1996 (when the matter was finally resolved): i.e. that the goods supplied under the debt arrangement were priced by India at a rate higher than the market tag on these goods in dollars. This difference in rates was deemed unfair by the Russian government.[17]

Variations in the list of goods to be supplied under the arrangement were renegotiated repeatedly, since, with time, the initial range was considered to be restrictive—a short list including soya meal, pharmaceuticals, and tea.[18] Again, difficulties in handling the debt on the Russian side[19] led to a variation in arrangements for its use. In October 1998, during a visit by Finance Minister Yashwant Sinha to Moscow, it was agreed that half of the debt would be used for the import of specific items and handled through the state. The rest would be auctioned to interested parties in the Russian Federation (a habit already begun in practice but not regularized by the two governments). Reasonable agreement also came to exist concerning some form of continuity in debt payments after 2005—when the repayments according to earlier exchange rates was to end. An amount of Rs. 9,500 crore, it was established, would be due from India in hard currency over a twenty-year period from 2005–6.[20]

Significantly, under the Putin administration (after 2000) as a result of later steps by the Russian government to withdraw benefits it granted debt-related commerce, a decline occurred towards 2002 in the advantages that rupee trade enjoyed in Russia, despite this continuous process of bilateral adjustment. For instance, although Russian authorities required payment of VAT on all imports, including those that came in under the debt trade, a convention existed until 2001 that the VAT would be paid later on goods obtained by use of the rupee debt. In practice, this payment was overlooked, and, hence, debt trade took place at a discount. Again, when the rupee was used for Russian purchases, a special discount of the order of 15 per cent was made available to the purchaser—i.e. goods were priced at a different rate when they were bought in rupees under the debt arrangement. By

2001 both conventions had ceased to exist,[21] and seeking out the rupees at BFTR auctions came to be regarded as a nuisance by companies who otherwise could arrange for purchases in hard currencies. The operation was to remain valuable to companies who were in the habit of using it, as in the case of the former FTO Medeksport, or the tea-trading organizations, but the significance of the strategy in the Russian market declined substantially by 2002.

By this time, while both governments were aware that the contribution of the debt to long-term economic collaboration could only be minimal, the debt did throw up new opportunities; and few ever took the view (occasionally expressed), that the matter should now be ignored since it was to India's advantage that the fund should not be used.[22] Debt rupees were of value to small companies who did not conduct large dollar transactions. Initiatives were taken by the ministry of commerce of the Government of India to promote small and medium business bearing this in mind, as were the efforts of Ambassadors S.K. Lamba and K. Raghunath to promote Indian trade in the Russian provinces. Only a few enterprises, however, responded to such overtures, as is clear from the later record of those who used the debt during 2002–5.

Arrangements were made to utilize the debt funds in other ways. Switch trade of sorts existed between the UK and Russia (perhaps with the concurrence of the GOI) whereby the UK dealt in the debt and was able to subsidize its coal machinery sales to the Russian mining industry. The records of these manoeuvres, though, do not specify the technical details of this arrangement—e.g. the way the details were worked out and the awareness of the GOI of what transpired. Meanwhile, methods of how to use the debt for Russian investments in India were to repeatedly be under consideration, although the later record indicates that the schemes that were involved ultimately contributed nothing to the improvement of the economic relationship between India and Russia.

The State and Indo–Russian Trade

The IRJC and Other Official bodies

Following the settlement of the exchange rate for the Soviet-era debt, the pivot, at the state level, of economic collaboration and scientific cooperation between the Russian Federation and India became the

Indo–Russian Joint Commission constituted in 1993. Equipped with numerous working groups in India and in Russia, this was the successor body to the Indo–Soviet Joint Commission. The institution worked by a routine procedure, established by previous practice: the evolution of plans based on the discussions of working groups that received suggestions from PSUs, subsequent vetting by the Commission, and final authorization by the government. In the circumstances, suggestions for MOUs were many, but in the context of privatization and dislocation in Russia, real work ran into heavy weather. Distinguished statesmen figured on both sides, but none gave the Commission their specific patronage. This was as true of those on the Russian side as on the Indian side. From 1994 to 1998, the chief Russian representative on the Commission was Anatolii Chubais, disinterested in government to government collaboration and engrossed with privatization. His successor, Yurii Maslyukov, Russian Prime Minister Evgenii Primakov's trusted deputy prime minister, was to be preoccupied with the problems of how to deal with the crisis of August 1998. On the Indian side, prominent figures such as Pranab Mukherjee were themselves concerned with problems of India's entry into the WTO, and gave routine attention to the Commission.

The bureaucracy on both sides, however, egged on by the lobbies inside and outside the state, breathed life into the work done by the Commission. Both strove hard to make public sector units and traditional arrangements prime factors in commerce; and in the decade that followed settlement of the rupee–rouble exchange rate, they stimulated the trade generated by the debt payments. This trade focused on business routed through FTOs in Russia that bought pharmaceuticals, tea, and foodstuffs on behalf of the Russian government, or deals directly handled by local governments who were given sections of the debt as part of federal grants. Officials also focused on various tie-ups between Russian ministries, FTOs, and Indian PSUs. Working groups on industry, coal, and other sectors featured some representation from the Russian or the Indian private sectors, as in the case of Kaka Benukidze, who took over Uralmash in the course of Russian privatization. Embassy officials in Moscow kept in touch with Indian entrepreneurs operating in Russia, and developed an Indian Business Association in Russia in 1994 to this end. While activity ran to keeping old channels of exchange alive, officials initiated steps to stimulate private trade through fairs, exhibitions, etc., and made piecemeal efforts to develop official contacts that might prevent

Russian legislation discriminating against Indian goods. The initiatives threw up dividends (as in the case of Ambassador Ronen Sen's long interactions with the Foreign Economic Affairs Minister Glazev). A still broader approach came with S.K. Lamba's appointment as Ambassador (1998), when a determined bid was made to create business lobbies that supported the India trade. Using a network among Russian Indologists linked to the Centre of Indian Studies of the Institute of Oriental Studies, Russian Academy of Sciences, Lamba set up meetings in Russian regions with local officials, and members of India's private sector went with him, paying their own way. The meetings threw up information concerning the requirements of regional governments, the funds at their disposal, and tenders that were being called. Lamba's initiative followed up information concerning a substantial interest in the promotion of close economic relations in the Centre for Indian Studies. The interest had manifested itself immediately after the disintegration, when the Head of the Centre, A.A. Kutsenkov—an economist who had a wide range of contacts in the Military Industrial Complex—had founded a chamber of commerce of sorts in the mid-1990s—the *Rossiiskii-Indiiskii Fond—Promyshlennaia Torgovaia Palata.*[23] A key figure in Lamba's initiative was Tatiana Shaumian, a leading scholar of Indo–Soviet and Indo–Chinese relations, one of the leading figures of the Centre of Indian Studies (later its Head), and one of M.S. Gorbachev's advisors on Indian affairs. Shaumian was (and continued to be) a figure whose personality and family background imparted its own prestige to whatever she did. She was the granddaughter of the Baku Commissar, Stephan Shaumian and the daughter of Lev Shaumian, one of the editors of the Great Soviet Encyclopaedia and a close friend of A.A. Arzumenian and others associated with the Soviet Central Committee.

From the side of the Government of the Russian Federation, except in the case of the arms deals, assiduous steps were taken to promote Indo–Russian trade only after Yevgenii Primakov became external affairs minister (1995) and later prime minister. The key figure here was the Russian ambassador in New Delhi, A. Kadakin. For initiatives, the Russian effort was able to call on a valuable range of property that the Federation inherited from Soviet days. This was partly concentrated in the hands of government and partly in the hands of the Houses of Culture, which fell under the direction of Valentina Tereshkova's *Roszrubezhtsentr*[24]—the successor to the old Houses of Friendship organization—which acted as an international autonomous body, but which was dependent on the Russian government for funds. Although this was a fraction of the property that had been devoted to Soviet-sponsored activities, it was able to provide opportunities for easy access to translation and interpretation, as well as space for accommodation in India.

Quasi-official Bodies and Associations Working with State Sponsorship

An important government channel that provided stimulus to private Indo–CIS (including Indo–Russian) commerce, throughout the decade, was the Indo–CIS Chamber of Commerce, even after the death of its great figure, Manubhai Shah, in 2000. Wholly unlike other Chambers of Commerce, and set up (in 1985), to promote private trade with the former Soviet Union the Chamber was not a representative of a fixed commercial interest. Rather, it was almost the equivalent of a semi-government agency which worked *in tandem* with sections of the private sector that had dealings with the USSR.

Throughout the post-disintegration period, the Chamber's activities were extensive. It arranged visits of delegations from Belorussia, the Ukraine, Russia, and the Central Asian Republics to India and vice versa. It organized fairs in Delhi. It maintained a regular newsletter in which it attempted to provide information concerning customs and tariffs. Its members included the leading entrepreneurs of the region (including the Khemkas), and it became a standard reference point for CIS companies wishing to do business with India and vice versa. True, with time, the Confederation of Indian Industry (again with some encouragement from the Ministry of Commerce), FICCI (which has its own CIS research unit), along with major bodies dealing with Small and Medium Enterprises took over some of the standard activities of the Chamber: but this did not decrease its vigour, which was significant for Indo–Russian commerce. FICCI, for instance, established a Joint Business Council with the Russian Federation for Commerce and Industry soon after disintegration: but it remained inactive during 1997–2003. The tie-up between the CII and the Russian Union for Commerce and Industry was also lacklustre. Hence, although the FICCI and the CII were often the first point of reference for large organizations that sought a foothold in India, as was the Russian Trade Office, information about business prospects in the RF came as much from the Indo–CIS as these organizations. Smaller enterprises referred often to the Indo–CIS Chamber, as did CIS enterprises outside Russia.

THE PATTERN OF TRADE AND THE ECONOMIC RELATIONSHIP

TRADE AND ITS STATISTICS

The statistics that chart the Indo–Russian trade that evolved against this background are a problem. UN Comtrade statistics in dollars, and WTO trade statistics in dollars do not exist in web format prior to 1996. Russian and Indian statistics do not coincide—partly since, unlike India, Russian data includes defence equipment and follows the calendar year. For the purposes of this study, UN Comtrade US statistics for the period after 1996, in Table 1 of the Appendix, and statistics (in US dollars) of the Director General of Commercial Intelligence and Statistics (Government of India) [DGCIS] for Indo–Russian trade (Table 2 of the Appendix), have been used to strengthen overall impressions available from rupee figures available in DGCIS figures (given below).

These figures present the following profile of trade. The nodal points of the commerce (Appendix Table 2) were: in the case of India's imports from Russia, fertilizer, newsprint, metal goods and machinery; in the case of Russian imports from India, foodstuffs, pharmaceuticals and ready-made garments. At first glance when compared with the last years of Soviet rule, figures for total trade appear to show a sharp downturn that was never reversed. To solely draw such a picture from them, however, is clearly untoward, even if it is the habit of reputable newspaper reports, official statements, Chamber of Commerce handouts, and Indian scholarship.[25] First, there is a crucial lacuna: there is no mention of services. In a situation where both sides benefited from Indian demand for servicing and modernizing of equipment installed under older arrangements, this is a crucial shortcoming of the data.

Important perspectives on the trade statistics emerge if we take note of specific aspects of the data for non-Russian CIS–India trade. This provides a gloss on the figures for Indo–Russian trade.

On the face of it, the figures for imports from and exports to Russia before and after 1991 indicate fall in trade. But clearly figures for the

TABLE 3.1: OF INDO-RUSSIAN TRADE 1989-2000

(Figures rounded off to the nearest crore of rupees)

	Imports into India from Russia	Exports from India to Russia
1989–90	2037	4458
1991–2	1796	4040
1992–3	737 (CIS)	1756 (CIS)
1993–4	806	2036
1994–5	1584	2534
1995–6	2864	3495
1996–7	2230	2880
1997–8	2501	3541
1998–9	2300	2975
1999–2000	2700	4108
2000–1	2364	4061
2001–2	2553	3807

Source: *Statistics of the Foreign Trade of India, by Countries and Commodities*, vol. 1 (Exports), vol. 2 (Imports). (Director General of Commercial Intelligence and Statistics, Ministry of Commerce, Government of India). Annual Figures as published in March.

Note: Crore of rupees – ten million rupees.

TABLE 3.2: EXPORTS FROM INDIA TO CIS STATES OTHER THAN RUSSIA

(to the nearest crore of rupees)

	1992–3**	1993–4	1994–5	1995–6	1996–7	1997–8	1998–9	1999–2000	2000–1	2001–2
Ukraine		414	203	215	160	226	147	184	323	387
Belarus		*	*	*	97	13	6	10	18	10
Moldova		*	*	*	2	3	4	3	4	9
Uzbekistan		5	22	25	29	65	54	43	43	31
Tajikistan		3	Under1	16	2	4	2	10	16	5
Turkmenistan		5	2	4	5	6	8	24	12	21
Kazakhstan		8	26	29	16	56	160	117	229	218
Kyrgyzstan		*	*	*	*	*	*	59	80	52
Latvia	1	7	19	21	15	25	40	56	63	29
Lithuania		2	4	4	13	8	15	42	40	31
Estonia	1	3	8	3	11	11	22	28	15	19
Armenia		Under1	Under1	Under1	2	4	Under1	3	6	6
Azerbaijan		Under1	Under1	Under1	2	11	17	31	53	50
Georgia		Under1	Under1	4	4	7	2	6	14	40

TABLE 3.3: IMPORTS INTO INDIA FROM CIS STATES OTHER THAN RUSSIA

(to the nearest crore of rupees)

	1992–3**	1993–4	1994–5	1995–6	1996–7	1997–8	1998–9	1999–2000	2000–1	2001–2
Ukraine		335	628	113	433	668	571	661	595	796
Belarus		*	*	*	4	Under 1	1	67	9	23
Moldova		*	*	*	Under 1	Under 1	*	*	Under 1	Under 1
Uzbekistan		4	26	36	9	10	70	56	48	82
Tajikistan		2	6	11	3	*	11	10	2	6
Turkmenistan		7	33	9	1	Under 1	Under 1	16	5	9
Kazakhstan		7	27	27	45	133	523	58	64	35
Kyrgyzstan		*	*	*	*	*	*	7	20	2
Latvia	*	24	5	23	28	51	47	3	20	4
Lithuania	*	2	Under 1	3	2	1	1	44	5	5
Estonia	*		9	Under 1	Under 1	Under 1	3	4	2	31
Armenia		*	Under 1	Under 1	Under 1	Under 1	Under 1	Under 1	3	2
Azerbaijan		*	Under 1	Under 1	Under 1	Under 1	17	2	Under 1	1
Georgia		*	Under 1	Under 1	Under 1	*	23	Under 1	3	Under 1

Source: *Statistics of the Foreign Trade of India, by Countries and Commodities*, vol. 1 (Exports), vol. 2 (Imports). (Director General of Commercial Intelligence and Statistics, Ministry of Commerce, Government of India). Annual Figures as published in March.

Notes: * No figure given

** Gross CIS statistics only available (excluding Russia, Lithuania, Latvia and Estonia)

period before 1991 deal with the Soviet Union as a whole (and include re-exports to Eastern Europe), while those for the subsequent period consider only one state of the USSR. The decline is less sharp if figures for trade with the FSU as a whole are borne in mind. Important also, all Russian export to India was conducted in hard currency or hard currency prices; and the huge fall in the value of the rouble against the dollar (from 0.5 in 1989 to 5,000 in 1995) and the *comparatively low* level of costs and prices in Russia implies that the low figure masks a high real value to Russia, as well as a high level of rouble trading and manufacturing activity. Even if we consider the fall in the rate of the rupee against the dollar (the value fell by over 100 per cent during the decade), the volume of goods were significant. The bulk of imports from India, meanwhile, was mainly made within the framework of debt repayment, and amounted to a considerable gain to the Federation (even if there were many scandals associated with its use).

True, a comparison with the Russian Federation's overall trade figures indicates that the India trade did not play a substantial part. Major trading partners were the United States. Western Europe, and, most important, the other CIS states. But notably, most of the exports to the West were of natural gas and petroleum or petroleum products: which, even if they made up 40 per cent of Russian foreign earnings, only spoke for one industry. Mechanical goods, manufactures and chemical items ranked low in trade with the west, at a time when these industries were those most affected by depression. On the other hand, exports to India (Appendix Table 2) at this time were on average, a more impressive proportion of the exports from the Russian Federation in these goods (steel, electrical goods, machinery, fertilizer, etc.) during the 1992–2000 period: an important indicator that the Indian customer may have been a more important factor than expected in a network that vouchsafed the survival of many industries. The statistics for imports from and to India also indicate that Indian manufacturers made important inroads into the Russian market in crucial areas in which they had had begun to make only a small showing in the past, pharmaceuticals especially.

Clearly the 'discourse' on decline in Indian writing comes from the overall change in the position of the former Soviet Union and the Russian Federation as India's trading partners, and the unstable characteristics of the trade (which led to periodic alarm). The increase in the significance of markets in the United States, Europe, and South-East Asia in India's external trade was responsible for the change in the status of CIS and Russian trade, however, rather than a decline in the volume and value of trade with the former Soviet Union. 'Decline' of trade in the strict sense, it must be stressed, must also be traced to changes which predate disintegration, when links between the public sector and Soviet industry were already in the doldrums. Again, the Gulf War (and the subsequent containment of Iraqi commerce) brought to an end an important commerce in oil and the end of special arrangements between Iraq and the USSR to supply India and other countries. Finally, with regard to vicissitudes in the Russian market, as the Tables on the commodity-wise breakdown of the trade indicates, there were wild fluctuations in the off-take of different goods, in the case of both exports and imports. This followed directly from the unsteady character of the Russian market, where consumer patterns were still to be firmly established, and where problems of capital and administrative interest (sometimes organized crime) often interfered with business. But the problems posed by this must be balanced against the fact that after 1991, alternative areas of commerce were opened up, which established a certain minimum in the trade. Even if the fate of these opportunities was uncertain, their existence could not be discounted.

The New Economic Relationship

Arguably, in fact, a new relationship emerged between the Federation and India which depended on the past, but which proceeded in a new direction. The range of this relationship is not easily established through the standard data, and its contours are best understood through a record of economic activity where the statistics are only a part of the picture.

CORPORATE STRATEGIES IN INDO–RUSSIAN TRADE

The Sample and the Main Trends in Trade

State corporations and private companies followed a number of routes as they put together the commerce and economic cooperation that is indicated by general figures and impressions. A common denominator in early years (1993–8) was the resort to debt-operations where Indian companies processed orders for FTOs such as Medeksport or Soiuzkhimeksport, who made purchases on behalf of the Russian government. These imports were pivotal to official policy—as for instance the maintenance of the public health system in the case of the purchases by Medeksport. Again, PSUs in India worked with the Russian private/state corporations and front organizations (often transformed FTOs) for the update of equipment and plant. Beyond this, how far the approach of companies coincided or differed can be established from material on the nature of corporate behaviour derived from a close examination of the 87 odd companies registered with the Embassy of India in Moscow (1998–2001) (Appendix, Table 4). Further data on other companies is available in the press and in the Newsletter of the Indo–CIS Chamber of Commerce; and additional information was also gathered during fieldwork in the Russian Federation.

The material fleshes out the story of how companies made trade once the guiding hand of the planned economy was gone. It shows how for some entrepreneurs such trade was part of international strategies where India and Russia were two spokes in a larger wheel of commerce where the work of the IRGC was an opportunity rather than a guideline. This is true of Indian entrepreneurs such as Ravinder Chamaria and Pramod Agarwal, who operated in such a manner as standard practice, well before 1992. The opportunities provided by the debt-trade and the chaos in the Federation paved the way for others to take this path—this time with close reference to the working groups set up by the IRGC. This was the route taken by the 'giants' of the Indian pharmaceutical industry, and similar enterprising concerns who set out to establish a foothold in the 'emerging market' of Russia and the CIS. Significantly, although the businesses treated these ventures independently of operations in Western Europe and the United States, company representatives in Russia agreed that interests in those markets had an impact on the strategy of the company as a whole, and led to ups and downs in interest in the Russia business. This followed from the chaotic circumstances of the transition. Almost all Indian entrepreneurs had to brave the vicissitudes of the Russian market, facing major difficulties on three major issues—warehousing, customs regimes, and shipment—even as their treatment of these indicated a host of problems that were contingent.[26] Organized crime was an additional problem: but business representatives are not keen to name names here.

Major exceptions exist to these standard methods of Indian intervention in the Russian market. One method was the direct use of the Federation as a hub of operations—a novel route that was followed most spectacularly by the Khemkas' Sun Group. The Khemka case had major spin-off benefits for India in that it led to the Sun Group's opening investment operations in New Delhi. Such ventures were a major contrast to those of Soviet times when the initiative was impossible until late perestroika. The Sun enterprise was probably the most remarkable case at the time of an Indian group, with feet firmly in India, developing formidable operations abroad that went well beyond a specific contract job. The second off-beat method of Indian intervention in the Russian market was the initiative of the ONGC to support oil and natural gas exploration in Sakhalin—an initiative that involved financial outlays from India.

PATTERNS OF COMPANY BEHAVIOUR

The following forms of corporate behaviour are noticeable from the data.

a. *Some Russian enterprises used links forged during the perestroika, and before, to establish business contacts or make arrangements for joint ventures, using standard FTOs, and connections at official levels.* A good example was Elektrosila of Leningrad (St. Petersburg), a traditional supplier of equipment to India which attempted to extend its direct links with Indian producers both within and outside the FTO network. However, the enterprise became involved early in the boardroom wars of the new Russia and the complications of privatization; and its interest in the Indian market was not to be sustained. Other companies attempted to work directly in India, using their established links. Immediately after disintegration, they or their representatives established contacts with former partners either through the Russian Trade Office (based at the Russian Embassy) or directly.[27] Information exists about repeated visits to India by Russian delegations in the early years after disintegration. In the case of Elektrosila, quick links were made with the Thermax Corporation branch in Russia, so that the latter could act as an intermediary with steel plants and machine-building units in India.

Two major FTOs who operated in India in the past and that were also quick to pick up threads post-disintegration were Technopromexport (in the power sector) and Tlazhpromexport (which dealt in heavy engineering goods, especially steel-making technology). Technopromexport reorganized itself under the new dispensation as a 'federal unitary enterprise', preserving its links with the government, and it constituted an association with some of its old customers. The organization then came into the Indian market with aplomb.[28] It figured significantly in modernization and construction at Neyveli in Tamil Nadu[29] and for units in Madhya Pradesh.[30]

Tiazhpromeksport[31] (TPE) prompted joint ventures and brokered rupee-rouble debt deals. The company quickly came to terms with disintegration and arrived at agreements with Magnitogorsk, Novolipetsk, Nizhnii Tagil Iron and Steel Works, JSC Uralmash, Irkutsktiazhmash, and the administrations of Tula, Cheliabinsk, and Tver, to undertake international trade—which included some with India. Here, TPE worked with TISCO for the import of steel into India and they also supplied regular teams of engineers to Rourkela for maintenance purposes. They were the main go-between for Russian customers who required Indian manufactured goods under debt arrangements. TPE was also to be in the bidding for some time to take over the Indian Iron and Steel Company (West Bengal), offering to use debt funds for its operations.

A number of other large firms displayed initiative and pursued old links with India. Russian companies worked with a number of coalfields—Djanjara, Talcher 15, Cobra, etc.[32] Gidroenergoprom constructed a power house on the right bank of the Bakra, and supplied equipment for units in the vicinity to the Balimela Power Plant.[33] A major initiative that came from such contacts was the formation of Romelt-SAIL (India) Pvt. Ltd. in 1997, after a long period of negotiation. This was a company established by SAIL with the Moscow Institute of Steel and Alloys, the Novolipetsk Iron and Steel Works and Amet Ltd (Moscow). It was concerned with the marketing of Romelt technology for steel mining in India and abroad, essentially working with slag to manufacture usable products.[34]

Except in the case of Tiazhpromeksport, none of these cases depended on rupee–rouble debt funds, even though all could have drawn on debt money once it was available after January 1993. Companies had to compete in Moscow for funds available to Russia, and in the hectic days of the early transition, there were no special arrangements made by the government to assist Russian companies to feel their way into ventures abroad. Even if traditional connections with officials could be used to gain advantage, debt funds were directed to immediate requirements for consumer goods—mainly tea and pharmaceuticals. Powerful 'newcomers' in Russian industry, such as the oligarch Kakha Benukidze, came to be involved in Indo–Russian trade as they bought into a traditional player which had a distinct Indian link. In Benukidze's case, this was the formidable Uralmash company centred on Ekaterinburg. But Benukidze remained a decoration on the IRGC and Uralmash made no use of debt funds for India business, a clear indication of how matters stood at the time.

Significantly, in all cases of major Russian businesses coming to India, even if debt funds did not promote the enterprise, it was the Indian public sector that was most directly involved, and public funds played their role. In the case of coal, all the units were part of the Coal India family, the pits received state grants for the Russian modernization and payment of Russian experts was covered by the trade protocol.[35] In the power sector, for instance, the National Thermal Power Corporation Ltd., the Power Finance Corporation, or state governments were crucial. Private companies were drawn in to assist (as in the case of Larsen and Toubro at Neyveli), but the work was for PSUs and there was some show of government involvement. This was the consequence of the direct connection between Russian technology and the public sector in the past, the slow rate of Indian privatization, and the poor productivity of heavy engineering units concerned with steel and coal machinery. Russian companies targeted Indian PSUs as a matter of course, and the case of new Russian entrants into India proved the point. Hence, the work of Rudgormach (a Joint Stock Company of Voronezh) showed a slightly different route of entry into the Indian market than that of Technopromeksport, but once again, the Indian public sector was involved. Rudgormach supplied machinery to surface coal units in India,[36] with a long-term perspective in view, after winning a tender for the use of World Bank funds in a competition in which the good offices of government certainly had some role.

Elsewhere, Technochim Holding (Russia) and Pigment Corporation (Russia) came to terms with Saraf Agencies (Kolkata) and Industrial Development Corporation (Orissa) to export pigment from India,[37] in a project that was certainly to be of long duration and which had local state backing. Both cases indicate the standard methods of operation of Russian business: out and out reliance on Indian partners, and, even when there was recourse to standard practices of tender, an orientation towards the public sector. Russian companies made surveys in India of various concerns (the Heavy Engineering Corporation for instance), with similar projects in mind, and similar terms.[38]

Not all Russian FTOs reorganized and preserved their stake in the Indian market, however. This was true of Exportlen, for instance, which used to do considerable jute buying; it was also true of others. Again, unlike firms such as Gidroenergoprom, new units did not make a determined bid for the Indian market, a fact recognized by all commentators and businessmen.

b. *In many areas of trade (whether debt trade or not), private Indian agents came to function as the middlemen, replacing FTOs and official agencies.* In fact, the new circumstances of commerce required a degree of international savior faire which official bodies did not have, which FTOs had not always developed, and which was often absent in the successors to FTOs, who were normally souped-up consultancy agencies that developed pretensions as 'holding companies'. The consequence was the rapid preeminence in Indo–Russian trade of Indian brokers who had been Russian traders in the past, or who had served a function as service-providers to FTOs. Such trading organizations now reached beyond the FTO circuit, preserving their connections with this old network. They themselves set up business between Indian and Russian enterprises. And, after 1997, when the debt-rupee came to be auctioned, they acted as consultants for enterprises using the debt route for trade.

The AGIO Corporation became a major actor in the Russian market in this regard. This Singapore-based trading organization of the academic-turned-entrepreneur Dharam Vir, and the Chamaria and (later) Chanderia families, ran a good number of deals in the post-1991 period, involving Indian business. The company split in 1997, but its offshoots (Agio Countertrade, Agiorus, Agio Image, etc.) and many of its operatives continued to act as traders and go-betweens (even in the defence sector). The latter-day Dubai-based tycoon, Ravinder Chamaria, was known for his exceptional savior faire during these days. He was said to have rented a dacha close to Boris Yeltsin's and entertained major officials of the Federation government, using Russian-speaking intermediaries for the purpose. The company developed an extensive network within official circles: an achievement associated with the name of Rajender Sethi—who formed his own independent enterprise after the disintegration of AGIO. Pointedly, the Company fulfilled FTO functions—making its profit from commissions and refraining from purchase of Russian business or partnership in new corporations.

The pattern repeated itself in other instances, though perhaps in a less spectacular manner. A prominent operator was Span Overseas,[39] a Pune based company which dealt in everything from plastics to wood pulp, acting as direct intermediaries for Russian producers in Archangelsk, Ust Ilimsk, and Solambala Pulp Mills. The CEO of the Company had some rough dealings with the mafia, however, and had to conduct the bulk of his operations from outside the Federation. More impressive was the Texcuna Group of companies, who ran early operations in the USSR from the 1960s. Smaller operations were associated with R. Goenka's Axiom Projects International of Calcutta, which dealt with export of bags;[40] Amtel Exports India,[41] which dealt in Software and had bases in Baroda and Singapore; Dina International,[42] based in Mumbai, and focused on pharmaceuticals. Raji Menon of MenonImpex and Menonpharma did some trading, but had to quit Russia operations after some deals turned sour. Rita Singh of Mesco was interested in trade as well as acting as a go-between for a collapsing Russian civil aviation sector which needed to sell or lease aeroplanes for non-military activity, including everything from crop spraying to short-distance executive flying. A series of scandals in India, though, ended her operations in Russia.

Thermax of Pune was an example of a standard Indian producer-exporter who moved into brokerage. A Pune based company set up by Rohinton Aga (d. 1996), Thermax specialized in chemicals, captive power, water and waste solutions, cooling, boilers, and heaters. It had established its fortune in its Indian and Russian operations before 1991, and had interests in Sri Lanka, Bangladesh, Indonesia, Malaysia, the UAE, Saudi Arabia, Kenya, Nigeria, USA, and UK, as well as the USSR. Until the onset of perestroika, the company's Moscow operations were centred on the sale of boilers, and its activities pivoted on the enthusiasm of the Soviet-trained engineer Gagan Patwardhan. The company picked up young Russian-speaking Indian students to man its enterprises. During perestroika, it attempted to develop its standard sales and also diversified into trade.

During late perestroika and immediately post-1991, the company became a standard reference for those who wished to enter the Russian market. Many agents consulted the Company, as did prominent Indian producers such as Mukund Iron and Steel. It had a number of contacts in the CIS, and its Moscow operatives conducted extensive business tours in the FSU. The post-disintegration scenario witnessed an interest among Russian enterprises to use Thermax for their export operations. In Sverdlovsk, in the St. Petersburg area, and in the Upper Volga region, invitations were sent by local managers to Thermax executives to visit plants and to conclude arrangements for trade with India and with third parties. The head of Thermax sales operations at this time, Narain Apte, was kept on the move, as were his colleagues Shankar Mukherji and Animesh Basu. Using the Company's long association with Russia, its executives had built-up a series of networks with Russian intermediaries operating at airports and ports, enabling them to bypass the difficulties of a varying customs regime. A strict code of payments was well-established for the Company's own reference, and why and how were seldom questions that were asked. This eased operations in the chaotic circumstances of the post-disintegration period.

A detailed examination of some of Thermax operations, during 1992–4 indicate the problems of doing business in Russia, and the success/lack of it in the face of the difficulties. They show that the main stumbling blocks to the successful conclusion of a deal involved the problems of liberalization itself, but cannot be limited to them: in the new context, use of India's rupee debt with Russia and payment via the direct rupee/rouble route provided opportunities, but also threw up a fruitful field for manipulation. Undoubtedly, it was this situation which led to a gradual move to hard currency dealings as an important part of operations.

Information is available for two Thermax initiatives in the period immediately after 1991. The first is business which involved a consignment of jute to be sold by Birla Jute Industries Ltd. in 1992–3 to Russia for use by P.P. Sakher, through the agency of Thermax (in Russia) and Ferrera Eco (a regional Chamber of Commerce of the Moscow region). Cargo worth almost one and a half million dollars was involved, and the first part was to be shipped during 1993. Rupee/rouble arrangements were bypassed, and the transaction was to be handled in hard currency. An LC was opened in London with the Moscow Narodyi Bank by the Incombank, Moscow, for the appropriate sum in dollars. Delays followed because of incorrect nomenclature in the LC, but finally, in June 1993, the consignment was delivered to Odessa. Two major problems arose in the course of the transaction: the Indian side asked for an extension of the LC at one point, and the Russian side refused; and the Russian side complained of a shortfall in delivery in Odessa at another point, while the Indian side showed that all goods had been present at the time of the departure of the consignments from Calcutta. Uncertainty was manifest about where the goods could be delivered: in Odessa, which was in the Ukraine, or in Illychevsk or Novorossiisk, Russian ports on the Black Sea.

Distinctive about the business is that the importer was not a standard FTO and had come into the picture as part of the new business operations prevalent in Russia. P.P Sakher had not approached an FTO, and if it had, it found it unsuitable. Thermax's role is distinctive. The Company was clearly now involved in serious brokerage rather than production and sale: its reputation was established sufficiently for Ferrera Eco to approach it in this capacity.

Among the difficulties that business faced, inflation was a major problem. Demands from the Indian side that the LC be extended were met with outrage: delays had already cost the Russians substantially as a result of the varying exchange rate of the rouble, they could not accept further delays. Disintegration also threw up the problems of shipment. The Russian Black Sea ports were not equipped to deal with large numbers of ships. Substantial (and costly) problems, however, were involved in the use of Ukrainian ports. Finally, the pilferage at Odessa is an important indication of both the helplessness of the parties involved and the increasing involvement of organized crime in any transactions of this time. It is worth noting, however, that the deal was ultimately successful, and that all parties were relatively content with the results: a clear indication of the advantages of India trade, irrespective of the losses and the variations in the exchange rate of the rouble.[43]

A subsequent, though unsuccessful attempt by Thermax to do business with the Birla group of companies indicates that whatever the search for non-traditional routes for commerce in Russia, standard routes persisted. Thermax' diversification into brokerage is again clear. In this second case, Thermax was negotiating on behalf of Vneshstrojimport, Promstrojmaterialy, Strojmaterialintorg, and Stroitechnoservice with Birla Linoleum and Vinoleum for purchase of linoleum from India. This followed the Russian government allocation of $15 million for purchases of linoleum from India against rupee payment. Significantly, all the buyers here were standard trading organizations which had been in foreign trade for some time. The idea of the 'opportunity' was clearly thrown up among the closed group which handled commercial transactions using the rupee debt payment. Thermax did attempt to use the occasion to see whether some business could be done with its Kazakh representative in the course of the transaction. All other aspects of the deal though went through standard channels: getting the Russian ministry to release the funds, etc. Ultimately, the transaction fell through because tea vendors in India and tea buyers in Russia were able to impress the government for special attention to their case; and also because the Indian price for linoleum was substantially higher than the world price. Use of the rupee debt for linoleum was unprofitable as far as the Russian government was concerned.[44]

Other companies that followed the Thermax path (with a greater stress on the sale of their own products) were: Delhi Cloth Mills (which worked through DCM Overseas Ltd.) and the Sri Ram group, which set up Usha Intercontinental[45] for such operations. Local companies were formed by Indians to act as on-the-ground brokers (as in the case of the small trading unit the Vijaya Corporation, which dealt extensively in the pharmaceuticals industry in the early 1990s).

c. *Strategies in the Russian market by 'old Russia hands' who were not interested in agency trading.* Significantly, in a step that indicated some of the problems of trading, among 'old Russia hands', Thermax International Ltd., even though successful with agency operations, moved out of trading (around 1994) and began to focus once again on its basic product, which sold well throughout the period—i.e. the medium-size heating unit that was used in the far north. The Company fell back on a product with a long-term reputation, and developed sales rather than focus on fix on a highly volatile post-disintegration market for consumer goods. It went into district heating, working with sections of the President's administration in unusual locales, and also taking on a World Bank project in Nizhnii Novgorod, where it already had experience and in Archangel, where it worked with the city authority. Operations were begun in Kazakhstan, where Commander Mathur, who had a navy man's experience of Russia, was set to direct business. And the company sold in Uzbekistan, Turkmenistan, and Azerbaijan, moving on also into Eastern Europe with some work in Poland.[46]

There was, though, no diversification into the production of small heating units for the 'cottages' (large private villas) of the 'new Russians', a departure that might have offered some competition to European manufacturers who entered the arena. Also, CIS operations gradually became less aggressive (the Kazakh branch closed in 1998). The sluggish approach was certainly the consequence of Aga's death in 1997, after which the various divisions ceased to coordinate their marketing strategies and the Company went through revamping in Pune. Russian operations lost the edge when both Animesh Basu and Narain Apte, who had spearheaded sales after 1991, left the firm. A fresh approach to expansion had to wait until Shankar Mukherji returned to Moscow in 2002 December, to put the firm's affairs on a sounder footing.

Meanwhile, among other Indian producers operating in Russia from Soviet times, debt arrangements were used by the pharmaceutical company, Torrent, which supplied the Russian government's front agencies in the drugs sector—the FTOs Medeksport and Sovkhimeksport. The gradual collapse of these two companies, owing to loss of staff and competition in health care from private drug distributors, weakened these operations until they had receded to the margins of Torrent's business by 1997, even if this form of commerce did enjoy a brief revival during the crisis of 1998–9.

Tea exporters who were oriented to the Soviet market in the past also used debt arrangements. J.V. Gokal of Kolkata took the lead, but other smaller concerns also profited from the trade. Former FTOs—the 'Grand' Trading House and Roschaikofe—were the go-betweens on the Russian side. A degree of scandal came to be attached to the trade—after proof was supplied that the statistics for tea imports did not match with the actual figures for tea purchases in Calcutta. On occasion, customs examinations in Russia revealed that refuse was exported in place of tea, against the LC in India. The trade had become a means of buying rupees cheap in Russia through a joint Indo–Russian enterprise. The Russian buyer obtained rupees notionally at the auction in Moscow at a rate lower than its prevailing value against the rouble and dollar, arguing that he would buy tea. An LC was opened against the RBI's debt fund. Goods of no value were exported, leaving the Indian partner with the money released by the RBI. Such manoeuvres, along with the invasion of the Russian market by cheap teas (from Sri Lanka and Kenya), led to a fall in demand for the Indian product, as indicated by the statistics in Table 3.4. Given the strong tea-drinking tradition in Russia, it was unlikely that imports from India would decline wholly, but waywardness in the tea trade, complicated by the entry of sundry importers, led to a

TABLE 3.4: TEA EXPORTS FROM INDIA TO RUSSIA

Year	Amt. (m.kg)	Value (Rs. crores)
1991–2	108	57
1992–3	502	68
1994–5	66	470
1995–6	92	865
1997–8	82	814
1999–2000	96	801
2000–1	78	540

Source: *Business Messenger* (Moscow), 2001, p. 52.

decline in the reputation of Indian teas, whatever the efforts of the Tea Board.[47]

The Sun group of industries, run by the Khemka family, who were old hands in Russia, took a different path in the new Russia. Sun became the most substantial investment firm of Indian origin operating in the Russian Federation by 2002. Unlike Thermax, Torrent, or J.V. Gokal, Sun did not generate Indo–Russian trade, but came to represent a link between Russia and India of long term strategic importance—a link that held out promise for the development of business between the two countries in the future.

Sun, along with Sudhir Gupta's Amtel, was one of the few Indian operations that took advantage of the privatization process, which did not initially intended to allow substantial control of Russian industry by foreign entrepreneurs, but ultimately permitted it.[48] From 1958 Sun had been associated with exports of machinery from the USSR to India, using rupee–rouble arrangements. The 'Sun Group' established itself thereafter outside India (although it had Indian operations and branches), with offices in London, Moscow, and Boston, specializing in investments and trading operations. In 1992, when initiatives began to privatize major Russian industries, Sun decided to involve itself in the process, avoiding the standard areas of foreign interest—the oil and natural gas sector, and other areas of extractive industry—to focus on areas of goods of mass consumption. From 1996, its operations were linked to the more elaborate operations of Sun Capital Partners, which had an investment fund of $155 million, set for direct investments in

Russia and the CIS and based on major state and corporate pension funds in the US and banks and investment funds in the Near East: enterprises that accounted for a sum of over US $300 billion. Merill Lynch, the investment bankers, were directly involved in the activities of the enterprise, and the fund directed investment into twenty units which dealt with beer production, confectionery, food processing, oil and natural gas, and hotels. The group utilized its connections with Foreign and Colonial (UK), which had extensive European experience, in handling such operations.[49]

The pivot of the group's operations in Russia came to be Sun Brewing, which became known for its achievement in the beer business in a broad belt. The reach included the Moscow area, parts of the Urals, and the Volga region, where Sun turned around major Russian outfits after taking charge of the lion's share of their interest. Many brands were concerned: Tolstiak (of the Saransk Brewing Company), Klinskoe (produced in the Moscow region), and Sibirskaia Korona were the most famous, but Pikur (from the Kursk Brewing Company, Kursk), Viking and Rifei (Perm Brewing Company, Perm), Premier and Vladimir Monomakh (Ivanovo Brewing Company, Ivanovo) Bavaria, Volzhanin, and Stalingradskoe (OAO Povol'zhe, Volzhskii) are also now manufactured by Sun. The beers were produced from initially five, later seven, breweries located in the cities mentioned as well as in St. Petersburg and Yekaterinburg. The decision to focus on these concerns came after a survey by the Khemkas of 150 breweries in Russia and Eastern Europe. Considerable effort went into 'equipping the enterprises with up-to-date technology, touching up the principles of management and accounting, incorporating new marketing technologies and systems of sale'.[50] Some US $70 million were invested in the breweries. A focus on producing 'world class beers'[51] for a national market was a clear part of strategy. At the same time, the firm prided itself on preserving 'local habits' in the factories and working with local tastes for beer in order not to forego the natural market for the product, i.e. the immediate vicinity of the brewery. An effective regional and national distribution system was evolved. To avoid the vagaries of the market, Sun set up Star Distribution, which, according to Shiv Khemka, was intended to integrate all-Russian and regional marketing strategies. Star had its own independent daughter companies (e.g. Star Kursk), and worked out of nine major centres to supply eleven important cities and over thirty other urban centres. The result of the enterprise was impressive. In 1998, Sun controlled 15 per cent of the Russian beer market and had increased the production of the breweries in its control from 3.96 million hectolitres to 12 million hectolitres. Combined sales of the product (including Interbrew figures) grew from US $39 million in 1994 to US $245 million in 2000. In 1999, Sun further developed their enterprises with a well-planned expansion in partnership with the Belgian brewery Interbrew (which had one brewery in Russia and one in the Ukraine): an expansion which led to control of 18 per cent of the Ukrainian and Russian beer production in 2000. According to Sun this permitted technological inputs from Interbrew into the Sun breweries.

The enterprise required considerable attention to regional politics in the Federation, since brewing, as a former CEO of Sun Brewing was to later explain, was an industry that paid the bulk of its taxes to local governments rather than to the central pool. Nor were other problems wanting. Again, as Sun's CEO pointed out:

> When you buy these breweries, they are in bad shape. But it doesn't take that much to improve them. Once you improve them, everyone wants to come and take them back. Fundamentally it's an issue you always have to deal with here. Anytime a company is unprofitable, nobody is interested. The minute you make it profitable, there are people who want it back.

Those who created such problems for brewing varied from the local management, who wanted to reassert control, to the local beer distributor and members of the regional administration. Sun had to face the normal problems of the time of privatization, including public doubt about the strict legitimacy of the acquisition. The company had to resort to a variety of tactics to maintain control: tribunals, courts, provincial governors, and regional administrations. It may have been possible that in dealing with situation, Sun was both benefited by its selection of senior management, which had long experience of Russia. But the jaundiced views of Russians by US managers that Sun recruited may have also been an added problem in the resolution of its difficulties.[52]

Sun also diversified into confectionery, took control of three enterprises and hoped to set up a national holding company with interests in the confectionery industry at a broad level. It found its existing commitments (and the problems of confectionery) too demanding to go ahead with the project, though, and sold two of its plants to Nestle and persevered with a major unit in Voronezh. The latter, the Voronezhskaia Konditerskaia Fabrika, was permitted to develop many of its old 'recipes' (which had fallen away under the pressure of the mass-production targets of the Soviet era). The enterprise gradually improved productivity, and was eventually sold off by Sun in March 2001 to the Babaeevskii Concern, Russia's largest confectionery holding, which included enterprises that produce quality chocolates rivaled only by the Korkunov enterprise.

A stake in the fishing industry came through Navenor Holdings Ltd., which was put together by Sun Capital Partners, the Swedish company Scandsea, and the Icelandic Freezing Plants Corporation. The 'holding' was meant to operate like other such ventures, to establish a pooling of resources for enterprises in fish harvesting, processing and distribution, and 'held' crucial shares in production and cold storage units in Moscow and Perm. Besides these concerns, Sun established a stake in computer software in Russia, where it had extended the operations of its London-based enterprises, e-start.com and Vesta Capital Partners, as well as its US enterprise Cybiko, through Vesta Eurasia. The latter focused on developing information technology strategies in Russia, while Cybiko dealt with entertainment computers. Sun's interests in the travel business (represented in Keysystem.com) extended to tour operators and travel agents working out of the Russian market.

For all its international connections, the group was treated as Indian in its own profile and the profile of its Chairman (Nand Khemka) and major directors (Uday and Shiv Vikram Khemka). In a discussion in New Delhi in November 2002, on the eve of Putin's visit to India, Nand Khemka made it clear that although dedicated to developing production in Russia (and elsewhere), Sun saw itself as a distinctly Indian company; and in all the articles written on the group in Russia, the Indian origins of the group are firmly and unequivocally stressed.

The Group had major Indian operations (Sun F&C Mutual Fund and Sun Securities (India) Pvt. Ltd.). Here, the Mutual Fund brought into India a major partner of the Sun Group abroad—Foreign & Colonial Emerging Markets Ltd (FCEM),[53] which managed assets of the order of US $4 billion and was firmly connected to Eureko BV—a finance group based on Portuguese, Dutch, and other European insurance funds. Sun F&C Mutual was run by Uday Khemka, and had on its board a number of prominent Indians (besides competent professionals and representatives of FCEM) including B. Bhattacharya,[54] P.R. Khanna,[55] Dipankar Basu,[56] F.C. Kohli,[57] and former Foreign Secretary S.K. Singh.

The group provided a route for bringing Indian expertise and capital into Russia, and taking capital and international expertise into India. Its Russian operations could be compared with the organization of L.N. Mittal in Karaganda in Kazakhstan, though the latter had no spin off for India except in terms of goodwill. Sun was also clearly, like Thermax, a source of information for Russian companies operating in India.[58]

d. *Companies with little or no experience of the Federation entered the Russian market in their own right.* Trade witnessed the arrival of a number of new entrants who made headway rapidly. Some had a major reputation in India, while others were swashbucklers inspired by the opportunities of an emerging market and saw themselves as pioneers. The engineering and construction firm Larsen and Toubro was an important instance of the large Indian company's arrival in Russia; but the real innovation was in pharmaceutical exports. Here, almost all the big players in India, Ranbaxy, Lyka, and Dr. Reddy's,[59] came into the market with some vigour, following the standard players, Torrent and Cadilla. They wished to establish a foothold in the market during perestroika; and they moved deeper in after 1991. Acquisition and local production then became a focus, as it became clear that the stake in the market could be large (even 30 per cent in the case of some exports[60]) and required aggressive engagement.

Cadilla itself had set the example, moving quickly under Dr. Brij to equal Torrent's business of US $70–80 million at the time of late perestroika. The company came to terms quickly with the disintegration of the Soviet health system, the collapse of the automatic supply of producers to hospitals and consumers, and the emergence of the three big distributors, Protek, SIA, and Shreya. Cadilla initially sold to the FTO Medeksport; but then developed a network of Medical Representatives in Ekaterinburg, Cheliabinsk, Perm, Moscow, St. Petersburg, Kazan, Samara, Voronezh, Rostov, and Krasnodar. These established a demand for the Indian product, and Shreya (a distributor headed by an Indian entrepreneur) acted as the middleman, guaranteeing payment for local orders. The organization occasionally stretched beyond this safe system of operations to deal with smaller distributors and consumers; but it ran into difficulties and had to resort to long-drawn judicial suits to get what it was owed when it did so. Its authority in the Russian market was broken somewhat during the restructuring of 1995, when this major player was split and the prominent offshoot Zydus Cadilla was created. The latter remained significant in Russia, though, as the fourth largest pharmaceutical company in India, with a turnover of about US $250 million by 2002. The initiatives were handled by men with a Russian background (such as Jaideep Kapoor) or those who monitored the CIS market extensively for major pharmaceutical organizations, such as S.C. Choubey who worked with Glenmark from 1995 in this field.[61]

Ranbaxy began operations in Russia during 1993–6, when the head of the company's export division, Dr. Brar,[62] worked to develop this market. Lyka Laboratories entered the country in 1997–9 and worked independently until its acquisition by Heterodrugs. Both used small organizations to front for them. Lyka worked with the services of Lucky Exports under the management of four Indian students, among them Vinay Singh and Ashish Obeisi. Ranbaxy used Sanjiv Singh's Intercare and the Vijay Corporation, whose proprietors, Sujit and Shekhar Singh, eventually became the tycoons of the Shreya Corporation. In both cases, the focus was initially sale to Medeksport, and rupee–rouble purchases, with some attention to convertible currency business with LCs. The latter became the prime focus after 1997 when the companies began to restrict themselves to dollar operations, following government default on purchases through Medeksport (Anup Banerji, who was in charge of Lyka's operations, cleared the company's fraction of $70 million only in 1999). Dr. Reddy's was to avoid such a course, focusing primarily on standard sales. By 2002, though, its turnover here was the same as what the company made in Europe.

Other than the older businesses (Torrent and Cadilla) who restricted their operations to sale of formulations, all the companies attempted to work with local producers, if only at the level of packaging. This was considered the equivalent of local manufacturing, and could bring registration costs ($15,000 per product) and duties down. Russian facilities came to be used by Dr. Reddy's (whose Reddy–Bismet was promoted by Deve Gowda when he was prime minister). Ranbaxy went into collaboration with Protek to market Cifran. Lyka, under Anup Banerji's management, went into collaboration with Nizhpharm. The local units were forward-moving organizations. Nizhpharm, and its lead entrepreneur, Andrei Mladinstev, for instance, were selected for special grants by the EBRD and had certification for Good Manufacturing and Good Laboratory Practices. The company worked with producers such as Nabros of Ahmedabad. Collaborators more often than not had special clout and helped the penetration of the Indian organization: a special case was that of Pharma Syntez of Irkutsk, run by the Indian student Punia with the benefactions of his father-in-law, the mayor of the town. The company worked with bulk imports of injections and anti-TB drugs, with Lyka, after the Irkutsk mayor put the project forward for consideration while Ambassador Satinder Lamba was travelling to promote Indian goods. Other companies, such as Nizhpharm, had their own special standing in their locality.

In all such cases, the Indian organizations sought to act like the Sun Group. Their manoeuvres were well-coordinated with government and local traders. Substantial coordination with Russian producers, however, eluded all other firms, and, significantly, there are no indications that any made the kind of commitments to local companies that the Khemkas did. When spurious goods were uncovered, consequently, they were unequivocally identified as 'Indian' and had no Russian back-up other than the Russian distributor who worked with them: an aspect of Indian pharmaceuticals' problems that attracted repeated attention during scandals in 1995 (when Ronen Sen dealt with it), 1998 and 2002 (when the repercussions were handled by Shreya and Intercare).[63] Since, unlike Eastern European products, Indian goods followed different pharmacoepia from the Soviet, and did not have the same international reputation as, say, Glaxo products, this was a considerable disadvantage. Despite excellent beginnings, the major Indian players faced stiff competition from Czech, Hungarian and Slovene producers, who returned to the Russian market with a vengeance after 2000.

The advance of Indian firms into a number of countries explains why they did not bite deep into the country and allowed such a situation to develop. In the case of Ranbaxy, revenues outside of India amount, in 2002, to about US $257 million compared to US $234 million in the previous financial year. Of this, revenues from North America stood at US $134 million and US $130 million respectively, revenues from Europe at US $17 million and US $31 million, and revenues from Russia at US $37 million and US $29 million respectively. Even acknowledging the high returns from Russia, the statistics show where the firm's main interest lay outside its India operations, i.e. in a growing market in the United States and Europe. Again, Torrent maintained strong Russian sales, but its focus clearly shifted elsewhere. By 2002 Brazil formed the launching pad for the firm's operations in Latin America, and US $1.5

million was invested in a wholly owned subsidiary, Torrent do Brasil Ltd., registered in Sao Paulo. From this, Torrent catered to 36 major distributors in Sao Paulo and Rio de Janeiro and the operation had the largest sales force outside India. There were ventures in Africa, where Torrent was one of the leading Indian companies in Zimbabwe by 2002 and planned to enter South Africa and Francophone Africa. Germany and Europe generally, as well as Sri Lanka and Vietnam were areas of the company's expansion over the previous decade. Hence, although Russia was one of the first and key markets for Torrent in the early 1990s, and Torrent was one of the largest Indian suppliers of pharmaceutical formulations to the Russian government tenders, its brands were widely accepted and the company enjoyed a good equity, focus began to move elsewhere by the beginning of the 2000s.

True, in the case of major adversity, the companies showed considerable staying power, indicating that they considered they were in the market to stay. In 1997–8, there were substantial defaults in payment, but none of the major businesses withdrew from Russia. Nor did litigation discourage them (even when it was backed by substantial international capital). This was true of Cadilla (as remarked earlier); it was also true of Dr. Reddy's. This company, which had entered the Russian market after 1991, made deep inroads (Russian sales came to 15 per cent of the company's total sales in 1999). It was bested in 1999 in a patent fight against the US giant, Pfizer, but persisted in litigation, unfazed by the complications of the Russian judicial system.[64]

e. *The Sakhalin 1 project. A major departure in government enterprise.* A major innovation in Russia–India cooperation, comparable to the extraordinary initiatives of the Sun Group, was the decision by the Indian agency to invest in the exploration and exploitation of the oil and natural gas field at Sakhalin 1. Following meetings of the working group on cooperation in energy issues (the most far-reaching took place in 1998), and the formulation of various schemes for Indian investment in the Russian energy sector, the agreement on Sakhalin 1 was signed in February 2001. The scheme was decided by Rosneft-Sakhalin, Sakhalin-Morneftgaz-shelf, and ONGC Videsh Ltd. of India. It focused on the exploitation of three fields: Chaivo, Odoptoo, and Orkutoondoghi and envisaged an output from 2005–6 of 8 million tons of oil and 9.5 cubic metres of natural gas annually. Basic development had commitments from a group of three: Exonmobile, an American company, Sodeco, a

Japanese consortium, and Rosneft (the mother company of Rosneft-Sakhalin). By the agreement of 2001, ONGC obtained 20 per cent of the Rosneft share (which was 40 per cent of the stake established by the first agreement of 1995 concerning the field)—involving some US $2 billion.[65]

Like the operation in the Sudan, the venture was an attempt to strengthen the energy base of a country that had inadequate resources in this area. However, how the production sharing agreement would operate when the field actually came into operation, and whether Russian laws would cause complications for Indian pricing was a problem that led to disquiet about the investment.

f. *Lack of initiative from Russian companies on the Indian market.* Throughout the period, Russian enterprises (other than old India hands like Tiazhpromeksport) showed little dynamism in the way they handled the Indian market. In the case of imports into Russia, the reason is evident. Links with an Indian producer were essential to work the rupee–rouble debt, and rather than waste funds on exploration, it was worthwhile to work through an Indian agent. Why Russian business did not adopt an aggressive posture in exports to India is still inexplicable and can be contrasted with Ukrainian and Belorussian companies. The continuance of rupee–rouble debt payments was important again here: it gave Indian agents an area of expertise which they worked on to develop an image for themselves in Russia as the key to India, the *sine qua non* through which all trade had to flow. Since Russian companies tended to be more concerned to make arrangements among themselves, and settle their home market and their management affairs in a period of corporatization and dislocation, this strategy of the Indian middleman worked well. Late in the period, Russian banks began to scout India to attract investment and to invest in joint ventures, though in a limited and piecemeal manner.

The importance of the 'Indian' initiative in making business in the early years of the post-transition period, and the corresponding weakness of Russian initiative, is illustrated from limited information that we have of a deal conducted between Bentimi Ltd., the Moscow branch of Vishal Exports of Ahmedabad, and the ballbearing company Kol'tso. The deal was substantial—an order for 2,160,000 ballbearings, which compared well with monthly orders of between two million and ten million for the whole of Russia and the CIS. Bentimi did most of the work in 'making' the business. Bentimi established links with Kol'tso trading branches, arranged operations with the principal in India, arranged LCs, etc. There was limited networking in Russia which was put together by Kol'tso. The business was conducted in 1993–4.

The reasons for the weak initiative from the Russians are clear. Although Kol'tso was a prominent company of the Soviet period, it had a number of commitments: producer units which dealt with abrasives, machinetools, and instruments, as well as those for making washing machines and toys (!). It had a fleet of 500 vehicles, and owned clinics, creches, farms, etc. Its commitments could not be met with the dramatic fall in sales which followed disintegration, when much of its funds were frozen and its production fell. Somehow, output of sorts was maintained at a level not much lower than those of 1990, but this was only because of existing stock of raw materials, 'paid' holidays for staff, quick networking among nearby customers, and acceptance of non-payment. Kol'tso's management had no sense of the broader market, despite the company's having had a thriving export sector before 1992. Once the strategies of 1992 had been exhausted, managers spent their time in attempts to extract subsidies from the Federal government in 1993 and making adjustments to control the company under privatization. The increasingly desperate situation threw up radical changes, getting the Gosplan list of erstwhile customers, setting up of marketing units in major urban centres, and various arrangements to deal with old debtors. The gamut of activities, however, did not leave time for finding customers, and much depended on being found. Nagging labour problems also pinned the management down even though these never erupted into full-scale strike activity. Inevitably, Kol'tso's position depended on business being set up by entrepreneurially-minded organizations. And, in a classic instance of such activity, Bentimi, and other firms moved in to establish the link.

g. *The caution of the small-scale businessman, and images of entrepreneurship in Russia. J.P. Kanoria's 'Business with New Russia'.* The Bentimi case is clearly an instance of a company that went about its business with a degree of care and resolution. It did not make wild commitments to its suppliers and there was to be no new activity. The activity of Indian firms such as Bentimi was far from comparable to that of US or European based firms staffed by Russians who wished to return during perestroika and its aftermath to build a new world, preaching sermons to businessmen in the country—a clear example being the US stockbroker Alexander Elder. Although Indians were aware of 'success stories' among their own fraternity (like the Khemkas), who could compare at a pinch with Boris Jordan, who, together with the New Zealander Stephen Jennings, made a fortune from trading shares in privatized units, they were careful about their situation and acted with circumspection.

This cautious approach, blended with a sense of enthusiasm, is evident from one of the few relics of the Indian entrepreneur's 'mind' at this time: a manual for businessmen written by J.P. Kanoria, a Calcutta businessman. Kanoria's manual indicates that primarily accustomed to a situation dominated by FTOs in Russia, or to the circumstances of operating in India, Indian entrepreneurs were thrilled by Russian prospects but wary about a world that had to be understood. Showing great enthusiasm for the state of Russia, Kanoria roundly criticised the Bolshevik past. Admitting the chaos of the present, he pointed out that Indians should take an interest in the diamond industry, consumer durables, textiles, footwear, and various forms of countertrade. In an eccentric manner he produced advice with a wild sense of what could be done. But he also outlined the main obstacles. Among the latter, Kanoria noted fluctuating currency exchange rates, random taxation, administrative arbitrariness, difficult transportation, uncertain customs duties and a self-contradictory regime of laws. He provided information about how to handle each (giving a reasonable account, for instance, of export duties and VAT levies on various products, the customs system, etc.), providing addresses, telephone numbers, and government agencies to help the businessman through. Kanoria also included random data on trends in the Russian economy, indicating the relative shrewdness with which a 'tenderfoot' went about his work, producing on the whole a picture of an uncertain landscape with many lifelines and great possibilities. Overall, like other instances, the manual indicates the caution which guided Indian business in the way it handled the Russian market, whatever be the sense that great profits could be made.

h. *Shuttle trade*. True, despite caution, some small-scale activity was important throughout the post-disintegration period, depending on operators who had links with customs agencies in Russia and dealt primarily in garments and luxury goods. The size of this trade is uncertain, and the scale for the Russian Federation probably decreased over time, given the increasing systematization of the Customs Code, and its rigorous application to these *chelnoki* (bagmen). Networks operated, though, and lived on legends of great profits to be made and the lack of economy with which Russians approach spending. Centres in Karol Bagh and Ludhiana occasionally came to appear as conduits for shuttle trade, neatly spliced with prostitution rackets where Russians played the chief role as suppliers and products. This seamy side of Indo–Russian economic relations of the time attracted press attention frequently, but it hardly ran to scale, facing stiff competition from Chinese, Turks, and Lebanese, who had better access to the Russian market than Indians. Like the case of tea scandals mentioned above, until there is proof to the contrary, shuttle trade cannot be considered an important part of the India–Russia relationship of this time.

THE SOCIAL STATUS OF INDO–RUSSIAN TRADE

The involvement of official agencies, and regional governments (in India and Russia) in the trade brought it important advantages. It opened up avenues where many problems of the 'transition' (customs, excise duties, etc.) were ironed out by official intervention, even if the smoothness of commercial operations could not be compared to Soviet times. The affluence of traditional 'Russia hands' such as Nand and Shiv Vikram Khemka, and their active inclusion of members of the New Delhi elite in the activities of such agencies also added a dimension to improvements in the standing of the trade. Both trends had important broader consequences. For without them, in India and Russia, Indo–Russian trade would have suffered a major status decline. That, given the increasing ascendancy of trade in other global theatres, would probably have led to its general neglect by public bodies, and in its turn would have removed from the trade the official benediction that was important even in the circumstances of a dilapidated Russian state.

In this, it should be noted that while many companies that were the go-betweens for small producers in India (AGIO, Texuna, etc.) exhibited exceptional dynamism and developed an international reputation, they were based in the CIS or elsewhere (Dubai, Singapore, and London) and their profile had little weight in India, despite the existence of local branches and affiliated companies in the country. This is true for businessmen such as Sujit Singh, Ravinder Chamaria, and Pramod Agarwal, who distinguished themselves by their enterprise, but who had a subdued persona in India, and did not have the international reputation of other Indian CIS hands based abroad such as L.N. Mittal. On the other hand the Khemkas, despite their foreign base, evolved major social links in India, making them minor legends in the country, just as they became minor legends in Russia and internationally. Their standing and activity added to the status of Indo–Russian trade that was constituted by the reputation and authority of other players in the business—corporations such as Larsen and Toubro, ONGC, or BHEL or influential technocrats in the Russian Federation and powerful bodies like Technopromeksport. This reputation was further developed by the success of firms such as Ranbaxy, Dr. Reddy's, Cadilla, and other major Indian pharmaceutical enterprises in the Russian space.

The profiles of prominent Indian businessmen associated with the Russian market require some note in this regard.

- *Sujit Kumar Singh* b. Patna, Bihar. MBBS student in Kiev. Initially worked with a small trading organization—the Vijaya Corporation—immediately after Soviet disintegration. Founded the Shreya Corporation, reputedly the third largest pharmaceutical distribution and marketing company in the RF in 2000 (turnover of US $210 million). Initiator of Shreya Life Sciences (India) (reputed turnover in 2001 of US $600 million), which specializes in exports from India to Russia and the CIS.
- *Pramod Agarwal* b. Bombay, Maharashtra. Began business in Bombay in 1975 in a family firm, which dealt with textile exports to the USSR. Handled Company business in Hong Kong. In 1981, founded Texuna International Limited to trade commodities (cement, cotton, grain, etc.) throughout Asia. Entered the Soviet market during perestroika. Post-disintegration, opened first CIS branch in Tashkent in 1992. Moscow office set up in 1993, then branches in Almaty, Ashgabat, Baku, and Odessa, with turnover reputedly reaching US $200 million by 1995. In the mid-1990s, the company was reputedly one of the world's ten largest cotton dealers, trading some 300,000 tonnes annually. Also reputedly one of major Asian buyers of CIS steel, upwards of 1 million tonnes per year and a leading oil trader, shipping some 2 million tonnes of

crude to Europe from Central Asia. Trader also in grain. Worked with wheat purchases from Kazakhstan and deliveries to Russia and the Ukraine. Reputedly a major supplier of CIS cotton to the Russian textile industry in Ivanovo, near Moscow. Collaborator with Japanese company Matsushita Electronics for distribution of all its National and Panasonic brands in most of Central Asia. One of the region's leading direct investors. Initiator of the US $25 million joint venture outlet, Tvoy Dom in suburban Moscow, with 16,000 square metres of shopping under one roof (opened March 2001). Other projects: construction of a US $73 million wheat silo in Turkmenistan, the commissioning and supply of a US $54 million baby food plant in Uzbekistan, the development and the purchase of an industrial complex consisting of a phosphate mine, a fertilizer plant, and a chemical plant in Kazakhstan, under the Republic's privatization scheme. Partnership activity with governments of Uzbekistan, Kazakhstan, and Turkmenistan, Germany's Veba and the UK's Cairns Energy (with whom Texuna is exploring for oil in Central Asia.) Agarwal was the founding Chairman of the Asian Russian Trade Association in 1994.

- *Ravinder Chamaria* b. Calcutta, West Bengal. Moved from India to Singapore in the 1970s. Prominent figure in the AGIO group of companies. Resident in Singapore and later Dubai. Founded a dot.com company in addition to his trading activities. Bought into silos in Kazakhstan. Active outside the Indian Ocean–CIS area, with interests in the UK.
- *Nand Khemka,* Founder of the Sun Group of Industries. Chairman and Managing Director, Indag Rubber Ltd. and Director, Unipatch Rubber Ltd. Graduated from Columbia University (USA) in 1956. Dealt with servicing operations for Indian heavy engineering collaboration with the USSR.
- *Shiv Vikram Khemka,* Executive Director, Sun Group of Companies, Russian Federation, 1985, BA in Economics, Brown University, USA; 1990, MBA in Finance, Wharton School of Business; Master's in International Studies, the Lauder Institute. Member of the Board of Governors, The Lauder Institute. Member of the Advisory Board, Centre for Business and Management, Cambridge University. Member, Brown University Young Alumni Board. Member of the Visiting Committee, Davis Center for

Russian Studies, Harvard University. Member, Young President's Organization. Member, Wharton European Board.

An important dimension to the Khemka profile here was the Group's concern with business-knowhow that compared with the best in the world and in Russia, and close connections with the more important businessmen and statesmen of the Federation. The image that the company valued such attributes was cultivated even while the firm maintained clear Indian credentials; and it was an image that was firmly asserted in staffing policy. Here, among senior personnel, Sun had Indians with a good record such as Vaidyanathan Sivakumar,[66] Amarjit Singh Soni[67] and Dinesh Sood,[68] who had eminent backgrounds in Indian business in terms of training (Indian Institute of Technology, Institute of Chartered Accountants, etc.) and experience (senior management in the case of Soni). The group also had Russians with impressive backgrounds such as Salavat Rezbaev,[69] Roman Nagaev,[70] Igor Goundobin,[71] and Valentin Romanov,[72] who had graduated from institutions such as the Moscow State Institute for International Relations (MGIMO) and had good records of service either with important international firms (Goldman Sachs in the case of Rezbaev) or the diplomatic service (in the case of Goundobin and Romanov). A number of senior personnel with good US backgrounds worked for the firm, including Maxwell Asgari Andrew Baxter,[73] and Barbara Duvosin.[74]

The kind of rhetoric employed by Sun's senior directors indicated the group's assertive commitment to the Russian market in the long term. In the firm's promotional literature Nand Khemka hammered this point home.

> The Sun Group has worked in Russia for more than 40 years and we have grown to love the country. During this time we have learned that mutually beneficial and prosperous business in Russia is possible. The Sun Group creates modern, stable and successful companies. We create them for the benefit of investors and employees, for the regions in which we operate and for Russia. Our multinational team consisting of high caliber experts actively participates in the financing, restructuring and managing of Russian companies. We always strive to adhere to the highest standards of quality. We are pleased that by investing our capital in Russia, we are strengthening Russia's economy and contributing to international economic cooperation.

This position was followed up by other statements in the promotional literature such as 'Sun Group feels that it is a part of Russia' and 'We believe it is our duty to help this great country by supporting cultural, public and educational programmes and initiatives'.

Deliberate links with Russian functionaries, and support to regional governments as well as associations with philanthropic activities in the Federation, reinforced this image. Hence, the Khemkas' inclusion in President Putin's Council on Foreign Investment is reflective of the kind of confidence the organization cultivated in the regions. It is also indicated in the pointed reference of V.N. Tikhomirov, Head of the Administration of Ivanovo region concerning the way Sun had been important to the local administration's finances—sentiments echoed by other functionaries in regions where Sun had a presence.[75]

> The Administration and the Legislative Assembly of Ivanovo region are thoroughly satisfied that under the most difficult circumstances the stable and highly efficient work of [the enterprise] makes a valuable contribution to the financial improvement of the state's budget by way of timely payment of taxes . . . ZAO Ivanovo Brewery accounts for 13% of all tax payments in the city of Ivanovo.

Sun's philanthropic and cultural activity strengthened this image of benevolence and commitment. It covered a variety of activities from sponsorship of youth marches,[76] funding of charity concerts,[77] and assistance for special surveys of the changing status of the young and the old under the travails of Russia's transition. True, the activity was limited in scale; and the most substantial endeavour was Sun Interbrew's support for a Moscow regional psychoneurology hospital for children. And even this was limited to providing medication, toys, and education materials. Yet the list of activities left an impression that the company was on call when such needs arose; and since other enterprises were not forthcoming with major acts of charity and philanthropy, the company did not measure up badly in its environment.

Continuous state-to-state cooperation through working groups of officials on both sides provided an added respectability to Indo–Russian commerce and supplied an important dimension to the achievements of an enterprise such as Sun. Even if India–Russia business-to-business links were established and measured in terms of profit and loss, and were determined by the rules of the chaotic market, they carried with them an aura of association with a friendship that went beyond the commercial. In discussions of this, the old rhetoric of friendly mutual assistance survived, and, despite several problems, such cooperation displayed a degree of vitality, and was used as a badge by even commercial organizations. Hence, the Indian Business Association proudly included a list of such ventures in the *Business Messenger*, its official journal. Along with an interview with the Embassy official associated with scientific and technical cooperation, the following 'achievements' were mentioned.

Under the aegis of the Integrated Long Term Programme between the two countries, the *Business Messenger* pointed out, a broad programme of collaboration had led to:

- The establishment at Bharat Immunologicals and Biologicals Cooperation Ltd., Bulandshahr, of a unit for the production of polio vaccine, with the use of technology provided by IPVE, Moscow. This was to provide vaccine to the National Immunization Programme of India and to UNICEF, and to be supplemented by other schemes to use Russian technology for vaccines to deal with Measles, BCG, Hepatitis B and Rabies.
- The establishment of an Indo–Russian Centre for Advanced Computing Research (IRCACR) in Moscow, the sale of a new generation of Indian supercomputers to the Institute of Computer Aided Design, Moscow and the installation of an advanced Indian computing system at the IRCACR, Moscow, for assistance in applications concerning Computational Atmospheric Sciences, Computational Fluid Dynamics, Seismic Data Processing, etc.
- The integration of Russian seismic sensors with Indian digital recorders and location of these at various points for observations by the Indian Meteorological Dept.
- The development of industrial and medical lasers.
- The development of porous silicon luminescent devices and detectors.
- The development of special linear accelerators for industrial application.
- The development of a special microtron for therapy.
- The development of joint gamma ray experiments.
- The development of a payload jointly for dispatch on a Russian rocket.
- The development of an imaging unit for a gamma ray telescope.
- The development of a multipurpose light transport aircraft.

The impressive list was supplemented with a substantial record of a host of MOUs for collaboration at various levels between the Department of Science and Technology, the Council for Scientific and Industrial Research, the Indian National Science Academy, the Russian

Academy of Sciences, the Indian Council for Agricultural Research, the Russian Academy of Agricultural Sciences, and a number of other bodies in Russia and India. All the agreements indicated a thriving industry of public cooperation designed for social benefit, with a minimum eye to commercial issues and were witness to the friendship between the two states.[78] They fleshed out the bonhomie that was recorded in the working groups where officials of the Central Bank of Russia and other agencies (who had clout in Russian government) met their Indian counterparts to establish the rhetoric of Indo–Russian friendship. The same goodwill was indicated in intentions to cooperate in the construction of a nuclear power plant at Kudamkulam in Tamil Nadu (announced in November 2001), despite the prevailing displeasure with which the Indian nuclear programme was viewed in international circles following the Pokhran tests of 1998.

Significantly, as the Indian Business Association publication itself indicated, the limited commercial application of many of the targets of collaboration, where half the products were confined to files, set fixed boundaries to the value of state to state friendship for the trader and the entrepreneur. And for most of those concerned, there appeared to be little chance of a change in the situation, given the unadventurous behaviour of government in Russia and India and the way the prime movers in the Russian economy took steps to prevent any return to patterns of the past. Even if entrepreneurs were directly included in government working groups, it was questionable whether the circumstances would alter. Besides, in fields such as nuclear energy, the role of the private sector was clearly to be limited, all major activities being normally undertaken by state agencies such as the Nuclear Power Corporation of India, which, as official sources for the early 2000s indicate, had no room for entrepreneurial activity.[79]

Again, despite a degree of respect that Indian operations attracted in the Federation, many entrepreneurs who came to Russia from India for business remained, socially speaking, in a ghetto of sorts, unlike their European or American counterparts. Indians did not make determined bids to participate in elite Russian entrepreneurial forums, although they were adept at making contacts and retaining them. They were not associated with the various clubs that grew up in Moscow in those times—the Golden Club, the VIP Club, or the International Russian Club. Nor were their names associated with the various lobbies that developed. The stagnation of FICCI's initiatives is a good indicator of the state of affairs, as was the utter lack of interest displayed by the Indo–CIS Chamber of Commerce in this form of activity. The Khemkas stood out as the sole case of Indian entrepreneurs establishing an interface with the Russian establishment.

Outside the rank of the elite, Indian businessmen and business-representatives who had a strong Indian profile, like their Turkish, Lebanese and Korean counterparts, restricted themselves to the immediate requirements of work and the Indian community in Moscow. Here, the term 'old Russia hand', when applied to Indians who worked for the new entrants into Russia, seldom had the same connotations it had when applied to Europeans or Americans, who had gone beyond the community circuit to adopt a network among powerful Russians. Among Indians, the term indicated a long stay, a sense of the peculiarities of the country, some savior faire, and a list of business contacts. It did not imply a deeper involvement with the social and political life of the land. The larger Indian community in Russia itself may have provided some back-up, consisting as it did of individuals who had married in Russia or had been associated with the Communist Party in the past, and who consequently had links that were valuable. But by themselves, businessmen stuck to the small Indian bridge party on weekends, and the get-together with Indian friends around a cook-up, Indian style. The Embassy and the Indian Business Alliance traditionally organized the odd meeting, and the Bengali Puja had been running for twenty years or so by the early 2000s—but there was no other centre of general congregation, even if figures like Sujit Singh were a cynosure of sorts.

By and large, businessmen who had not developed Russian families (and many who had), who arrived in Russia during the new wave of trade, like almost all Americans, Europeans, Turks, etc., did not think of themselves as primarily Russia specialists, even if they had excellent knowledge of the region. They formed an excellent reservoir of expertise that Indian companies used: but their eyes were not trained on Russia primarily. Anup Banerji, who was responsible for Ranbaxy and Lyka in their teething stage and moved on to Universal after Lyka was taken over by Heterodrugs, was a good example of the businessman operating in the market. He had good Russian gen but he also had some African experience and had worked in Eastern Europe, and was not opposed to dealing with operations outside Russia. The same applied, on a more limited scale, to Rajesh Sharma of Usha Continental, who began working on his own after DCM left Russia. Young operatives in charge of Dr. Reddy's and Ranbaxy ventures were even less Russia-driven. The Russian market did not throw up the standard responses to advertisement and marketing that young Indian professionals were trained to expect—responses that the Indian market provided with all its limitations. Little wonder that a pharmaceutical expert like Jaideep Kapoor,[80] who worked well for Cadilla, decided to go on to the West to 'improve himself' there with an MBA and access to its opportunities by 2002. Among professionals and businessmen in India the Russian market was regarded as an opportunity to make money and go further. Few regarded it as the principal opportunity.

The case of the Indian-owned newspaper, *The Russian Journal*, provides the example that proves the rule. Launched from Moscow in 1998 by Ajay Goyal, a non-resident Indian based in the United States, and run by his brother Sandip Goyal in the Federation, the 'journal' was well-established and competed with the *Moscow Daily Times* and other papers for the English reader. Goyal took a serious interest in Russian affairs and his leaders intervened in national debates on the Russian nation, Russian elections, changes in the Russian economy, etc. His vantage point was external to Russia, though, with a lifestyle, partially in the US and partially in Russia. Goyal asserted his rootlessness:

> Like Russians, we Indians – from a failed national system with little to speak of except corrupt politicians – see our pride in those who have made it big . . . overseas.[81]

Despite their popularity and Russia-orientation, though *The Russian Journal* and Goyal, like most Indian businessmen and professionals, specialized in remaining on the fringes of Russia and her politics—involved but cautious, with feet firmly planted in another environment.

A brief note on the publication must indicate that in 2000, *The Russian Journal* was run with a business magazine. It came out from Moscow from 1998. The publications contained a wide range of translated articles, commentaries and invited articles and columns.

Goyal described his venture in the normal style of most newspaper men 'a voice on all things Russian to the world uncolored by bias, fear or partisanship'. He was involved in Russian business for 15 years. He described himself as 'a veteran of Russian business . . . an independent thinker and writer on the Russian economy, business culture and media.'

He considered himself an expert on the Federation, deeply committed to an understanding of its culture and standing for the cause of democracy in the country. He himself ran a column in the journal on 'Intellectual Capital'.

Undoubtedly such a situation had advantages. For the Indian businessman was not associated with any group or lobby in a fluid political and economic environment. It restricted the reach of entrepreneurship, though, as the Chairman of the Indian Business Alliance in 2002, Rajesh Sharma was aware, as he attempted to create a dynamic and special aura for the organization through a degree of exclusivity and high rates for membership.[82]

PERSPECTIVES ON INDO–RUSSIAN TRADE: FOUNDATIONS AND CONTEXT

The Alumnus Factor

In many companies, the sales and marketing limitations which were the upshot of a 'ghetto' mentality were compensated by the activities of an informal community of Indian students in Russia. These were University goers who had come to the country during perestroika and who were driven to jobs when the value of state scholarships plummeted and prices sky-rocketed. Well endowed with Russian friends who faced similar problems, and equipped with a sound knowledge of language and country, this group worked for Indian entrepreneurial units and extended the range of the latter's operations. In the case of the pharmaceutical industry, as the links between the drug stores and producers collapsed, Indian students allowed Ranbaxy, Cadilla, and others to step in, through behind-the-scenes lobbying with the FTOs Medeksport and Soiuzkhimeksport, and with government agencies and hospitals at a time when the steady flow of funds into health care from the state was drying up. Sujit Singh of the Shreya Corporation was the most distinguished of these facilitators: but a number of others (such as Sanjay Singh of Intercare) have also been mentioned.

The Shreya Corporation was established by Sujit Singh in 1993. It began as an Indian company located in rooms in the Izmailovo Hotel, importing pharmaceuticals and allied goods. The company worked primarily with foreign pharmaceutical agents operating in Russia, and state purchases against the rupee debt from Indian companies. In 1994 the company moved more firmly into the Russian pharmaceutical market, focusing on distribution and establishing a network with pharmaceutical enterprises inside Russia. The network extended outside the country after the corporation received a license for pharmaceutical activity. Affiliated units developed (it had representations in 34 cities by 2002) and the organization used the web extensively from 1996 for its activities, advertising prominently at the autumn exhibition of pharmaceuticals of 1995. Investments were duly made in warehousing and the profile of the company was strong enough for its management to play a major role in 1997 in the Moscow municipal social programme for free and preferential medical service. Adjustments ensured that Shreya survived the 1998 crisis, and in 1999 its position was strong enough for the Corporation to open 33 drugstores in Moscow Eastern Administrative District within the framework of free and preferential medical service programme, and to participate in another, the Dialysis Centre in Moscow. The corporation had a staff of 2,000 at the beginning of the 2000s. By 2001, the corporation marketed about 4,500 products, where the Indian product share was only 10 per cent. The products were drawn from 25 countries. The organization served 5,000 clients, including 350 suppliers and 150 Russian manufacturers. It had no stated interested in production in Russia, though its spokesman did not rule out the possibility.

Shreya was linked to Shreya Life Sciences (India) which acquired the pharmaceutical division of Rallis India Ltd., a Tata pharmaceutical unit, which was then incorporated as Amadeus Biotech and Pharmaceuticals Pvt. Ltd., a company that worked closely with the CIS market. In 2003, the Indian company acquired Plethico Pharmaceuticals as part of a bid to establish itself as a major player in the Indian pharmaceutical industry—a bid which, according to Sujit Singh, could have involved further acquisitions. Significantly, though, Singh diversified in investments in India thereafter, rather than broaden his base in Russia.[83]

Intercare was founded in 1996 by Sanjiv Kumar Singh, who qualified in medicine in Russia. Probably the fifth largest distributor of pharmaceuticals in the Russian market by the beginning of the 2000s, it had a wide range of products (a list of 5,000) at its disposal (from a number of manufacturers) and worked by a distinctive philosophy of pricing, according to Singh. It set up an extensive network of partners

(35 nodes) and was frequently quoted on Russian TV on pharmaceutical matters.

In the years immediately following disintegration, students like Sujit Singh set up units that worked closely with Indian companies. Hence, Anup Banerji of Ranbaxy worked with the members of the Vijaya Foundation, with young alumni of Soviet universities. The students in turn were able, in time, to provide their partners access to the Russian market as government orders collapsed. They also provided back-up services with the mafia and low level officialdom in circumstances where only Sun was able to do without their assistance.

A prominent alumnus who went in a different way was Sudhir Gupta of Amtel, who had business links with India and worked as an assertively patriotic NRI.[84] Post-1996, the connections of this organization with India diminished as Gupta moved firmly into the Russian business world.

The Amtel Group was founded by Sudhir Gupta as a Trading Company, and had Indian connections. Initially the enterprise provided rubber from Singapore to Russian companies and dealt in a series of goods (tea, fruit juices, vodka, etc.). Gupta was involved in financial speculation during the early phase of reforms—and Amtel is recorded as one of the investors in the Tokobank. He ventured into production and manufacture-financing in 1996, and established control over various companies under 'Amtel Holding'. At the beginning of the 2000s, in Siberia the main units associated with the group were in Krasnoyarsk (JSC Krasnoyarsk Plant of Industrial Rubber Products and JSC 'Tire Complex Amtel-Siberia') and Kemerovo (Chimvolokno Amtel-Kuzbass); in central Russia in Voronezh (OOO Voronezhskii Shinnyi Zavod), Kirov (Kirov Tire Plant) and Volgograd (Volgograd Plant of Carbon Black); and in the Ukraine, in Chernigov (JSC Chernigov Plant 'Chimvolokno') and Kiev (JSC JV Rosava). By Gupta's own admission, Amtel did not construct plants. This was clear also from the public relations statements of those who ran the various factories. Amtel attracted scarce finance (often from abroad) for limited ventures within existing plants (focusing on retooling). The company worked in close collaboration with major Russian vehicle producers such as Logovaz and foreign tyre and automobile producers interested in the Russian market. Amtel had important collaborations with the Vneshtorgbank, the Joint-Stock Commercial Innovation, UkrSibbank, and KPNU Sibtekhmontazh. And it had a link up with Nokian Tyres PLC of

Finland. Its shares were held by Alfa Bank, Troika Bank, Mez Prom Bank, and Nikoil. Its total assets came to $300 million and it had an annual turnover of $350 million.

Amtel maintained a cultured public face—with participation in seminars on quality management systems and support for the contest for the car journalist award. The Company commanded high respect on the Russian stock exchanges and was quoted on the New York Stock Exchange.[85] The complications that Gupta had to live with came to the fore in November 2002, when there was an attempt on his life.

Like Ranbaxy and Torrent, the alumnus firms sought a field of play broader than Russia. Hence, the Shreya Corporation established interests in India, and had close links with distributors in the Ukraine; while Sudhir Gupta had interests in the Ukraine, the United Kingdom and the United States. Their authority rested firmly in Russian business, but neither involved himself solely in the Russian business world.

There were exceptions, but their enterprise was small scale. They included figures such as A. Chakrapani, of JSC Solar Corporation, a former medical student from Kiev who married in the USSR, had a family and turned to commission work after the disintegration. There was Anil Jain of Nadia Impex, who also married in the USSR, had a family, and, at the time of disintegration was working for Moscow Radio's Hindi service after completing his education. Jain found his salary inadequate and went to work for a South-East Asian group that was moving into a textile unit and wanted a non-Russian manager who knew the language to reshape the unit's workforce. He later went into trading, using a large network of local contacts. Both perestroika students had a firm and clear personal commitment to India—and travelled to the country regularly to keep in touch with their families. Jain had an exceptional obsession with Hindi and for a while brought out a newspaper in Moscow in Hindi. Chakrapani's and Jain's primary moorings, clearly, were in the Russian business world and being essentially small-scale entrepreneurs with excellent local reputations, they had no real intention to move out of the Federation. As Jain's business showed, however, he was willing to work with any company that could provide business, Indian or not. He advertised on the Embassy website, but his trade was not solely with India. Chakrapani kept in touch with information concerning a range of non-resident Indian operations while he had a clear link with the community of Indian perestroika students.

CIS Context

The market of the neighbouring CIS states that acted as a support for Russia business was a source of possible long-term destabilization for the Indian connection with Russia. The cohort of India's perestroika students was able to work throughout the Soviet space and draw Indian business into the area. For this reason and for others, almost all the companies mentioned in the corporate survey above developed trading operations throughout the CIS, and were able to take advantage of rupee–rouble arrangements and India connections for transactions there, if and when this was permissible. Inevitably, Indian operatives in Russia not only established connections, which were bilateral, they looked to prospects further afield when they contemplated their ventures. Indian tie-ups in Russia had a spin-off benefit for India's exports to the CIS region and business in the latter initially strengthened the former. In the period immediately after disintegration, Agio undertook a number of enterprises in the Ukraine, using its position in Moscow as a base. Axiom Projects International focused as much on Kazakhstan and Ukraine as it did on its Russian operations. In pharmaceuticals, there was regular business coming into Cadilla, Dr. Reddy's and Ranbaxy from the CIS, though the Moscow operation was clearly the most important.

The likelihood was clear by 2002, though, that with the revival of Russian production and steady competition from Eastern Europe, Indian ventures would retreat into the more peripheral CIS market—into Kazakhstan, Kyrgyzstan, and Belorussia, which had tariff agreements with Russia. It was also likely that Indian organizations would face stiff competition from Russian ventures in these countries thereafter, as they used Russophone connections. The promise of the CIS, a less competitive market, had a tendency to weaken the Russian initiative in the circumstances, even while giving Indian enterprise no great stability in the region. Until the early 2000s, the route had not acquired significance substantially because of the poor banking arrangements in most CIS countries (where LCs required the deposit of almost the whole sum before the letter was issued, and where Indian banking operations were in a fledgling state). In Belorussia and Uzbekistan there were tight state controls with no special arrangements such as the debt-trade with Russia whereby the Indian businessman had a point of entry. Infrastructural access to Kazakhstan still left much to be desired, as did the standard problem of warehousing.

Poor exploitation of the market by Western companies and the low per capita income, though, indicated that the region remained a major market for Indian goods, especially pharmaceuticals, which could use Russian networks as a point of dispatch if direct access and funding was a problem. Clear connections between distributors, as in the case of Shreya and its Ukrainian partner, made easy access using Russia a possibility.

Market Support for Indian Business: Long-term Problems

It became questionable whether the intangible factors that supported Indian business in the Russian market would hold out in the long term. This refers to the positive image of the Indian businessman and his goods in the Federation. Interviews with Indian entrepreneurs in Moscow during this period elicited a uniform opinion that Russians were more happy to do business with Indians than with Europeans and Americans. Not because Indians afforded greater opportunities and funds, but because Euro–American attitudes towards business and management were regarded as 'non-Russian', while Indian perspectives were not regarded as exceptionally alien. Indians were seen as a lesser threat when business arrangements came up: less aggressive, and less well-heeled. They were respected as employers, and seldom associated with the behaviour of their Euro–American counterparts (who have a reputation for ruthless treatment of both white-collar and blue-collar workers in Russia). Again, Indian business still had some aura of a government-to-government link, even if it had been common among Indian entrepreneurs operating in Russia to argue that there was a gap of trust (and a superiority complex) which lay between Indian businessmen and Indian officials, whatever the apparent desire of the latter to improve trade. The same cannot be said about entrepreneurs of EU or US provenance, who acted with independence, even if they received assistance from their governments.

Significantly, Russians did not pass up opportunities to collaborate with Americans and Europeans, despite such sentiments. Hence values probably had little significance when it came to brass tacks. Again, it is questionable whether such sentiments were shared by a new generation of businessman and consumers, for whom the image of India was poorly formed and who, as Ajay Goyal was to point out,[86] worked with racial stereotypes concerning the inferiority of India's sense of technology. For many 'sophisticated' new Russians, moreover, India meant cheap goods of uncertain provenance (the unfortunate image of Indian pharmaceuticals and readymade fabrics). It was this that prevented the consumption of Indian drugs in consciously 'up-market' (and prosperous) locales such as St. Petersburg.[87] Indian pharmaceuticals were popular at the lower-income end of Russia's population and in far-flung areas where market-awareness was less developed.

The Instability of the Russian Market

The instability of the Russian market that encouraged the maintenance of large off-shore holdings by Russian oligarchs was a major factor in keeping not only small operations such as JSC Solar but also larger Indian operations on their toes, preventing a major build-up in Russia. At one level, economic crises such as that of 1998 encouraged trade operations with India. The crisis came from a shortage of hard currency in the Federation, and difficulties of interest payments on short-term high-interest bonds, rather than any fundamental change in Russia's manufacturing economy; and it affected Russia's capacity to import Western goods very substantially,[88] even if the banking crisis itself did not affect a large number of major producer units.[89] In the circumstances, Prime Minister Primakov asked the Government of India to increase its payments, in order to assist the Russian government; and the concurrence of the Government of India brought Indian goods into renewed focus on the Russian market. It also encouraged the import of Russian goods into India.

Equally, though, the crisis of 1998 destabilized organizations such as Chakrapani's, as well as more substantial operations such as the Russian Torrent operation, since much business was dependent on non-debt trade and the crisis led to a collapse of purchasing power and savings. Since such upsets were common in Russia in the 1990s, Indian entrepreneurs treated the region gingerly—which did not bode well for their future commitments. Since various categories of goods had problems preserving their ascendancy in Russia (such as pharmaceuticals), the caution led to an uncertain position which could, literally, go anyhere.

NOTES

1. When I visited *Demokraticheskaia Rossiia* offices at 22 Petrovka in May 1992, they were clearly unused to dealing with Indians of any persuasion or profession.
2. *The Statesman* (Calcutta), 20 and 21 August 1991 for details of the equivocal position of the Indian prime minister.
3. *Business Messenger* (Moscow), 2001, p. 11. There seems to be a common strain in all official pronouncements of this time, which stress the watchwords of democracy and reform. Iurii Khlebanov, deputy prime minister and member of the IRJC, was more clear about geopolitical interests. During the Vajpayee visit, he took a similar position to the deputy FM with this minor addition: 'We proceed from the ground that geopolitical and national interests of Russia and India coincide, both countries are adherents to democratic principles of social development and both have interest in securing propitious external environment and internal stability for carrying out social and economic reforms. It is also very important that the principle of protecting territorial integrity is one of the basic principles of foreign policy for both Russia and India.' Ibid., p. 7.
4. This perspective on the Russian economy is now standard in the Federation and is the staple diet of students of economics. See for instance the discussion on transition in a standard textbook for university students, E.V. Krasnikova, *Ekonomika perekhodnogo perioda* (Moscow: Omega-L, 2008).
5. Mr. Vohra discussed this with me on a number of occasions during 1998–2001. Those who made the material available charged exceptional rates—a fact that later caused scrutiny by the CAG!
6. The best account of the circumstances in which the decision on the rupee debt was taken is Nirmal Chandra's 'India's Rouble Debt and Depreciating Rouble', *EPW*, 3–10 July 1993.
7. Discussions with Animesh Basu, of the Thermax Corporation in Moscow, in early 1992.
8. The move to subsidize India trade in Russia on the part of the Government of India was evident early after disintegration, but it took shape haltingly, and Montek Singh Ahluwalia (Secretary, GOI) and J.N. Dixit (Foreign Secretary GOI) were not in favour of the step. These are conclusions I draw from a discussion with J.N. Dixit on 22 July 2002.

   There are reasonably clear stages to the way in which Indo–Russian trade relations came to be regularized, and the final settlement of how India's debt to the USSR came to be handled. Initially the Agreement on Trade and Economic Cooperation of 22 February 1992 established a regime for trade in a specific set of goods 'on a balanced basis': for export from Russia, for petroleum products, various metals, wood pulp and newsprint, books, records, etc., asbestos, rubber, polyethylene; for export from India, tea, coffee, pharmaceuticals, books, etc., tobacco, bags, freight containers, garments, leather products, etc. The Agreement was not clear, however, about what exchange rate was to be used if the Russian side was to pay through debt-settlement arrangements. Commerce found a more sound footing following the introduction in India of the Liberalized Exchange Management System on 1 March 1992, and the RBI's Notice to Exporters (no. 3 of the RBI) that made it clear that trade would not be guided purely by the Trade Protocol. The position was that 'besides the trade which can be carried out under the clearing mechanism of the Trade Protocol, imports and exports of goods and services may also take place in any freely convertible currency, in accordance with the trade regulations and exchange control regulations of the two countries'.

In these circumstances, Indian traders avoided the Trade Protocol and came to follow the standard regulations that guided export trade. Such rules included the requirement that 40 per cent of export earnings be surrendered to the RBI, exchanging the balance at official and market rates and allowing companies to retain 15 per cent of their earnings. Like all traders, they had to deal with the wild fluctuations of prices in Russia and day-to-day variations in the exchange rate of the rouble.

The GOI took pains to maintain good relations with the Federation during this period of uncertainty concerning the working of the Trade Protocol. It took steps to ensure that India could not be used as a conduit for export of capital in these difficult months. Under the February 1992 Agreement, it was stated clearly that the 'RBI shall permit the Russian exporters to India and/or their banks to open Special Accounts designated in US dollars with commercial banks in India upon presentation by the exporters/their bankers of certificates issued by the Central Bank of the Russian Federation, which shall, *inter alia*, indicate the percentage of export earnings which, according to the laws and regulations of the Russian Federation should accrue to the Centralized Foreign Exchange Fund of the Russian Federation. These Special Accounts shall be credited with export earnings of Russian exporters in India less that part which, according to laws and regulations of the Russian Federation should be allocated to the Centralized Foreign Exchange Fund and should be transferred by the order of the respective exporters through commercial banks in India to the Central Account of BFTR with RBI.' This introduced the Central Bank of Russia as a player in judging what was to be exported from Russia at what price, preventing speculators from following here the practice they followed in Western and Eastern Europe, i.e. exporting goods at artificially low prices, and receiving reimbursement at a higher rate, to deposit the balance abroad in convertible currencies. The commendable approach of the GOI, however, meant that India was not a preferred export target at this time. Links that could have developed did not develop (except in cases where the practices followed in Europe could be replicated in India in a clandestine manner, through the use of accounts outside India for payments that were not legitimate).

The trade agreements and the RBI notices that guided trade are reproduced verbatim in Ramesh Behl and L.D. Mago, *The Indian Businessman's Guide to CIS* (Delhi: Global Business Press, 1994), pp. 256–8, 263–5.

9. Ibid.
10. To make sure that India was not affected in this arrangement by the varying course of the rouble, the Memorandum of Understanding made it clear though that use of this technical credit would follow the principle that the contracts would be 'in internationally competitive prices and denominated in US dollars'. Also, to limit outflow of currency, it was made clear that while 'payments of these transactions . . . shall . . . be made in US dollars', 'there shall . . . be no outflow/inflow of US dollars from/to India on account of the trade transactions . . .'. The regime that was set up was that 'the BFTR shall open a Central Account with the RBI and one or more accounts with commercial banks in India in US dollars with the approval of the RBI. These accounts will be used only for carrying out trade transactions arising out of Trade Protocol, and balances standing to the credit of these accounts shall not be allowed to be transferred from India. In case of exports to Russia under the Trade Protocol, reimbursement will be received in US dollars by the exporters' bank from the banks maintaining the account of BFTR or from the RBI maintaining the Central Account of BFTR. In case of imports from Russia, the importers' bank will have to transfer US dollars to the Nostro accounts of banks maintaining special accounts of Russian exporters/their bankers or to the Nostro accounts of banks maintaining the account of BFTR.' The regime was confirmed by the RBI's notice to exporters, no. 4, which also specified the various allocations under technical credit and restated the basic requirements of notice no. 3. See Behl and Mago, op. cit.
11. *Payment Procedures: Exports to Russian Federation* (Reserve Bank of India, December 1995), pp. 5–7.
12. On 28 January 1993, at a meeting between Indian Prime Minister Narasimha Rao and Russian President Boris Yeltsin, an arrangement was agreed regarding the rupee–rouble exchange rate taking into consideration the rate at which debt was to be determined as well as prevailing prices. The arrangement followed discussions between Finance Minister Manmohan Singh, Russian Deputy Prime Minister Mr. Shumeiko, and Minister for Foreign Economic Relations (Russia), Mr. Glaziev. The agreement on the exchange rate, following the Yeltsin–Rao meeting, was signed by Manmohan Singh and Vladimir Shumeiko. The agreement noted that Soviet-era debt was to be paid by India 'in Rupees by means of export of Indian goods'. It also noted that the rate of exchange for 'determining the payment schedule' was established hitherto by an Indo–Russian Protocol of 1978. This Protocol had worked with a formula that 'provided for changes in the value of the Rupee in relation to a 16-currency basket . . . but assumed that the value of the Rouble to be invariant.' On 31 March 1992 the debt stood at 9,871 billion roubles or Rs. 31,342 crore. This figure was treated in different ways according to the Agreement. It was noted that it was a figure that emerged from the exchange rate of 1 April 1992, shortly after the rupee had been devalued. By an earlier exchange rate (1 January 1990) the figure would have been Rs. 19,660 crore. The overall sum would be repaid

bearing this difference in mind. The difference in the two amounts (Rs. 11,682 crore) would be fixed in rupees and would be rescheduled. This rescheduled portion would carry no interest and it would be repaid in annual instalments over 45 years. According to the agreement, this sum 'would have no protection against any fluctuation in the value of the rupee for a period of five years. Thereafter it would be indexed to the SDR if the average annual depreciation of the Rupee exceeds 3 per cent over this 5-year period. Similar reviews would be conducted at the end of every 5-year period.' The non-rescheduled sum, meanwhile, (Rs. 19,660 crore) would be repaid over 12 years carrying an annual interest of 2.4 per cent. By the agreement, 'this amount would . . . be denominated in rupees and repayments of the principal and interest of this portion of the debt would be effected by India in accordance with the schedule in force for each of the relevant inter-governmental credit agreements. The rupee payments of the principal and the interest on this non-rescheduled portion of the debt would however, be protected by adjusting the rupee amounts in line with future changes in the rupee value of the SDR basket of five currencies.' See Behl and Mago, op.cit. for material from the agreement. The terms of the agreement are also noted in outline in *Payment Procedures: Exports to Russian Federation*, op. cit., pp. 2–5. Specific clarification is set out in *The Economic Times*, 30 January 1993. See also Chandra, *India's Rouble Debt*, op. cit.

13. Ibid.
14. Interview with J.N. Dixit, New Delhi, July 2002.
15. This point was stressed by Shiv Vikram Khemka in his presentation at the Rajiv Gandhi Foundation on the eve of the visit of Vladimir Putin to India in November 2002.
16. 'Protocol of the First Session of the Inter-Governmental Russian-Indian Commission on Trade, Economic, Scientific and Technological Cooperation' (hereafter PRIC[I]). Moscow 13 and 14 September 1994, p. 5. 'Protocol of the Second Session of the Inter-Governmental Russian-Indian Commission on Trade, Economic, Scientific and Technological Cooperation' (hereafter PRIC[II]), New Delhi, 9–12 October 1995, p. 3, para. 4.1.4.
17. PRIC[I], pp. 5, 3, para. 4.1.5. In the course of 1995, the GOI considered a list of goods for which the value addition for debt transactions was to be waived, and the matter was solved to the satisfaction of both sides.
18. PRIC[I], p. 4. PRIC[II], p. 3, para. 4.1.3. In 1995, for instance, the Russians were interested in adding sugar to the list of goods to be imported.
19. 'Protocol of the Third Session of the Inter-Governmental Russian-Indian Commission on Trade, Economic, Scientific and Technological Cooperation', 10–11 February 1997, Moscow, p. 3, para. 2.1.5. The problems were not felt on the Russian side only, and the transfer to the auction system was for mutual benefit, despite an impression to the contrary in the Indian press of the time. Hence, the Protocol in 1997 is clear about Indian annoyance. 'The Indian side pointed out that allocation of rupee funds continued to be characterized by

delays. In several cases, rupee allocations were being made to Russian organizations with no experience in trading in India.'

20. *India-Russia: The Road Ahead*, p. 3 (Confederation of Indian Industry, 2000).
21. Interviews with A.K. Sinha and A. Kohli, Embassy of India, Moscow, December 2002. The point about the decline in interest in rupee dealings was stressed by Anup Banerji, a former President of the Indian Business Association and a businessman well versed in the ways of Indian pharmaceutical dealings in the former Soviet Union and Eastern Europe. Interview with Anup Banerji, December 2002, Moscow.
22. This view has been expressed to me in confidence by an official of the Ministry of Commerce.
23. Interviews with A.A. Kutsenkov in 1992 (May), 1995 (July), and 2002 (December). The Chamber brought together various influential figures in local government and in industry to try and promote Indian trade. It was one of a small number of organizations that developed at this time with such ends in view. Interview with A. Kohli, Counsellor Economic, Embassy of India, Moscow, December 2002.
24. Valentina Tereshkova, 'Cultural and Educational Links between Russia and India', in *Vladimir Putin, President of the Russian Federation, Official Visit to India, December 2002* (Moscow: RIA, 2002).
25. This downturn is the subject of a number of articles. For the standard view see a variety of articles in Shamsuddin (ed.), *India and Russia: Towards Strategic Partnership* (Delhi: Lancer's Books, 2001); Gulshan Sachdeva, 'Indo-Russian Trade and Economic Relations: Present Realities and Future Possibilities', R.G. Gidadhubli, 'India–Russia Economic Relations: Challenges and Opportunities' and Tahir Asghar, 'Indo–Russian Trade: An Overview', as well as Jyotsna Bakshi, 'India Russia Cooperation in Economy, Science and Technology'.
26. The statements of S.P. Das, Working President of the Indian-CIS Chamber of Commerce and Industry, in a latter day report on the state of commerce, summarizes many of the complaints of individual entrepreneurs. The range of solutions that were agreed on (including intergovernmental action) indicate the intensity of the problems. Regarding shipment, Das commented: 'Absence of adequate shipping facilities have created a major bottleneck and have become serious disincentive for boosting trade to a desired level. During USSR, all goods were transported to Russia through the Black Sea port of Odessa and Illychevsk and the duration was about 3 weeks. Today, goods are being transported to Moscow through St. Petersburg and also Novorossiysk ports and the total duration is about 50–60 days. The Novorossiysk is at present not suitable for handling containerized cargo. This port is required to be upgraded to match the requirement of handling both bulk and containerized cargoes. Russian government agreed to upgrade this port from the debt repayment fund to be paid by India. Further, Russian government had also signed an agreement with shipping corporation of India to run a joint stock shipping line in 1997.

This should be expedited without further delay. At present exporters are experiencing enormous difficulties to transit the goods by land to Moscow from St. Petersburg. In fact, transportation of goods from St. Petersburg to Moscow by road is highly unsafe and costly due to under-world activities.' Problems with wharehousing were substantial according to Das: 'Under the present hurdles and helpless conditions, concept of maintaining a warehouse at Moscow and St. Petersburg are ideal and will avoid many difficulties that we are facing in boosting trade in Russia'. Regarding customs (again in echo of many other statements), Das pointed out: 'Tariff and non-tariff barriers under the present global market economy are in constant conflict for the development of free market economy for slowed down investment process and growth of trade. In the national interest, Russia should review its policies and take effective measure to simplify the customs duties, entry procedures rules and regulations ensure clear and transparent laws and give wide publicity among the exporters-importers and arrange for speedy release of goods from tariff barriers.' *ICCCI Newsletter*, June 1999, pp. 5–6.

27. I am grateful for this information as well as other insights into company behaviour to Joysree Mukherjee, who was associated with the Indo–CIS Chamber of Commerce until 2002. Ms. Mukherjee gave me this information during a number of interviews in 2002.
28. See Valentin A. Kouznetsov, 'Technopromexport: Long-standing Cooperation in India's Electric Power Sector', in *Vladimir Putin, President of the Russian Federation, Official Visit to India, December 2002* (Moscow: RIA, 2002). Technopromeksport has had a long association with India. Information on the FTO can be found from its website—www.tpe.ru—which shows how the FTO adapted to modern times.
29. Technopromeksport in association with the Indian ABL won the tender for modernization of three units at Neyveli TPS in a competition with BHEL-Siemens. Ibid.
30. This involved the Narmada Hydroelectric Development Corporation at the Indira Sagar Hydropower Project. Ibid.
31. See the website of the organization which details its various enterprises on the Indian market from the mid-1990s. (www.tyazh.ru)
32. Arun Mohanty, 'Indo-Russian Cooperation in the Sphere of Energy Security', in *Business Messenger*, December 2002.
33. Information for Gidroenergoprom (fdd. 1990 under Managing Director Vladimir Loshak) is available from the company's website www.gidroenergoprom.ru
34. *Steel Authority of India, Annual Report*, especially 1996–7, 1997–8, and 2000–1 (Steel Authority of India Ltd., New Delhi, 1997, 1998, 2001 respectively). The information concerning Romelt occurs in the Director's Report section.
35. See the Department of Coal (GOI) site http://coal.nic.in/ The section on foreign collaboration provides the information.

36. Information supplied by Alexander Prokhorov, Trade Representative in India of Rudgormach, Calcutta, October 2001.
37. The Russian agencies proposed, in March 2002, to set up a Rs. 1,000 crore titanium dioxide pigment production plant in Orissa (where 75 per cent of the 50,000 tonne output was to be exported to Russia). Russia had little titanium for pigment production: and the Orissa material was compatible with Russian technology. Triple super phosphate fertilizer (130,000 tonnes) and iron oxide pigment (500,000 tonnes) were also to be produced. The agencies were to work with Saraf Agencies of Kolkata, who would process beach sand in Ganjam, and supply ilminete, which is an important component in pigmnent production. The venture included participation by IDC (Orissa), which held the mining leases. Half the 250,000 tonne production was for the Russians, while the rest was to be exported to various countries including Ukraine, Korea, etc. *Business Standard*, 11 March 2002.
38. A. Prokhorov of Rudgormach used to work for TPE and supplied me with this information. Interview with A. Prokhorov in Calcutta in 2001.
39. Internet information has linked this company to M. Shivnani of Moscow and Dubai, V.M. Deshpande of Pune, and business in a variety of goods: autore-conditioning and garage equipment, building materials, plastic processing machinery, packaging machines and electrical and metal machine-making equipment, bags and wood pulp.
40. Information on Axiom has been available at their website, www.axiom.ru which shows the company to have entered Russia in 1994, and operating in the Federation, Kazakhstan, and UK. Its Calcutta office has been at 28B Shakespeare Sarani, and its specialization has been machines and bags.
41. This is the Indian branch of Sudhir Gupta's Amtel Group in Russia. Internet information on this organization indicates that it is based in Baroda (R.C. Dutt Rd.), and related to Amtel Exports of Singapore. This Indian company has been functioning in Russia since 1989.
42. Internet information on Dina has linked the company to Rajesh Verma of Mumbai, and to outlets in Delhi. The company is said to have had a long connection with Russia, and to deal in pharmaceuticals.
43. The material on this transaction is available in the Archives of Industrial Export Services, Calcutta, Thermax file. The papers were generously made available to me by Mr. P. Guha Thakurta, and Mr. S. Ghosh, Managing Partners of the organization. The basic contract for the transaction was executed in Moscow on 9 October 1992. Correspondence is available on pilferage and various other problems of the transaction in letters and other correspondence of 1993.
44. Archives of Industrial Export Services, Thermax file, Letter of 8 April 1994 to Thermax Moscow, concerning allocation of Russian rupee funds for linoleum and subsequent correspondence.
45. See www.ushain.com Besides pharmaceuticals, the company works with processed foods, leather and engineering equipment.

46. Interview with Shankar Mukherji, Moscow, December 2002.
47. T.K. Chakraborty, 'Indian tea in Russia', *Business Messenger*, 2001. Chakraborty, the Director of the Tea Promotion Board in Moscow, points out the problem. 'The tea market internationally is becoming more and more price competitive, Russia being no exception. With setting up of various blending and packaging facilities locally, there has also been an increasing tendency for import of low quality teas at cheaper prices from available sources.' The Tea Board and the Ministry of Commerce strategy has been to go on a quality tea promotion campaign using an international consultancy agency (M/S Accenture).
48. Interview with Surojit (Bunt) Ghosh, 1993, a member of the EBRD and CSFB team that conducted the first auctions in Russia in the winter of 1992–3. In the early stages, buyers were sought even as the auction began. To enhance the kudos of the process, many of those sought out were foreign entrepreneurs. The Singapore entrepreneur Rajan Pillai, for instance, was one of those involved in auctions for the Bolshevik Biscuit Factory.
49. Ekarerina Ballerina, 'San Grup v Rossii: 40 let aktivnoi raboty', *Rossiiskaia Federatsiia*, no. 2, 1999, p. 5.
50. 'Kak Vesti Uspeshnyi Biznes v Rossii', in *Chelovek I Kar'era*, no. 5, 1999, p. 8.
51. This is clear from the fact that effort did not simply go into increasing output and improving marketing. In the case of the Kursk brewery (KPK), for instance, while installed capacity was raised from 720,000 to 1,200,000 hectolitres and a malt factory was established in the brewery complex, measures were also taken to ensure improved levels of cleanliness and hygiene, primarily through the installation of a new generation of filters and innovations in water-treatment. See 'Kak Vesti Uspeshnyi Biznes v Rossii', op. cit.
52. Both advantages and disadvantages are clearly evident in the case of Maxwell Asgari, who was Sun's CEO in the mid-1990s, and who made the statements noted above. The Khemkas hired him from the huge Swedish-Swiss corporate Asea Brown Boveri in 1997. Asgari had come to the Russian market in the 1980s, with Combustion Engineering of the US, when he was one of those instrumental in setting up Applied Engineering Systems, a US-Soviet joint venture with the USSR's Ministry for Oil and Petrochemicals. The company was merged into Asea Brown Boveri and, when the latter finally pulled out of the joint venture and began speculation in Russian privatization, Asgari was their main operations chief and went on to set up twenty companies associated with the energy industry in various ways. Asgari evolved a keen sense of the Russian market, its emerging system of shareholdings, and the necessity to make a firm commitment and not to expect fast profits when it came to investment in producer industries. And he provided Sun with this vast experience. But his various prejudices are equally clear. 'The concept of ownership is still not intimately understood here. If you bought something cheap three years ago and added value, they say "You bought it cheap". The Russians are so paranoid about what you paid and what it is worth today. The fact that you've spent money on it and never taken money out is not considered. . . . When

you buy something and it's unprofitable, you own 60%. Then suddenly they say you own 27%, and then suddenly you own nothing.' Rose Brady, op. cit., pp. 192ff.

53. The mother company here was Foreign & Colonial Investment Trust PLC, an old investment company that originated in Britain and moved into investments in Japan, Thailand and Korea.
54. Chairman of Spectrum Power Generation Ltd. and Ginni Financial Services Ltd.
55. Member of various bodies set up by Reserve Bank of India and a Trustee in Unit Trust of India. On the Boards of State Bank of India and SBI Capital Markets Ltd.
56. Chairman of the Boards of Securities Trading Corporation of India Ltd. and Rain Calcining Ltd. Non-executive Director on the Boards of Industrial Development Bank of India and various other companies. Until 1995, the Chairman of State Bank of India where he set up SBI Capital Markets Ltd. and SBI Mutual Fund. Formerly the Chairman of State Bank of India until retirement.
57. Served in senior positions with the Tata Electric Company and Tata Consultancy Services. On the Boards of various Tata and other companies.
58. Material on the Sun Group is available in various sources. Besides the information mentioned above in *Chelovek I Kar'iera*, and Ballerina's interview with Khemka in, 'San Grup v Rossii: 40 let aktivnoi raboty', Shiv Khemka provided his own perspectives on management in 'Ob ymenii rukovodit', in *Perspektiva*, Autumn-Winter 1999, pp. 10–11. The Sun Group's own promotional information is useful (*The Sun Group in Russia: A Story of Success.*); and the Group puts out a lot of information about itself on the Internet: www.scp.ru is the main site. The Indian operations can be seen in www.sfc.com which deals with some of its investment activities. A report on Uday Khemka appeared in *The Wall Street Journal* (27 November 2000) by Stepanie Gruner, 'Businessman finds new ways to increase value of his work'.
59. The exceptions appear to be Cipla, Standard Organics, Unichem, and JB Pharmaceuticals. If we are to follow the record of JB Pharmaceuticals, though, a large amount of the Company's exports were targeted towards Russia, and the lack of presence in the Federation was probably an indication only that the company is not interested in producing locally.
60. *Indian Pharmaceutical Guide* (Bombay: Pamposh Publications, 1994), pp. 7–8.
61. Interview with S. Choubey of Zydus Cadilla, Moscow, December 2002. Also Zydus promotional literature—*Zydus Cadilla: Dedicated to Life*. Information is also available at www.zyduscadila.com
62. D.S. Brar developed the Pharmaceutical exports business of the company in early 1980s. This was the main area of the company's growth and expansion. In addition, Brar looked after the Animal Healthcare & OTC businesses. In

1986, he took over the Pharma business in India along with Chemical Manufacturing Operations. In early 1990s he led the company's expansion into overseas markets, creating joint ventures, affiliates, and subsidiaries in major countries like China, Russia, UK, South Africa and the USA. In 1996, he took over as the President of the company and was appointed CEO & Managing Director in 1999.

63. NTV Television broadcasts in Moscow, December 2002, when Sanjiv Singh of Intercase was repeatedly on air.
64. Pfizer accused Reddy's of violating its patent on a heart curing product, Noravsk. Reddy's claimed that its product, Stamlo, was manufactured using a different method. The Federal Arbitration Tribunal concluded in favour of Pfizer. Reddy's appealed the matter to the Supreme Arbitration Tribunal, *Indian Express*, 16 November 1999.
65. Arun Mohanty, 'Indo-Russian Cooperation in the Sphere of Energy Security', *Business Messenger*, December 2002.
66. Mechanical Engineering graduate from IIT, with MBA from IIM. Worked with research in India and South-East Asia as Head of Research for Crosby Securitities and Peregrine Securities in India, before going on to join Sun Capital Partners in 1998.
67. Student in USSR 1961–6, when he completed an M.Sc. in Petroleum Engineering. Later worked with ONGC for 30 years, and was on the board of the company. Briefly Chairman and Managing Director of Gas Authority of India Ltd. joined Sun in 2000.
68. Degrees in Computer Systems and Law and Chartered Accounting degree from the Institute of Chartered Accountants of India (New Delhi). Joined Khemka group in 1988 and Russian operations in 1992. Crucial to introduction of Western accountancy practices into Sun's Russian enterprises.
69. MGIMO and Harvard Business School, 1994–5, worked with Russian equity portfolio at Tiger Management (New York). Later experience in investment banking with Goldman Sachs and Co. (New York) Donaldson, Lufkin and Jenrette (New York), during 1997–9 and Moscow (from 1998). *The Sun Group in Russia: A Story of Success.*
70. BA from State Academy of Finance, Moscow, MBA Harvard Business School. Investment Banking background with Lehman Brothers (New York and London). 1993–5, McKinsey and Co. in Russia and Western Europe. *The Sun Group in Russia: A Story of Success.*
71. MGIMO, Ph.D. in Economics, took Executive Development Programme at the Wharton School of Business. Ministry of Foreign Affairs (RF). 1995–9, Vice-President of Sun Brewing.
72. MGIMO and UN University of Peace (Costa Rica). Ministry of Foreign Affairs (RF) until 1991. With Sun from 1995. *The Sun Group in Russia: A Story of Success.*
73. In Russia since 1994. Formerly Acting Financial Controller of CS First Boston Russia, Senior Financial Officer of US Russia Investment Fund and Finance

Director of Renaissance Capital. Then Chief Financial Officer of Navenor Holding. From May 2000, Chief Financial Officer of the Sun Group. *The Sun Group in Russia: A Story of Success.*

74. MBA Wharton School of Business, MIA from School of International and Public Affairs, Harriman Institute, Columbia University. In Russia since 1990. Managing Director and Chairman of the Board of W.R. Grace and Co.'s Russian operations, Manager for Corporate Finance/Privatization Services Division of Price Waterhouse (Russia). CEO of Sun Confectionery Ltd. from October 1997. *The Sun Group in Russia: A Story of Success.*
75. A member of the Indian Embassy, Moscow, pointed out that after Sun's withdrawal from Voronezh, local officials expressed sincere regret, since the organization had proved a prop to the administration while it had worked in the region. Interview with A. Kohli, Councillor Commercial, Embassy of India, December 2002. Sun's regular payment of taxes brought it closer to other administrators elsewhere, where it contributed to local taxes in a manner disproportional to the size of the enterprise. Interview with Valentin Pavlov, Moscow, December 2002. In 2000, the Sun group paid almost US $100 million by way of taxes to the Russian state budget. *The Sun Group in Russia: A Story of Success.*
76. In association with the New Prospects Fund.
77. In Moscow, St. Petersburg, and the US, involving the Moscow Chamber Orchestra, the Kremlin Chamber Orchestra and the American-Russian Youth Orchestra, with other groups.
78. Hari Mohan Saxena, 'Indo-Russian Cooperation in Science and Technology', *Business Messenger*, 2001.
79. See www.IAEA.org the website of the International Atomic Energy Organization, which gives the main institutions concerned with nuclear energy in India in its 'Nuclear Energy Handbook', and the website of the Nuclear Power Corporation of India, www.npcil.nic.in
80. Kapoor worked for Cadilla and left to do an MBA in the UK. The study was self-financed.
81. Ajay Goyal, *The Russian Journal*, 13 April 2001.
82. Interview with Rajesh Sharma, Moscow, December 2002.
83. *Business Messenger*, 2001. Interview with Shekhar Singh, Deputy General Director of Shreya. See also the website of the organization, www.shreya.ru . *Business Line*, 28 January 2003 carried a story on the acquisition of Plethico. The acquisition of Rallis was covered in Hindu's *Financial Daily*, 13 February 2001.
84. The 'patriotic element' was clear in the interview with Gupta to the Indo–Asian news service. Speaking of launching Amtel on the NYSE, Gupta stated: 'And the only dream that I have today is to put my brainchild into the New York stock market that would bring glory to my nation and to me.' The nationalist element is also evident elsewhere: 'If everything goes well according to plan,

Amtel would be the first Indian company in Russia whose shares would be traded in the coveted New York stock market by the end of the year.' See *The Hindu Business Line*, op. cit.

85. The main source on the company's factories and their performance is www.amtel.ru See also Indians Abroad in Hindustantimes.com 7 April 2003 for an interview with Gupta and an account of Amtel's venture on to the NYSE. Nriol.com 14 November 2002 also has a write up on Gupta.
86. Goyal provides an excellent example of this. 'Some months ago, I received some Russian visitors in San Jose, California: a group of technical geniuses, the best programmers in their field. They had some excellent products under their belt, and were seeking a paltry $2 million in investment. I had arranged a meeting for them with some potential investors, a group that manages nearly $600 million and knows its business—especially when it comes to software and technology. However, when the Russian visitors arrived, most of whom I was meeting for the first time, I couldn't help noticing the disappointed look on some faces as they entered the room. There were six Indians sitting around a dark conference table laden with the latest gadgets and—the room smelled of curry. "How the fu*k could these n*g**s know anything about software; how will these beggars give us money?" was the instant reaction from one of them in his blessed mother tongue.'
87. A marketing survey of the period before the 1998 crisis indicates this prejudice in St. Petersburg. See Minkevich op. cit. The major brands in demand were from Eastern and Central Europe: Gedeon Richter (Hungary); Polfa (Poland); KRKA (Slovenia); Bayer (Germany); Lek (Slovenia); Hoechst (Germany); Sandoz (Switzerland); UPSA (France); CIBA (Switzerland); AWD (Germany); Meuselbach (Germany); Glaxo Wellcome (Great Britain); Galencia (Yugoslavia); Pharmchim (Bulgaria). This was despite the known inclination of physicians to prescribe cheap rather than quality drugs. The survey made it clear that 'Although many products from India, Turkey, and China are represented in the market, they are not in great demand.' Even in the cheap drugs market, Eastern European and German companies were trusted names and held the field. A survey for the Russian Far East, on the other hand, notes that in the immediate post-disintegration period, until 1996, Indian drugs were important here. Once again, though, trust was clearly a factor, and 'quality' and 'poor assortment' apparently led to a decline of Indian pharmaceutical take in the region, giving way to Bulgarian, Polish, Hungarian, and Slovenian producers. See A. Dee and Olga Efremova, *Russian Far East Drugs and Pharmaceuticals Market* (US Dept. of Trade, 1999).
88. Jaques Sapir, *Le Krach Russe*, op. cit.; interview in 1999 with Arnab Das, J.P. Morgan's main negotiator in Moscow for purchases of the Russian debt, 1996–2000.
89. *1998, Banking Crisis*, op. cit.

CHAPTER 4

Indo–Russian Relations After 1991: Military–Technical Cooperation

THE RUSSIAN MILITARY INDUSTRIAL COMPLEX AFTER 1991, AND INDIAN DEFENCE PURCHASES

In the case of Russian armaments exports to India, it must be stressed, important differences from the general pattern of bilateral trade are noticeable. Certainly, Indian companies with international contacts were key intermediaries between Russian suppliers and Indian purchasers for a brief period after disintegration. But from 1996, these middlemen became marginal actors in the trade, often acting as minor facilitators. Direct government initiative became crucial to the way deals were made. Most important, unlike important areas of Indian activity such as pharmaceuticals or beer production, where the Indian role was significant but not essential, Russian armaments exports, India became central to the sector.

This followed from the fact the military industrial complex did not make the transition to the market economy as decisively as other branches of Russian industry that made some success of the new dispensation. True, from 1992, when President Yeltsin permitted arms industries of the Tula region to sell to foreign buyers in an 'independent' manner, private initiatives became normal in the MIC.[1] An attractive prospect opened up for a range of industries which produced well-reputed goods.[2] However, despite the changes, the complex had to submit to the dictates of the Interdepartmental Commission for Military Technical Cooperation with foreign countries (according to the Presidential decree of May 1992). Hence, although two major FTOs, Oboroneksport and Spetsvneshteknika, were given a role in issuing licenses to enterprises to sell armaments (August 1992), a major bureaucratic hurdle had to be crossed when making use of the license.[3] The creation of Rossvooruzhenie (State Corporation for Import and Export of Armaments) in November 1993 as a concern which would handle exports directly, made independent activity difficult.[4] The situation was further complicated by rigorous Presidential supervision over exports for a brief period under the aegis of the State Committee of the Russian Federation on Military Technical Policy (December 1994–December 1996). Although there was a return in 1997 to a system centred on a monopoly company, this time with Rossvooruzhenie sharing its authority with a new entity, Promeksport, a Presidential decree of 1 December 2000 restored rigorous control through a new export-control giant, Rosoboroneksport,[5] which took over Rossvooruzhenie and Promeksport. Such control coexisted with vigorous maintenance by the state of its stake in the armaments industry, as indicated by its *de facto* control over 80 per cent of concerns.[6] Cuts in defence spending within the Federation (from 25 per cent to 5 per cent of GNP over a ten-year period, 1992–2002), in such circumstances, made for an extremely tough position for the vast complex associated with the MIC, i.e. 11 million workers and their dependents (15 per cent of the Russian population) strung out in 2000—4,000 industrial plants, 500 research centres, and a number of 'closed cities' (Sverdlovsk 44, Sverdlovsk 45, etc.).

Various possible solutions were attempted. Some were the unplanned upshots of circumstance: many personnel emigrated, and this 'trimmed' the complex (they moved to the United States, Western Europe, China, North Korea, etc.). Conversion was considered by a number of plants: as for instance in the case of the Saratov Aircraft Plant, which went into civil aviation, or the Iantar Shipbuilding Enterprise, which went into merchant shipping. There are a number of cases of profitable ventures, often supported by US initiative.[7] Overall, however, there were clear problems. A Presidential decree of summer 1992 and the complex procedures set out in the decree on conversion (March 1992), made this path difficult.[8] Official policy in principle was in line with 'democrat' arguments, propounded from the time of perestroika, that conversion was important and necessary. But functionaries were not in favour of a pell-mell conversion policy without controls or safety net, since members of the MIC continued to be very influential in the presidential cohort and Parliament. Their caution came from the global experience of conversion. Countries where conversion was relatively easier, such as the United States, had not taken to the path decisively,[9] indicating a poor prospect. Russia's position was substantially more difficult, also, since the MIC had never been oriented to commercial attitudes. The complex government programme that was devised against this background quickly ran into heavy weather, and had only marginal success.[10]

Baidya Bikash Basu gives a fair account of the experiments and retreat that featured at this time, as the MIC was oriented in different ways at different times to conversion. With little sense of the scale of the impending financial crisis, in 1993–5 the Economic Ministry planned conversion within the framework of 14 programmes for Goskomoboronprom. These dealt with civil aviation, shipbuilding energy (including the plant of the Ministry of Atomic Energy, Minatom), forestry, housing, road-construction, agriculture, textiles, food-processing, .trade, consumer durables, communication and information technology, ecology, and medical equipment. The scheme had the support of the Presidency and was allotted a budget of 1.67 trillion roubles (at 1989 values). But it failed to get off the ground, clearly due to the chaos in public finances.

In December 1995 a scheme for 1995–7 was adopted—this time exercising restraint and circumspection, fixing on seven programmes for Goskomoboronprom: civil aviation, shipbuilding, fuel and energy-sector equipment, medical equipment, electronics, consumer goods, and communications and information technology. For Minatom, 18.6 trillion roubles was allocated. Now there was greater care in the financial planning, indicating only a 7.3 trillion rouble provision from the budget, conversion loans of 6.3 trillion roubles, and non-budgetary sources of five trillion roubles. But finding even this scheme beyond government resources, both economic and political, in late 1997 the Ministry set out a 'Federal Programme for Restructuring and Conversion of the Defence Industry' for 1998–2000. This conceived of a reduction in the number of arms industries from around 1700 to 670 by the year 2000, and by a further 35 more by 2005. This was to be the result of a 'rationalization of arms production, through vertical integration within industrial sectors and a limited number of horizontal mergers', even while there would still be some public financial assistance for conversion. In February 1998, a Commission for the Financial Improvement of the Defence Industry Organizations was set up, it was followed, in the next month, by a law on Defence Industry Conversion. The state of finances was indicated by the reduction of the scale of assistance for 1998–2000—25.5 billion roubles (at 1998 prices), only half to come from the central budget.

The upshot of vicissitudes in policy and the subsequent confused situation was dislocation and desperation. Consumption of stock in the MIC became normal, and personal survival became a problem. Almost inevitably, a 'black market' in military products developed in the Russian Federation at this time, and a wild search for foreign markets followed.[11] Where there was no demand, there was resort to subcontracting to get into the global market. Hence, in 1994, the US government agreed to provide $20 million to four MIC enterprises to enter into collaborative ventures with American producers. A degree of cooperation is also known to exist between Russian manufacturers and producers in France and Israel. The initiative had the advantage of equipping producer units with the capacity to stand up to international competition. A decisive attempt was made to acquire orders through advertisement and display. Hence the impressive Russian presence at a number of major displays: Abu Dhabi in November 1993, the LIMA-93 exposition in Malaysia in December 1993, the FIDAE-94 exposition in Santiago de Chile in March 1994, the Aviation Africa 1994 fair in Johannesburg in 1994, the DEFENDORY-94 exhibition in Greece, and the IDEX-95 in Abu Dhabi. Important orders began to come from the Middle East and Malaysia as a result of these ventures. Formidable performances were also given at the Farnborough and Paris (1996).[12] The Russians emerged on the world market as major players. During 1995–8 the United States had a share of 23.4 per cent in global arms transfer agreements with developing nations. Russia, meanwhile, had overtaken France and become the second supplier with a share of 21.5 per cent.[13] The trend was not stable, however, and was affected by the Asian financial crisis and the Russian collapse of August 1998. The value of Russian deals with developing nations fell from *c.* $3.2 bn in 1997 to $ 1.4 bn in 1998, and Russia's share of arms sales to developing nations fell from 18.9 per cent in 1997 to 10.6 per cent in 1998.

The Significance of Indian Purchases for the MIC

In the final analysis, innovations in marketing techniques helped the MIC to achieve stability to a limited degree: if the complex had to depend on them, it would have died quickly. This is as true of the 'success' stories of the transition, Sukhoi, and Ilyushin, as it is of the 'slow movers', MiG and Tupolev. The major success of the MIC came through ventures where deals were brokered by governments in the old pre-1991 style, against credits and special payment arrangements in the case of India and China. This is clear from the Table 4.1, which allows comparison of arrangements made in this way.

The sale of arms to India from 1998 figures in this category; and, like a similar set of arrangements with China, its importance to the MIC is clear from the above information. The negotiations with the Russian government, which attained its high point in the series of agreements on military cooperation that were signed by President Putin in September 2000 were the end-point in negotiations that took place between the two governments in the previous decade. For a prolonged period, accords took place, but supplies were limited and sluggish. This was the upshot of the administrative reorganization of the MIC, and uncertainty about its future until 1997. Reports of the visits of various Indian ministers and prime ministers to Russia confirm the problem: the Narasimha Rao (Moscow, July 1994) and Chernomyrdin (Delhi, December 1994) visits; the Primakov visit as Foreign Minister (Delhi, March 1996); the Gujral visit (February 1997); the Deve Gowda visit (March 1997). It was only when the Russian economy (and the MIC) came into sudden crisis over 1997–8 (culminating in the 1998 August crash) that the final tilt to old customs and habits occurred in this area. From then, the India–Russia Joint Commission passed firmly from the hands of supporters of 'private trade' and liberalization, such as Anatolii Chubais, to figures such as Yurii Masliukov (Prime Minister Primakov's

TABLE 4.1: SUPPLIES OF ARMS TO DIFFERENT NATIONS FROM THE MIC (1992–9)

	Russia	India	China	Kuwait	Syria	Columbia	S.Korea	Malaysia
Planes	7	85	101	70			4	18
Helicopter	8	16	6	6	12	12	30	6
Tanks	31	175	140	60	60			
Subs	2	6	4					
Ships	2	4	3				2	

Source: A.Z. Egorin, *Rossiia-Indiia: sostoianie I perspektivy voenno-tekhnicheskogo sotrudnichestva* in *Rossiia – Indiia: Perspektivy regional'nogo sotrudnichestva (g. Nizhnii Novgorod)*, Moscow, 2000.

protégé and a supporter of old-fashioned state controls), or, after 2000, those who were wholly controlled by President Putin's administration, and supported a regime of official regulation. A degree of regularity and intensity also began to mark arms deals. By the time of Primakov's visit to India as prime minister (December 1999), the new course had been set, and its strength was only to be confirmed at the time of the visit of President Putin to India in 2000. The role of the state in organizing and directing manufacture, it appears, was set to grow in the future, as the flow of funds from government to the sector increased (as it promised to do), and a rigorous cartelization was enforced by government in the industry.[14]

The Character of the Russian MIC: MiG and Sukhoi

A brief examination of the performance of two members of the Russian aerospace industry, MiG and Sukhoi, in their competition for the Indian market, and their different levels of success confirms the importance of the state. In both cases, survival strategies of conversion, rationalization, and private initiative on the global market characterized the period after 1991: and in the case of both, these strategies were successful only to a limited degree. Sukhoi, however, consistently had an eye to the assistance of the state and did very well in its competition with MiG. In neither case could the state serve as the main consumer of the product, given the bankruptcy of the Russian treasury. Sukhoi's experience, however, indicates that government could still be of use.

At MiG, following General Director Rotislav Belyakov's support for the Yanaev putsch leaders in 1991 August, the company (the Mikoyan OKB) had to fend for itself quickly with little support from government. It resorted to a team-up with its main producer unit, the Moscow Aircraft Production Organization (MAPO) No. 30, to form a Military Industrial Group (MIG-MAPO), which was associated with Kamov Helicopters. It focused on the family of MiG-29 Fighters and Kamov Helicopters, as well as small aircraft projects and upgrades of early generations of MiG. Production was at Aircraft Producer Unit 30. The long-term objective was to make the new consortium a MNC, with the help of financial institutions and foreign capital. Cutbacks in staff were quick. Unprofitable subdivisions were closed down, marketing became focused, and means were sought for credit arrangements for customers.

The new corporation even went into business with the Singapore-based Indian Company, AGIO Countertrade, to work out methods for better marketing and production or assembly outside Russia. A major shake-up in the leadership took place.[15]

The operation was a limited success, and, in conjunction with a sloppy trade in spares and inventory that was available in plenty, the Company managed to improve its MiG-29 designs, which were its standard stock in trade, while working on MiG-31 improvement. The unit was supported from the side by the independent manufacturing plant at Nizhnii Novgorod, which belonged to the original Mikoyan Design Bureau but failed to join the merger. Under contract, this plant manufactured one MiG-31 'Foxhound' per month, and also managed to innovate on MiG-31 models, with an eye to the future. Some limited income from a conversion drive (production of gliders, motorboats, ski poles, pots and pans) helped pay salaries.

Sukhoi, however, did better. Tightly oriented around production units in Komsomolsk-on-Amur in the Russian Far East (Khabarovsk), the Irkutsk Aviation Production Association (IAPA), and a production facility in Novosibirsk, the Company's chairman, Simonov, intervened at the highest levels of the Yeltsin administration, and helped the armed forces with their funding problems. The top brass in turn offered the Research and Development or production contracts to his corporation. To beat inflation, Simonov traded sport aircraft for used Toyotas, and then used the Toyotas (whose value appreciated) to trade for goods and services. He kept his own costs low by minor adjustments in salary paid in roubles. This eliminated any new-product tax losses. Any dollars that were received were kept abroad in the West and the interest was used. Having maintained the plant in order in this way, Simonov was able to use his clout with the Presidency (rather than, as in Belyakov's case, with Parliament) to pick-up scarce funds. He had however to give way to a successor, Alexei Fedorov, the head of the Irkutsk Plant and a business management graduate from Oklahoma University (1996) who developed Simonov's work. Their efforts obtained a special status for the Company. On 30 December 1996, the Sukhoi Aviation Military Industrial Complex (AVPK) was given life and validated as both a State Enterprise and a Joint Stock Group by the Russian Government. From this vantage point, Sukhoi came to terms with Rossvooruzhenie for a series of export arrangements.[16] With its enormous authority, it was able to push its case with India and the PRC to obtain the contracts which gave it first rank in the Russian aircraft industry,[17] as well as a degree of competitiveness against major forces such as Mirage, Boeing, and Lockheed.

INDO–RUSSIAN RELATIONS AFTER THE SOVIET REVOLUTION OF 1991: INDIA'S DEPENDENCE ON RUSSIA RECONSIDERED

An important footnote to this course of development in Russia's interests in the Indian economy, however, is that although Russia's dependence on the Indian economy grew to a degree that was unprecedented at this time, the terms of India's engagement with the Russian economy seriously changed. If the figures cited in the previous section indicate serious supplies to India of military hardware, and much is said about the dependence of the Indian arsenal on Russian inputs, the experience of the 1990s was not without effect in India. During the 1992–8 period, when Russian suppliers were sluggish or poor, Indian buyers exercised considerable acumen in finding access to individual Russian firms through private parties in Eastern Europe or Yugoslavia,[18] and through planned trips to the Russian Federation to pick up parts in the arms bazaar as and when they could.[19] They also resorted to a variety of producers in the former Soviet Union and in Israel to supply the deficit in Soviet parts. Thus at the level of the defence industry, India came to have greater flexibility in the way she used her options than had been the case before. The arrangements of 1999–2001, moreover, indicate crucial departures in the character of interaction between the Indian and Russian sides from the situation before 1991. As in the past, there was a transfer of manufacturing technology to India as weapons agreements were concluded. Hence, much of the actual process of assembly in the case of T-90 tanks and missiles was to be done in India (at the Heavy Vehicles Factory, Avadi, and by Bharat Dynamics).[20] Systematic upgradation of MiG-21s and MiG-29s was to be done on site in HAL, and going on earlier experience, such work involved complete transfer of computer data concerning the installation of new parts, and so on.[21] A novel feature of the interaction, however, was that Indian agencies were permitted to specify the changes they wished to make in aircraft (a point often mentioned in favour of India's acquisition of the Su-

30).[22] The Russians also expressed their willingness to turn a blind eye to any alterations in arms which contravened the terms of START.[23] Cooperation with an eye to production in India and exports were also seriously discussed.[24]

Again, various aspects of the MIC's cooperation with military enterprises based outside Russia meant the possibility of India's obtaining supplies and spares from sources other than the MIC in the Federation. Israel was one such source, and various arrangements were concluded over time in the early 2000s.[25] The situation coincided with a trading relationship that looked after itself, and which promised to provide major rewards because of its self-sustaining nature.

The most visible aspect of this trend, where Indian know-how supplemented Russian in military technical cooperation, allowing space for the inflow of different traded inputs, was the formation of the Brahmos venture—which originated in an agreement of 1998 between FSUE NPO Mashinstroeniia of the RF and the Defence Research and Development Organization (DRDO) in India—to produce a supersonic missile. The company that was formed (Brahmos Aerospace Private Ltd.) test-fired its product (the DO3) in 2003—and suggested the possibility of new ventures thereafter.[26] The missile used the research inputs of the Russian MIC and also independent missile work conducted in India that had shown its strengths in the Agni series of missiles. It was a binational creation to the core. Again, although the product of state initiatives, Brahmos was assertively a product that was meant to be marketed internationally, and its producers not only articulated specific national security interests but also the orientation of such interests to demand on a global scale

Clearly, the upshot of the situation that developed in the Russian MIC in the 1990s, and the circumspection that this situation forced on the Indian military technical establishment, was that Russia's junior partner had come to a point when it could exercise real authority in its relations with the Federation. This consequence of Soviet disintegration and liberalization in Russia had important implications for the character of security arrangements in South Asia and the terms in which they were negotiated.

NOTES

1. In May 1992, a Presidential decree set up procedures for licensing companies to undertake independent ventures. Third-country sales by Russians and their manufacturing partners was envisaged at this time. Parliamentarily approved privatization in the armaments industry should be traced to the Statute on Certification and Registration of the Right of Enterprises to Export Arms, Military Equipment, and Works and Services for Military needs. Registered armaments enterprises were allowed to search for customers abroad, directly and through advertisement unless the Cooperation Commission forbade it. The enterprises could independently negotiate contracts, and export arms produced in excess of State orders if they possessed proper licenses. See Baidya Bikash Basu, 'Trends in Russian Arms Export', *SA*, February 2000 for the resume of the decree.
2. Su and MiG family of aeroplanes fit into this category. Other products of international reputation include: diesel electric submarines of the 877EKM and 636 models, 'Smerch' multi-launch fire systems, 'BMP-3' infantry combat vehicles, 'T-80U' and 'T-90S' tanks, air-defence systems 'S-300-PMU-1', 'S-300-V' 'Buk-M-I', 'Tunguska self-propelled SAMs' and 'Igla'. See Baidya Bikash Basu, 'Trends in Russian Arms Export', *SA*, February 2000.
3. See *Vedomosti S"ezda Narodnykh Deptatov RSFSR I Verkhovnogo Soveta RSRSR* (no. 28, 1992) for the text of the law.
4. Interviews with operatives in the MIC in St. Petersburg in March 1998. My sources pointed out that Rossvooruzhenie's permission to export was very difficult to come by. F(the decree on Rossvooruzhenie, see Baidya Bikash Basu, op. cit.
5. This followed Vladimir Putin's dismissal of Alexei Ogaryov, head of Russia's major arms exporting company Rosvooruzhenie, in November 2000. The President also sacked the head of Promeksport, Sergei Chemezov. The two companies were merged to form the Federal State Unitary Enterprise Rosoboroneksport under Promeksport's former Deputy General Director Andrei Belyaninov, who was appointed General Director of the new concern. See *Pravda*, 7 November 2000.
6. The nature of privatization in the military industry is dealt with well by Baidya Bikash Basu in 'Reforms in Russian Defense Industry', op. cit., though there is a tendency in the account to overstress the impact of privatization. Basu deals with the conflict between Minoboronprom (the Ministry for Defence Industries) and plant managers who wanted greater flexibility, and eventual moves to privatization. Even after structural change, though, control was exercised by the government through its hold of shares. By Basu's own admission, the composition of the Military–Industrial Sector in terms of the nature of ownership is as follows (in per cent):

	Type of Property	1998	2000
1.	State run enterprises	41	42
2.	Joint stock companies State capital	34	42
3.	Private companies devoid of state capital	25	16

See Baidya Bikash Basu, 'Trends . . .', op. cit.

7. Julian Cooper, who has studied conversion extensively, points out a number of interesting examples other than the Iantar. MIC companies dealing with fuel and energy production quickly found markets. Hence, the Severodvinsk State Centre for Atomic Ship Building provided rigs and special vessels for drilling and other work off the Pechora and Barents seas. AO Rosshel'f was the main initiator of the project. Some factories adapted to making coal-mining machinery—to make up the requirements of Russian pits from factories in the Ukraine and Kazakstan—as in the case of Yurga machine-building works (Siberia), AO Nizhne-gorodskii mashinostroitel'nyi zavod, Volgograd Barrikady and 17 other companies, all formerly specialists in the manufacture of missiles, launchers or nuclear equipment. Fifty companies came to work on fast railway connections from Moscow to St. Petersburg. Minatom's conversion success came from investment from the West. Under the Nunn-Lugar programmes, the US defence department provided funds ($1.2 billion of the Defence department budget for 1992–4), for this among other ends. Other sources included: The US–Russia Investment Fund (TUSRIF), the Overseas Private Investment Corporation (OPIC), the European Union's Programme for Technical Assistance to the CIS (TACIS). See Julian Cooper, 'The Future of the Russian Defence Industry', in Roy Allison and Christoph Bluth (eds), *Security Dilemmas in Russia and Eurasia* (London: Royal Institute of International Affairs, 1998) and Baidya Bikash Basu, 'Reforms . . .', op. cit.
8. The Law on Conversion was signed by President Yeltsin on 20 March 1992. The full text is available in *Vedomosti S"ezda Narodnykh Deptatov RSFSR I Verkhovnogo Soveta RSRSR* (no. 12, 1992). The relevant details are given in English in Baidya Bikash Basu, 'Reforms . . .', op. cit. Basu points out that the 'main principle' governing conversion was 'the use of high-technology capacities of the defence industry to produce output capable of competing on the foreign market' (Art. 2:2). There would be 'priority targeted state programmers for socio-economic development' and those were to be appropriate to the scientific and technical level of the industry and to the professional skills of the workforce (Art. 2:3). The defence industries would be compensated for keeping their mobilization capacities even for creating ones (Art. 2:4). Defence plants would be given at least two year's notice before receiving any cutbacks in orders (Art. 3:3). Defence industries were to be protected against circumstances that reduced their profits (Art. 8:3). The defence industries in some cases, would be subsidized so that prices on their conversion products would remain below world market prices' (Art. 8:5).

The visionaries of conversion conceived of a staggering scheme which the bankrupt Russian exchequer could not have undertaken. Basu quotes Mikhail Malei, Yeltsin's advisor on defence, who apparently argued that 'in order to introduce new technology and equipment there should be an overall plan, second, to halt the production process, third to remove the old equipment, fourth to acquire new equipment, fifth to assemble it, sixth to teach the workforce how to use it, seventh to start up the new production process'. Malei argued that the process had to have systematic financial support, and worked out a programme for 70 per cent conversion of the industry, involving a bill of $150 billion over 15 years.

9. For a Russian critique of military expenditure, see S. Veselovskii, V. Potapov and O. Salkovskii, *Insane Squandering* (Moscow: Progress, 1988). A good resume of the arguments is in to be found in the articles on conversion in *Armiia I Obshchestvo*, in the series *Perestroika: glasnost', demokraiia, sotsializm* (Moscow: Progress, 1990)
10. Unfortunately, Basu fails to provide information (or assessment) on the financial problems indicated here. And, by all accounts, not only the early stage (for the period up to 1995) but also most plans for the later stage did not get very far, owing to poor funds. Government subsidies went essentially into maintaining staff. Little came of the investment in terms of profitable conversion, and foreign assistance did little to help in terms of scale. This seems to be the unavoidable conclusion which follows from Julian Cooper's evaluations (see n. 42) as well as SIPRI data in the *Yearbooks*.
11. Good general accounts of policy concerning the defense sector are Richard F. Starr, *The New Military in Russia* (Annapolis, Maryland: Naval Institute Press, 1996), Baidya Bikash Basu, 'Russian Military-Technical Cooperation: Structures and Processes', op. cit.; Andrew J. Pierre and Dmitri V. Trenin, *Russia in the World Arms Trade* (Washington: Brookings Institution Press, 1997); Gary K. Bertsch and William C. Potter (eds.), *Dangerous Weapons, Desperate States* (New York: RKP, 1999). The early history of the arms industry are well dealt with in Stephen J. Blank, *Challenging the New World Order: The Arms Transfer Policies of the Russian Republic* (Pennsylvania: Strategic Studies Institute, US Army War College, 1993) and *The Nuclear Black Market* (Washington: CSIS Task Force Report, Center for Strategic and International Studies, 1996).
12. Richard F. Starr, op. cit., pp. 99 ff. See also Easy Tartar's accounts of the Russian Arms industry quoted below. Tartar is critical of Rand Corporation surveys which underestimate the capacity of the Russian industry to innovate in market techniques.
13. The precise breakdown with regard to 1998 armament deliveries by the Russian Corporate Defence Enterprises is as follows: Air Force Weaponry, 49.2 per cent; Army Weaponry, 25 per cent; Naval Weaponry, 15.9 per cent; Air-Defence Weaponry, 8.1 per cent; Other Weapons, 1.8 per cent. See Basu, 'Trends . . .'.
14. First Deputy Prime Minister Ilya Klebanov, who looked after state-

owned defence enterprises, outlined such a process of intervention, arguing that the sector needed to be overhauled and duplication cut down. Government intervention would partly be through funding: the state began to settle its 25 bn roubles debt to the industry from May 2000; the budget for the year 2000 set aside 48 bn roubles for R&D, repairs and new equipment. Basu points out in his evaluations of what was happening that forced mergers would be quick in coming (including that of MiG and Sukhoi). See Basu, op.cit. The general demand for the state to take a more forceful role and the willingness of the state to take that role is highlighted in Nikolai Semenov's interviews with leading defence-industry specialists and Duma personalities. See 'Kak ozhivit' Otechestvennyi VPK' in *Nezavisimaia Gazeta, Politekonomika*, Supplement no. 11, 12 September 2000. The article shows how personalities as well as industrial functionaries agreed on the need for state intervention.

15. MAPO-MIG was headed in 2002 by Vladmir Kuznetsov, who was born in October 1937, and graduated from the Tomsk Military AA Artillery School and the Moscow Aviation Institute. In 1959, he began working at MAPO as an Assistant Foreman. In 1987, he was appointed Deputy Director for Production, and became the General Director of MAPO in 1991. He was crucial to the MAPO-MIG merger and was supported by a replacement to former Deputy General Director/Commercial Director Belosvetov, Aleksandr Nikiforovich Bezrukov. At other levels, the subsidiary head (Director of Likhovitsky Machine Building Plant) was Vladimir Ivanovich Nungezer, First Deputy General Director. The Chief Engineer was Victor Mikhailovich Puzanov, Advisor to the General Director on International Marketing & General Representative in Germany. Easy Tartar dossier on MIG at the Web Site *Fighter Tactics Academy*, consulted in 2003.
16. The focus was on variants of the Su-35, Su-30, and MiG-29'M'. The equipment was suggested to the PRC, India, Indonesia, Syria, Algeria, Pakistan, Vietnam, Burma, Iran, Libya, Brazil, Peru, Argentina, North Korea, South Korea, and in the long term, Iraq. The price was about $30 million, sales were in small lots, and some form of credit was clearly available. See Tartar, op. cit. *Sukhoi 30* and *Sukhoi 37*, consulted 2003.
17. The Indian Air Force formally inducted its first eight Su-30 aircraft in early July 1996. The supply was quick and efficient: six months after the $1.8 billion contract to supply 40 aircraft was confirmed. The planes were an enhanced Su-27'PU' variant which became the Su-30'K', modified again with an India-particular navigation kit. The agreement with India was flexible: and reports indicated that the Indian Air Force would return them in the future or over 1997–2001, Sukhoi would upgrade these eight aircraft to full Su-30'MKI' status while delivering the other Su-32'MKI's in three batches. Indian pilots for the Sukhoi were trained in groups of ten at the Zhukovski Test Center. India bought 40 Su-30'MKIs' for $1.2 billion ($30 million each). The deal was uncertain because it was concluded by the Narasimha Rao government just

before it left office (paying $145 million in advance). However, a joint Indian Air Force/Defence Research & Development Organization Team found the Su-30'MK' to be superior to the Mirage 2000–5 in both range and payload, and the Deve Gowda government accepted the deal, after the Russians dipped the cost. The deal put paid to French ambitions for the Mirage 2000-5 in the region. According to *Jane's Defense Weekly* (October 1996), India got a reasonable bargain. For the Su-30'MKI' would be fitted with the advanced Phazotron Zhuk-27 fire-control radar, unlike earlier versions of the Sukhoi. See Tartar, op. cit.

18. Interview with former Secretary of Defence, Government of India, N.N. Vohra, April 2001.
19. *The Asian Age* 28 March 1999. In May 1994, July 1995 and June 1997, members of the Indian Navy made regular trips to the Russian Federation for such on the spot purchases. After 1998, such trips became unnecessary due to a greater degree of stability in the Russian MIC sales system, and its respect for Indian orders. A report by Josy Joseph in *The Rediff Specials*, 24 March 2001, mentioned Joint Secretary Vinod Rai's promotion of similar work for the air force. The report also mentioned the activities of various 'middlemen'. These included the Makalu Corporation, Machinery Sales Corporation, HC Supplies, and Dynatron. Russian companies such as AO Kompressor were involved in the operations and the mark-ups were apparently very high.
20. *Hindustan Times*, 15 February 2001.
21. *The Hindu*, 10 February 2001.
22. This was indicated in statements made by the Designer and Department Chief in Charge of the India deal at MIG. *The Hindu*, 10 February 2001.
23. This was made clear at the time of negotiations for leasing of Tu22M3 bombers (armed with KH-22 missiles). *Hindustan Times*, 19 February 2001.
24. *The Times of India*, 5 November 2000. This was the pith of discussions on Ilyushin's scheme for cooperation on aircraft in India with HAL.
25. A.Z. Egorin, *Rossiia-Indiia: sostoianie I perspektivy voenno-tekhnicheskogo sotrudnichestva* in *Rossiia – Indiia: Perspektivy regional'nogo sotrudnichestva (g. Nizhnii Novgorod)*, Moscow: Institut Vostokovedeniia, 2000. There was active consideration of upgradation of Russian-built 'Pechora' missiles in collaboration with Poland. *The Hindu*, 5 December 2001.
26. See the Brahmos Company's website, www.brahmos.com for basic details. The site describes the missile as 'a Supersonic Cruise Missile that can be launched from submarine, ship, aircraft and land based Mobile Autonomous Launchers (MAL)'. The missile is launched from a Transport-Launch Canister (TLC), which also acts as storage and transportation container. It is considered to be 'an anti-ship missile. It has the capability to engage land based targets also. The missile can be launched either in vertical or inclined position and will cover 360 degrees'.

HS Code		1996–7	1997–8	1998–9	1999–2000	2000–1	2001–2
62	Articles of Apparel and Clothing Accessories, Not Knitted or Crocheted.					0.00	
63	Other Made up Textile Articles; Sets; Worn Clothing and Worn Textile Articles; Rags.	0.04		0.01	0.01	0.01	0.08
64	Footwear, Gaiters and the like; Parts of Such Articles.				0.00		0.01
66	Umbrellas, Sun Umbrellas, Walking-sticks, Seat-sticks, Whips, Riding-crops and Parts Thereof.					0.01	
67	Prepared Feathers and Down and Articles Made of Feathers or of Down; Artificial Flowers; Articles of Human Hair.			0.02			
68	Articles of Stone, Plaster, Cement, Asbestos, Mica or Similar Materials.	0.01	0.00	0.01	0.01	0.01	0.01
69	Ceramic Products.		0.00	0.03	0.04	0.09	0.05
70	Glass and Glassware.	0.31	1.50	1.67	1.76	0.39	4.57
71	Natural or Cultured Pearls, Precious or Semi-precious Stones, Pre-metals, clad with Pre-metal and Articles Thereof; Imit.jewellery; Coins.	4.49	5.20	43.93	10.79	20.21	72.12
72	Iron and Steel.	88.81	163.24	75.65	85.99	108.39	49.65
73	Articles of Iron or Steel.	5.50	9.47	10.27	5.68	11.19	9.65
74	Copper and Articles Thereof.	61.76	39.27	13.34	20.01	5.06	0.86
75	Nickel and Articles Thereof.	28.67	45.12	26.71	26.67	38.50	37.35
76	Aluminium and Articles Thereof.	60.23	44.45	8.11	15.17	10.89	6.53
78	Lead and Articles Thereof.	0.16	0.84	0.60	0.30	0.10	0.04
79	Zinc and Articles Thereof.	15.66	18.82	13.02	11.59	10.17	13.52
80	Tin and Articles Thereof.	0.18		0.03			0.11
81	Other Base Metals; Cermets; Articles Thereof.	1.82	1.89	2.89	3.28	3.01	5.46
82	Tools, Implements, Cutlery, Spoons and Forks, of Base Metal; Parts Thereof of Base Metal.	0.00	0.02	0.02	0.02	0.05	0.05

HS Code		1996–7	1997–8	1998–9	1999–2000	2000–1	2001–2
83	Miscellaneous Articles of Base Metal.	0.05	0.15	0.11	0.08	0.00	0.02
84	Nuclear Reactors, Boilers, Machinery and Mechanical Appliances; Parts Thereof.	27.73	34.17	21.84	30.40	15.98	17.89
85	Electrical Machinery and Equipment and Parts Thereof; Sound Recorders and Reproducers, Television Image and Sound Recorders and Reproducers, and Parts.	5.96	9.94	4.75	9.64	13.16	7.02
86	Railway or Tramway Locomotives, Rolling-stock and Parts Thereof; Railway or Tramway Track Fixtures and Fittings and Parts Thereof.	2.23	0.90	3.71	5.02	0.16	0.18
87	Mechanical vehicles other than Railway or Tramway Rolling Stock, and Parts and Accessories Thereof.	0.08	1.97	0.61	0.11	0.02	0.00
88	Aircraft, Spacecraft, and Parts Thereof.	31.19	10.13	1.26	1.23	27.74	5.56
89	Ships, Boats and Floating Structures.	4.05	3.80	0.32	1.07	2.31	0.56
90	Optical, Photographic Cinematographic Measuring, Checking Precision, Medical or Surgical Inst. and Apparatus Parts and Accessories Thereof.	1.58	1.12	1.59	2.71	1.68	2.71
91	Clocks and Watches and Parts Thereof		0.01	0.01		0.02	0.05
92	Musical Instruments; Parts and Accessories of Such Articles.	0.05					
93	Arms and Ammunition; Parts and Accessories Thereof.		0.13		0.02		
94	Furniture; Bedding, Mattresses, Mattress Supports, Cushions and Similar Stuffed Furnishing; Lamps and Lighting Fittings not Elsewhere Specified or inc.	0.00	0.13		0.02		

HS Code		1996–7	1997–8	1998–9	1999–2000	2000–1	2001–2
95	Toys, Games and Sports Requisites; Parts and Accessories Thereof.	0.02	0.02				
96	Miscellaneous Manufactured Articles		0.04	0.01	0.06		
98	Project Goods; Some Special uses	9.26	1.18	18.32	17.79	4.44	3.09
99	Miscellaneous Goods	0.19	0.16	0.01	0.01	0.85	0.02
	Total	527.85	643.12	545.54	623.18	517.66	535.51

Source: Dept. of Commerce, Govt. of India Statistics Database http:nic.commerce.in

TABLE 3: INDIA–RUSSIA TRADE: EXPORT FROM INDIA

(*US $ millions*)

		1996–7	1997–8	1998–9	1999–2000	2000–1	2001–2
02	Meat and Edible Meat Offal.	0.21	1.19	0.30			0.11
03	Fish and Crustaceans, Molluscs and other Aquatic Invertabrates.	1.72	0.87	0.04	0.10	0.24	1.73
04	Dairy Produce; Birds' Eggs; Natural Honey; Edible Prod. of Animal Origin, not Elsewhere Spec. or Included.	0.24	1.09	0.10		0.03	
05	Products of Animal Origin, not Elsewhere Specified or Included.	0.03		0.19			
06	Live Trees and Other Plants; Bulbs; Roots and the Like; Cut Flowers and Ornamental Foliage.	0.14	0.00		0.00	0.02	0.00
07	Edible Vegetables and Certain Roots and Tubers.	0.32	0.30	0.33	1.86	0.70	0.41
08	Edible Fruit and Nuts; Peel or Citrus Fruit or Melons.	2.59	4.62	1.35	2.21	1.31	1.79
09	Coffee, Tea, Meat and Spices.	129.66	228.56	201.71	186.76	131.19	92.77
10	Cereals.	97.68	41.60	33.54	38.05	0.52	5.79

HS Code		1996–7	1997–8	1998–9	1999–2000	2000–1	2001–2
11	Products of the Milling Industry; Malt; Starches; Insulin; Wheat Gluten.	7.28	0.38	0.01	0.03	0.01	0.01
12	Oil Seeds and Olea. Fruits; Misc. Grains, Seeds and Fruit; Industrial or Medicinal Plants; Straw and Fodder.	2.95	8.90	1.79	3.74	6.62	5.48
13	Lac; Gums, Resins and Other Vegetable Saps and Extracts.	0.13	0.20	0.27	0.19	1.60	0.83
14	Vegetable Plaiting Materials; Vegetable Products not Elsewhere Specified or Included.		0.26	0.11	0.00	0.00	0.04
15	Animal or Vegetable Fats and Oils and their Cleavage Products; Pre-Edible Fats; Animal or Vegetable Waxes.	2.29	2.10	1.38	11.57	10.89	12.01
16	Preparations of Meat, of Fish or of Crustaceans, Molluscs or Other Aquatic Invertebrates.						0.20
17	Sugars and Sugar Confectionery.	18.22	5.82	0.02	0.02	0.00	0.16
18	Cocoa and Cocoa Preparations.	0.13	0.00				
19	Preparations of Cereals, Flour, Starch or Milk; Pastry Products.	0.14	0.09	2.45	0.01	0.07	0.04
20	Preparations of Vegetables, Fruit, Nuts or Other Parts of Plants.	0.84	1.42	0.86	0.40	0.88	0.84
21	Miscellaneous Edible Preparations.	40.17	78.16	62.93	42.88	53.92	61.38
22	Beverages, Spirits, and Vinegar.	0.38	0.25		0.05		0.01
23	Residues and Waste From the Food Industries; Prepared Animal Fodder.	3.47	10.93	2.80	5.42	10.29	0.07
24	Tobacco and Manufactured Tobacco Substitutes.	31.14	62.36	25.54	47.35	27.77	21.99

HS Code		1996–7	1997–8	1998–9	1999–2000	2000–1	2001–2
25	Salt; Sulphur; Earths; Stone; Plastering Materials, Lime and Cement.	0.42	0.52	0.25	0.03	0.32	0.39
26	Ores, Slag, and Ash.	2.73	8.36		0.00	0.58	0.75
27	Mineral Fuels, Mineral Oils, and Products of Their Distillation; Bituminous Substances; Mineral Waxes.	2.37		0.05			0.08
28	Inorganic Chemicals; Organic or Inorganic Compounds of Precious Metals, of Rare-earth Metals, or Radi. Elem. or of Isotopes.	31.89	1.54	16.17	6.15	21.81	0.42
29	Organic Chemicals.	15.19	13.39	13.15	23.20	10.95	11.34
30	Pharmaceutical Products.	98.14	98.42	41.68	101.69	100.49	92.36
31	Fertilizers.						5.55
32	Tanning or Dyeing Extracts; Tannins and their deri. Dyes, Pigments and Other Colouring Matter; Paints and ver; Putty and Other Mastics; Inks.	3.46	4.57	1.31	1.23	1.92	2.44
33	Essential Oils and Resinoids; Perfumery, Cosmetic or Toilet Preparations.	16.81	19.62	7.54	6.60	5.56	7.33
34	Soap, Organic Surface-active Agents, Washing Preparations, Lubricating Preparations, Artificial Waxes, Prepared Waxes, Polishing or Scouring Prep.	2.15	0.39	0.43	0.55	0.61	0.63
35	Albuminoidal Substances; Modified Starches; Glues; Enzymes.	0.02					0.00
36	Explosives; Pyrotechnic Products; Matches; Pyrophoric Alloys; Certain Combustible Preparations.	0.22					
37	Photographic or Cinematographic Goods.	2.52	4.44	5.71	0.90	0.04	0.03
38	Miscellaneous Chemical Products.	1.02	4.03	0.98	8.88	4.99	2.57

		1996–7	1997–8	1998–9	1999–2000	2000–1	2001–2
39	Plastic and Articles Thereof.	22.95	19.85	7.11	17.33	14.51	10.57
40	Rubber and Articles Thereof.	4.20	3.76	3.81	5.78	4.73	2.49
41	Raw Hides and Skins (Other Than Furskins) and Leather.	2.61	3.55	1.72	1.19	2.58	5.39
42	Articles of Leather, Saddlery and Harness; Travel Goods, Handbags and Similar Articles of Animal Gut (other than Silk-worm).	13.99	17.49	10.03	16.86	22.25	9.37
44	Wood and Articles of Wood; Wood Charcoal.	1.07	0.07		0.06	0.13	0.06
45	Cork and Articles of Cork.				0.58		
46	Manufactures of Straw, of Esparto or of Other Plaiting Materials; Basketware and Wickerwork.		0.00	0.02	0.07	0.05	
48	Paper and Paperboard; Articles of Paper Pulp, of Paper or of Paperboard.	1.27	0.37	1.52	0.97	1.84	1.50
49	Printed Books, Newspapers, Pictures and other Products of the Printing Industry; Manuscripts, Typescripts and Plans.	0.05	0.11	0.10	0.20	0.08	0.10
50	Silk.	0.08	0.38	0.11	0.16	0.20	4.42
51	Wool, Fine or Coarse Animal Hair, Horsehair Yarn and Woven Fabric.	0.56	0.20	1.26	0.19	0.53	0.10
52	Cotton.	27.98	47.36	44.84	64.91	63.26	22.71
53	Other Vegetable Textila Fibres; Paper Yarn and Woven Fabrics of Paper Yarn.	1.22	0.64	0.31	0.96	1.12	0.62
54	Man-made Filaments.	1.84	1.89	0.92	0.94	1.57	1.36
55	Man-made Staple Fabres.	4.47	2.20	0.77	2.43	3.87	2.32
56	Wadding, Felt and Non-wovens; Special Yarns; Twine, Cordage, Ropes and Cables and Articles Thereof.	0.04	0.49	0.65	2.37	1.09	0.13
57	Carpets and other Textile Floor Coverings.	1.49	0.87	0.59	0.57	0.33	0.28

		1996–7	1997–8	1998–9	1999–2000	2000–1	2001–2
58	Special Woven Fabrics; Tufted Textile Fabrics; Lace; Tapestries; Trimmings; Embroidery.	0.32	0.57	0.44	0.30	0.26	0.57
59	Impregnated, Coated, Covered or Laminated Textile Fabrics; Textile Articles of a Kind Suitable for Industrial use.	3.00	2.98	1.18	0.12	0.44	0.64
60	Knitted or Crocheted Fabrics.	1.41	1.57	2.93	2.46	2.86	2.72
61	Articles of Apparel and Clothing Accessories, Knitted or Crocheted.	47.86	51.89	60.53	134.86	206.82	236.57
62	Articles of Apparel and Clothing Accessories, not Knitted or Crocheted.	35.83	49.67	78.91	110.70	106.64	96.45
63	Other Made up Textile Articles; Sets; Worn Clothing and Worn Textile Articles; Rags.	45.88	30.01	4.35	2.95	2.23	1.54
64	Footwear, Gaiters and the Like; Parts of Such Articles.	13.81	30.46	14.01	10.45	6.94	1.60
65	Headgear and Parts Thereof.			0.02	0.04	0.01	0.00
66	Umbrellas, Sun Umbrellas, Walking-sticks, Seat-sticks, Whips, Riding-crops and Parts Thereof.						0.01
67	Prepared Feathers and Down and Articles Made of Feathers or of Down; Artificial Flowers; Articles of Human Hair.			0.02		0.07	0.00
68	Articles of Stone, Plaster, Cement, Asbestos, Mica or Similar Materials.	0.18	0.53	0.28	0.65	0.53	0.63
69	Ceramic Products.	0.10	0.21	0.01	0.28	0.38	2.31
70	Glass and Glassware.	0.57	2.20	0.00	0.15	0.16	0.15

		1996–7	1997–8	1998–9	1999–2000	2000–1	2001–2
71	Natural or Cultured Pearls, Precious or Semi-precious Stones, Pre-metals, clad with Pre-metal and Articles Thereof; Imit.jewellery; Coin.	4.82	4.70	2.00	2.10	2.88	0.82
72	Iron and Steel.	0.85	0.81	0.01	0.07	0.38	1.50
73	Articles of Iron or Steel.	0.48	0.43	0.41	0.70	0.60	0.89
74	Copper and Articles Thereof.	0.12	0.13	0.36	1.58	0.44	0.20
75	Nickel and Articles Thereof.		0.01	0.95	0.56	0.30	0.14
76	Aluminium and Articles Thereof.	0.77	0.19	0.14	0.59	0.93	0.41
78	Lead and Articles Thereof.	0.04					
79	Zinc and Articles Thereof.	2.96	2.98				
80	Tin and Articles Thereof.				0.75	0.00	
81	Other Base Metals; Cermets; Articles Thereof.		0.02	0.00	0.06	0.04	
82	Tools Implements, Cutlery, Spoons and Forks, of Base Metal; Parts Thereof of Base Metal.	0.48	0.63	0.56	0.34	0.66	0.51
83	Miscellaneous Articles of Base Metal.	0.27	0.83	0.59	0.69	0.46	1.06
84	Nuclear Reactors, Boilers, Machinery and Mechanical Appliances; Parts Thereof.	9.65	15.88	16.07	18.83	8.33	12.75
85	Electrical Machinery and Equipment and Parts Thereof; Sound Recorders and Reproducers, Television Image and Sound Recorders and Reproducers, and Parts.	22.93	16.96	7.07	8.74	12.79	9.60
86	Railway or Tramway Locomotives, Rolling-stock and Parts Thereof; Railway or Tramway Track Fixtures and Fittings and Parts Thereof.	0.11		1.31		0.00	0.00
87	Mechanical Vehicles other than Railway or Tramway Rolling Stock, and Parts and Accessories Thereof.	3.69	3.48	1.43	1.45	2.10	1.32

		1996–7	1997–8	1998–9	1999–2000	2000–1	2001–2
88	Aircraft, Spacecraft, and Parts Thereof.	0.02	0.76	1.19	2.03	0.11	4.35
90	Optical, Photographic Cinematographic Measuring, Checking Precision, Medical or Surgical Inst. and Apparatus Parts and Accessories Thereof.	6.44	7.01	2.38	32.06	9.43	14.31
91	Clocks and Watches and Parts Thereof.	0.11	0.09	0.11	0.05	0.36	0.27
92	Musical Instruments; Parts and Accessories of Such Articles.	0.00	0.01	0.01	0.01	0.03	0.04
93	Arms and Ammunition; Parts and Accessories Thereof.						0.01
94	Furniture; Bedding, Mattresses, Mattress Supports, Cushions and Similar Stuffed Furnishing; Lamps and Lighting Fittings not Elsewhere Specified or Inc.	0.01	0.02			0.00	0.04
95	Toys, Games and Sports Requisites; Parts and Accessories Thereof.	0.34	0.12			0.12	0.19
96	Miscellaneous Manufactured Articles.	6.55	7.32			6.20	6.22
97	Works of art Collectors' Pieces and Antiques.	0.01					
98	Project Goods; Some Special Uses.		15.02				
99	Miscellaneous Goods.	1.08	1.84			4.04	9.45
	Total	811.16	952.97	709.42	947.92	889.01	798.18

Source: Dept. of Commerce, Govt. of India Statistics Database http://commerce.nic.in

TABLE 4: INDIAN COMPANIES OPERATING IN MOSCOW
(LIST COMPILED BY THE EMBASSY OF INDIA)
1992–2002

Chemicals United Phosphorus Ltd.
Yukos Oil Co.

Construction, Engineering Goods and Steel Products
Larsen & Toubro Ltd.
Fortune International
Magnum International Trading Co. (P) Ltd.
Thermax (P) Ltd.
Span Overseas Ltd.
Star Way
Lotus International

Cosmetics, Toileteries
Lakme Lever Ltd.
Paints Industry
Food Enkay Texofood Industries Ltd.
Mm International
Intern.
Unilever N.V.

Allied Groceries
'Pizza Express Ltd.'

Garments
Oswal Woollens Ltd. (Nahar)
City Impex
Saluja Fabrics

General Trading
Axiom
Adani Exports Ltd.
Agiorus
Agioz Su
Agio Rus
Agio Image
Alfa Pat
Aska International
Amigo International Ltd.
Amtel Exports
Amtel Su Armas International
Benco
Bentimi
Caprihans Ltd.
DCM Overseas Ltd.
Dina International
Indigo
Inter Front Trading Co.
J.F.K. International
Volga International
Khanejas
Khemka Group (Sun Group)
Lucky Exports
Lucky Su Liberty Footwear Co.
Magnum Exports
New Technology
Nadex Corporation
Phoenix
Pix Transmissions
R-style Int. Ltd.
Ruchi International
Everest Trading
Data Pvt. Ltd.
Santa Rus
Sun Group
Thame's Int.
Texcomash Export
Texuna Group of Companies
Usha Intercontinental
Vijay Int. Ltd.
Green Mos International

Pharmaceuticals, etc.
Cadilla Healthcare
Core Healthcare
Dr. Reddy's Lab.
Ipca Laboratories Limited
Orlionok
Ranbaxy Laboratories Ltd.
Sun Pharmaceutical Industries Ltd.
Unique Pharmaceutical Lab.
Coral Med.
Pharmacare
Shreya Corporation
Transatlantic

A.E. Option
Inter Care
Novartis
Promed Exports
Wockhardt
Hoechst Marion Roussel
Cadila Pharmaceuticals
Lupin

Leather Items and Shoes
Bremco Exports
Savaria Trading

Linoleum & Floor Covering
Caprihans Int. Impex Pvt. Ltd.
Omega Su
Premier Vinyl Flooring Ltd.

Tea, etc.
J. V. Gokal & Co.
Saraf Trading Corporation
Beeye Overseas Ltd.
Tea Board Of India
State Trading Corporation (STC)

Cargo & Freight Services & Travelling
Awia Rus
Rao Intour
Vega Travels
Jay Kay Travels

TABLE 5: RUSSIAN INVESTMENTS OUTSIDE RUSSIA

Russian investments abroad by form (US $ million)

	1995	2000	2001	2002	2003	2004
All investments	226	15154	16841	19891	23264	33773
Direct investments	20	382	495	303	283	2064
Payments as capital	14	301	332	134	103	1868
Credit from partners					31	137
Other	6	81	163	169	149	59
Portfolio investments	0.1	31	70		4	76
Other	206	14741	16276	19588	22977	31633
Trade credits	36	2165	6944	7658	14039	17826
Other credits	1	11	257	480	385	2313
Bank deposits	167	12558	8998	11364	8543	11350
Other	2	7	77	86	10	144

Russian investments abroad by sector (US $ million)

	2000	2001	2002	2003	2004
Total	15154	16841	19891	23254	33773
Industry	1376	5820	6485	10546	17254
Energy	246	5007	4867	8215	10500
Oil extraction	108	4891	4722	8037	10304
Oil refining	8	12	7	18	
Gas					2
Coal	129	1044	5	5	194
Ferrous and non-ferrous industry	877	137	133	155	2386
Light industry	183	194	843	1144	2738
Chemical	24	299	149	213	822
Machine Tools	14	44	400	424	468
Food processing	15	47	45	167	25
Agriculture		1	45	131	6
Construction	0.1		12	10	266
Transport	142	56	112	5	4701
Trade	1087	2103	2059	178	607
Commercial activity	550	639	1024	4251	607
Finance, credit, insurance	11590	8218	10193	366	10665
Other	409	4	5	7860	274

Russian Investments abroad. CIS and non-CIS (US $ million)

	2000	2001	2002	2003	2004
Investments outside CIS	15154	16841	19891	23254	33773
Investments in CIS	131	310	240	544	713

Russian investments abroad (US $ millions)

	2000	2001	2002	2003	2004
Total	15154	16841	19891	23264	33773
US	12085	8545	10677	7400	10330
Cyprus	80	3483	3573	5943	7513
UK	86	1372	1686	3602	3630
Germany		544	863	1341	1858
Switzerland		443	982	952	1351
Bermuda		307			
Lithuania		302	295	1223	1316
Netherlands	69	267	457		
China		259	247	776	1545
Gibraltar		224			
Liberia	25				
Latvia	15				
Finland	2				
Yugoslavia	53				
Iran			112		280
Ukraine			126	261	194
Belorussia				243	

Source: Tables compiled from *Investitsii v Rossii* (*Federal'naia sluzhba gosudarstvennoi statistiki*, Moscow, 2005).

Bibliography

UNPUBLISHED SOURCES

Archives of Industrial Export Services, Kolkata

D'Mello, B., 'Foreign Collaboration in the Public Sector Steel Industry', unpublished PhD dissertation, Indian Institute of Management (Calcutta), December 1986.

'Protocol of the First Session of the Inter-Governmental Russian-Indian Commission on Trade, Economic, Scientific and Technological Cooperation', Moscow, 13–14 September 1994.

'Protocol of the Second Session of the Inter-Governmental Russian-Indian Commission on Trade, Economic, Scientific and Technological Cooperation', New Delhi, 9–12 October 1995.

'Protocol of the Third Session of the Inter-Governmental Russian-Indian Commission on Trade, Economic, Scientific and Technological Cooperation', Moscow, 10–11 February 1997.

'Protocol of the Fourth Session of the Inter-Governmental Russian-Indian Commission on Trade, Economic, Scientific and Technological Cooperation', New Delhi, 17–18 December 1997.

'Protocol of the Fifth Session of the Inter-Governmental Russian-Indian Commission on Trade, Economic, Scientific and Technological Cooperation', Moscow, 26–8 November 1998.

'Protocol of the Eighth Session of the Inter-Governmental Russian-Indian Commission on Trade, Economic, Scientific and Technological Cooperation', New Delhi, 7 February 2002.

'Protocols of Agreed Minutes of 1st Indo-Russian Working Group on Trade and Cooperation', 21–2 July 1994 (Moscow).

'Protocols of Agreed Minutes of 2nd Indo-Russian Working Group on Trade and Cooperation', 5–9 October 1995 (New Delhi).

'Protocols of Agreed Minutes of 3rd Indo-Russian Working Group on Trade and Cooperation', 23–7 January 1997 (Moscow).

'Protocols of Agreed Minutes of 4th Indo-Russian Working Group on Trade and Cooperation', 11–12 December 1997 (New Delhi).
'Protocols of Agreed Minutes of 5th Indo-Russian Working Group on Trade and Cooperation', 24–25 November 1998 (Moscow).
'Protocols of Agreed Minutes of 6th Indo-Russian Working Group on Trade and Cooperation', 12–13 January 2000 (New Delhi).
'Protocols of Agreed Minutes of 7th Indo-Russian Working Group on Trade and Cooperation', 11–12 January 2001 (Moscow).
'Protocols of Agreed Minutes of 8th Indo-Russian Working Group on Trade and Cooperation', 5–6 February 2002 (New Delhi).
'Protocols of Agreed Minutes of 9th Indo-Russian Working Group on Trade and Cooperation', 12–15 May 2003 (Moscow).

WEBSITES

www.axiom.ru
www.brahmos.com
http://coal.nic.in/
http://commerce.nic.in
http://comtrade.un.org/db
www.gidroenergoprom.ru
http://www.gks.ru
www.IAEA.org
www.interros.ru
www.shreya.ru
www.tpe.ru
www.npcil.nic.in
www.ushain.com
www.webapteka.ru
www.zyduscadila.com

PUBLISHED SOURCES

Afanasyev, V.G., *The Scientific and Technological Revolution: Its Impact on Management* (Moscow: Progress, 1975).
Aganbegyan, Abel, *The Challenge: Economics of Perestroika* (London: Hutchinson, 1988).

Ahmed, Muzaffar, *Myself and the Communist Party of India, 1920–29* (Calcutta: National Book Agency, 1970).

Akta Prezidenta I Pravitel'stva Rossiiskoi Federatsii (Moscow).

Allison R. (ed.), *Radical Reform in Soviet Defence Policy* (London: Macmillan, 1992).

Allison, Roy, and Christoph Bluth (eds), *Security Dilemmas in Russia and Eurasia* (London: Royal Institute of International Affairs, 1998).

Armiia I Obshchestvo (Moscow: Progress, 1990).

Arnett, Eric (ed.), *Military Capacity and the Risk of War* (Oxford: Oxford University Press, 1997).

Asghar, Tahir, 'Indo-Russian Trade: An Overview', in Shamsuddin (ed.), *India and Russia, Towards Strategic Partnership* (Delhi: Lancer's Books, 2001).

Aslund, Anders, *How Russia became a Market Economy* (Washington: Brookings Institute, 1995).

Azrael, J., *Managerial Power and Soviet Politics* (Cambridge: Harvard University Press, 1967).

Bailes, Kenneth, *Technology and Society under Lenin and Stalin* (Princeton: Princeton University Press, 1978).

Bakshi, Jyotsna, *Russia and India: From Ideology to Geopolitics, (1947-1998)* (Delhi: Dev Publications, 1999).

——— 'Sino-Russian Strategic Partnership in Central Asia: Implications for India', *SA*, May 2001.

——— 'Russia's National Security Concepts and Military Doctrines: Continuity and Change', *SA*, October 2000.

——— 'Russia-China Military-Technical Cooperation: Implications for India', *SA*, July 2000.

——— 'Russian Policy Towards South Asia', *SA*, November 1999.

——— 'Moscow Grapples with Political and Economic Crises: Implications for Foreign policy', *SA*, May 1999.

——— 'Russian Policy Towards Central Asia-I', *SA*, January 1999.

——— 'Russian Policy Towards Central Asia-II', *SA*, February 1999.

——— 'Russia's Post-Pokhran Dilemma', *SA*, August 1998.

——— 'No Single Power or Power Centre Can Have Exclusive Sway Over Central Asia: A Geo-Political Analysis', *SA*, April 1998.

——— 'India in Russia's Strategic Thinking', *SA*, January 1998.

——— 'India Russia Cooperation in Economy, Science and Technology', in Shamsuddin (ed.), *India and Russia: Towards Strategic Partnership* (Delhi: Lancer's Books, 2001).

Ballerina, Ekarerina, 'San Grup v Rossii: 40 let aktivnoi raboty', in *Rossiiskaia Federatsiia*, no. 2, 1999.

Balzer, Harley, *Russia's Missing Middle Class* (New York: M.E. Sharpe, 1996).

Basu, Baidya Bikash, 'Russian Military-Technical Cooperation: Structures and Processes, Strategic Analysis', *SA*, June 2001.

——— 'Russian National Security Thinking', *SA*, October 2000.

——— 'Trends in Russian Arms Export', *SA*, February 2000.

——— 'Reforms in Russian Defence Industry: Problems and Prospects', *SA*, January 2000).

——— 'The Private Sector and Defence Production', *SA*, June 1997.

Batchikov, S. and Iu. Petrov, 'The Formation of Financial Industrial Groups and the State', *Russian and East European Finance and Trade*, vol. 33, no. 1, 1997.

Behl, Ramesh and L.D. Mago, *The Indian Businessman's Guide to CIS* (Delhi: Global Business Press, 1994).

Belianova, E., 'Motivatsiia I povedenie rossiiskikh predpriatii', in *Voprosy Ekonomiki*, no. 6, 1995.

Berliner, J., *Soviet Economic Aid* (New York: Praeger, 1978).

Bertsch, Gary K. and William C. Potter (eds), *Dangerous Weapons, Desperate States* (New York: RKP, 1999).

Biznesmeny Rossii (Moscow: OKO, 1994).

Blank, Stephen J., *Challenging the New World Order: The Arms Transfer Policies of the Russian Republic* (Pennsylvania: Strategic Studies Institute, US Army War College, 1993).

Blasi, Joseph, Maya Kroumova and Douglas Kruse, *Kremlin Capitalism: The Privatization of the Russian Economy* (Ithaca, New York: ILR Press, 1997).

Botkin, O. and M. Kozlov, 'The Ural Plants Financial Industrial Group', *Russian and East European Finance and Trade,* vol. 33, no. 2, 1997.

Boeva, I., T. Dolgopiatova and V. Shironin, *Gosudarstvennye predpriiatiia v 1991-92 gg.: ekonomicheskie problemy I 'povedeniie* (Moscow: Institut Ekonomicheskoi Politiki, 1992).

Borisov, S.M., 'The Ruble Zone Without a Present and a Future ?', in *Russian and East European Finance and Trade*, September–October, 1995).

Bosworth Barry P. and Gur Ofer, *Reforming Planned Economies in an Integrating World Economy* (Washington: The Brookings Institution, 1995).

Boycko, Maxim, Andrei Schleifer, and Robert Vishny, *Privatizing Russia* (Cambridge Mass.: MIT Press, 1995).

Brady, Rose, *Kapitalizm* (New Haven: Yale University Press, 2000).

Budraj, V.S., *Soviet Russia and the Hindustan Sub-continent* (Bombay: Somaiya Publications, 1973).

Butrin, D., 'Who Owns Russia: Russia's Machine Building Industry', *The Russian Journal,* 12 April 2002.

Byelov, A., 'Who Owns Russia: Russia's Machine Building Industry', *The Russian Journal,* 15 March 2002.

Cambridge Encyclopaedia of Russia and the Former Soviet Union (Cambridge: Cambridge University Press, 1995).

Carter, J.R., *The Net Cost of Soviet Foreign Aid* (New York: Praeger, 1971).

Chandra, Nirmal, 'Russia's Sinking Economy: External Dimensions', *EPW*, 15 May 1993.

———, Dimensions of Social and Economic Crisis in Russia Today, *EPW*, 1 May 1996.

———, 'India's Rouble Debt and Depreciating Rouble', *EPW*, 3–10 July 1993.

———, 'USSR and Third World, Unequal Distributions of Gains in Trade', *EPW*, February 1977.

Chaudhuri, S., *The WTO and India's Pharmaceutical Industry* (Delhi: Oxford University Press, 2005).

Clarke, Simon, Peter Fairbrother, Vadim Borisov and Peter Bizyukov, 'The Privatization of Industrial Enterprises in Russia: Four Case Studies', *Europe Asia Studies*, vol. 46, no. 4, 1994.

Clarke, Simon, Peter Fairbrother, Michael Burawoy, and Pavel Krotov, *What About the Workers: Workers and the Transition to Capitalism in Russia* (London: Verso, 1993).

Chishti, Sumitra, *India's Trade with Eastern Europe* (Delhi: Indian Institute of Foreign Trade, 1973).

Chowdhuri, S.R., *Leftist Movements in India, 1917-47* (Calcutta: Minerva Associates, 1976).

Cooper, Julian, 'The Future of the Russian Defence Industry,' in Allison Roy and Christoph Bluth (eds), *Security Dilemmas in Russia and Eurasia* (London: Royal Institute of International Affairs, 1998).

Committee on Public Sector Units, 3rd Lok Sabha, 13th Report, *Management and Administration of Public Undertakings* (New Delhi: Lok Sabha, 1965).

Committee on Public Sector Units, 4th Lok Sabha, 30th Report.

———, Action taken on 22nd Report of 3rd Lok Sabha.

Connor, Walter, *Tattered Banners* (Boulder, Colorado: Westview Press, 1996).

Da Costa, A., *The Global Restructuring of the Steel Industry* (London: Routledge, 1999).

Datar, Asha L., *India's Economic Relations with the USSR and Eastern Europe 1953 To 1969* (Cambridge: Cambridge University Press).

Desai, Padma, *The Bokaro Steel Plant: A Study of Soviet Economic Assistance* (Amsterdam: North Holland Publishing, 1972).

Desert, Myriam and Gilles Favarel-Garrigues, *Les Capitalistes Russes* (Paris: Documentation Francaise, Problemes Politiques et Sociaux no. 789, 1997).

Djankov, Simeon and Caroline Freund, *Disintegration and Trade: A Study of Trade Flows Among and between Nine Regions and Fourteen Republics of the Former Soviet Union* (The World Bank Financial Sector Strategy and Policy Department, June 2000).

Dmitriev, M. and S. Vasiliev (eds), *1998: Russia's Banking Crisis and the Stabilization Phase* (Moscow: Carnegie Centre, 2001).

Dolgopiatova, T. and I. Evseeva, 'Ekonomicheskoe povedenie promyshennykh predpriiatii v perekhodnoi ekonomike', in *Voprosy ekonomiki*, no. 8, 1994.

Dolgopiatova, T.G., *Rossiiske predpriiatiia v perekhodnoi ekonomike: ekonomicheskoie problemy I povedenie* (Moscow: Delo Ltd., 1995).

Duncan, Peter, *The Soviet Union and India* (London: Routledge & Kegan Paul, 1989, Chatham House Papers, RIIR).

———, *Eastern Europe and the CIS, 1999. A Political and Economic Survey* (Europa Publications, 2000).

Elder, Alexander, *Rubles to Dollars* (New York: Institute of Finance, 1998).

Egorin, A.Z., *Rossiia-Indiia: sostoianie I perspektivy voenno-tekhnicheskogo sotrudnichestva* in *Rossiia – India: Perspektivy regional'nogo sotrudnichestva (g. Nizhnii Novgorod)* (Moscow: Institut Vostokovedeniia, 2000).

Ellman, Michael, *Socialist Planning* (Cambridge: Cambridge University Press, 1987).

Freeland, Chrystia, *Sale of the Century: Russia's Wild Ride from Communism to Capitalism* (New York: Crown Business, 2000).

Filatov, Anatoly 'Uralmash: India's Partner', *Soviet Land*, no. 2, 1976.

——— 'Expanding Cooperation for the Well-being of the Peoples of Two countries', *Soviet Land*, nos. 22–3.

Frydman, Roman Andrezej Rapaczynski and John S. Earle, *The Privatization Process in Russia, Ukraine and the Baltic States* (London: Central European University, 1993).

Gidadhubli, R.G., 'India-Russia Economic Relations: Challenges and Opportunities', in Shamsuddin (ed.), *India and Russia, Towards Strategic Partnership* (Delhi: Lancer's Books, 2001).

Gimpel'son, V., 'Novoe rossiiskoe predprinimatel'stvo: istochniki formirovanie I strategii sotsial'nogo razvitiia', in *IMEMO*, no. 6, 1993.

Goldman M., *Soviet Foreign Aid* (New York: Praeger, 1967).

Gurov, A., *Krasnaia Mafiia* (Samotsvet, MIKO, 1998).

Gurkov, I., 'Strategiia vyzhivaniia promyshlennykh predpriiatii v novykh uslovkiiakh', *Voprosy Ekonomiki*, no. 6, 1995.

Haksar, P.N. et al., *Studies in Indo-Soviet Relations* (Delhi: Patriot, 1986).

Hewett, A. and Victor L. Winston, *Glasnost' and Perestroika* (Washington: Brookings Institute, 1991).

Imam, Zafar, *Colonialism in East-West Relations* (Delhi: Patriot, 1967).

——— *Indian Drugs and Pharmaceuticals Ltd.* (Delhi: Patriot, 1968).

——— *Indian Pharmaceutical Guide* (Bombay: Pamposh Publications, 1994).

——— *India-Russia: The Road Ahead.* (Delhi: Confederation of Indian Industry, 2000).

——— *Indo-Soviet Coopertion* (Delhi: ISCUS, 1971).

——— 'Instructions on the application of import tariffs', in *Ekonomika I Zhizn'*, April 1994.

Johnson, Juliet Ellen, 'The Russian Banking System: Institutional Responses to the Market Transition', *Europe Asia Studies*, vol. 46, no. 6, 1994.

Johnson, William, *The Steel Industry of India* (Cambridge: Harvard University Press, 1967).

Jones, Kent, *Politics vs. Economics in the World Steel Industry* (London: Allen Unwin, 1986).

Kabalina, V.I. (ed.), *Predpriatie I Rynok: dinamika upravleniia I trudovykh otnoshenii v perekhodnyi period (Opyt monograficheskikh issledovanii, 1989-1995 gg.)* (Moscow: Rosspen, 1997).

——— 'Kak vesti uspeshnyi biznes v rossii', *Chelovek i Kar'era*, no. 5, 1999.

Khakhordin, Oleg and Theodore P. Gerber, 'Russian Directors' Business Ethic. A Study of Industrial Enterprises in St. Petersburg, 1993', *Europe Asia Studies*, no. 46, no. 7, 1994.

Khlebnikov, Pavel, *Krestnyi otets kremlia: Boris Berezovskii* (Moscow: Detektiv Press, 2001).

Kotkin, Stephen, *Magnetic Mountain* (Berkeley: University of California Press, 1995).

Kotz, David M., and Fred Weir, *Russia's Path from Gorbachev to Putin* (Oxford: Routledge, 2007).

Krasnikova, E.V., *Ekonomika perekhodnogo perioda* (Moscow: Omega-L, 2008).

Kucherenko, V., *Moskva—Imperiia T'my* (Moscow: Paleia, 1995).

Kukolev, Igor V., 'The Formation of the Business Elite', *Russian Social Science Review*, vol. 38, no. 4, 1997.

Kulev, I., 'Economic Cooperation between USSR and Developing Countries', *Soviet Land*, no. 5, 1977.

Kuznetsov, Andrei, 'Economic Reforms in Russia: Enterprise Behaviour as an Impediment to Change', *Europe Asia Studies*, vol. 46, no. 6, 1994.

Lampert, Nicholas, *The Technical Intelligentsia and the Soviet State* (New York: Macmillan, 1979).

Maksimova, Ludmilla, *Pharmaceutical Market in Russia* (Washington: US Department of Trade, 1997).

Mar'ianovskii, V., 'The Russian Economic Mentality', *Russian Social Science Review*, vol. 38, no. 4, 1997.

Matovnikov, M. Iu, L.V. Mikhailov, L.I. Sycheva and E.V. Timofeev, *Rossiiskie banki: 10 let spustia* (Moscow: Mak Tsentr, 1998).

Medvedev, Roy, *Kapitalizm v Rossii* (Moscow: Prava Cheloveka, 1998).

Mehrotra, Santosh, *India and the Soviet Union: Trade and Technology Transfer* (Delhi: Oxford University Press, 1991).

Mehta, Vinod K., *Soviet Union and India's Industrial Development* (Delhi: Manas, 1975).

Men'shikov, Stanislav, *Anatomiia Rossiiskogo Kapitalizma* (Moscow: Mezhdunarodnye Otnosheniia, 2004).

Michailopolous, Constantine and David G. Tarr (eds.), *Trade in the New Independent States* (Washington: The World Bank, 1994).

Minkevich, Mikhail, *Drugs and Pharmaceuticals in Northwest Russia* (US Department of Commerce Report, 1998).

Mohan, K.C., 'Mecon's Role in Building Heavy Industry', *Soviet Land*, no. 1, 1976.

Moonan, S., *Technology Transfer: Rejuvenating Matured Industries* (New York: Garland, 1997).

Mukherjee, Hiren, *Time-tested Treasure* (Bombay: Allied Publishers, 1975).

Mukhin, A.A., *Novye Pravila Igry dliia bol'shogo biznesa* (Moscow: Gnom ID, 2002).

Muravyov, Andrei, *Soviet Indian Economic Relations* (Delhi: Panchsheel Publishers, 1988).

Nanda, B.R. (ed.), *Socialism in India* (Delhi: Vikas, 1972).

Nayar, A., *The Steel Handbook* (Bombay: Tata McGraw Hill, 2001).

Nayyar, Deepak (ed.), *Economic Relations between Socialist Countries and the Third World* (London: Macmillan, 1977).

Neu, C. Richard, *Rand, Russian-American Business Leaders' Forum: Report on Inaugural Meeting* (Santa Monica: RAND, 1997).

——— *Rand, Russian-American Business Leaders' Forum: Report on the May 16-17 1998 Plenary Meeting* (Santa Monica: RAND, 1998).

——— *Rand, Russian-American Business Leaders' Forum: Report on the October 31-November 1 1998 Plenary Meeting* (Santa Monica: RAND, 1998).

——— *Rand, Russian-American Business Leaders' Forum: Report on the May 15-16 1999 Plenary Meeting* (Santa Monica: RAND, 1999).

——— *The Nuclear Black Market* (CSIS Task Force Report, Centre for Strategic and International Studies, Washington, 1996).

Osipov, G.V. (ed.), *Industry and Labour in the USSR* (London: Tavistock Publications, 1966).

'Ob ymenii rukovodit', *Perspektiva*, Autumn-Winter, 1999.

Payment Procedures: Exports to Russian Federation (Reserve Bank of India, December 1995).

Pierre, Andrew J. and Dmitri V. Trenin, *Russia in the World Arms Trade* (Washington: Brookings Institution, 1997).

Portyakov, Vladimir, *The People's Republic of China: Economic Policy of the 1990s* (Moscow: Institute of Far Eastern Studies, RAN, 1997).

Ranier, R., and J. Aylen, *The Steel Industry in the New Millennium* (London: IOM Communications, 1998).

Ravallhon, Martin and Michael Lokshin, *Who Wants to Redistribute?* (World Bank Development Research Group, Poverty and Human Resources, July 1999).

Regiony Rossii v 1998 (Moscow: Gandalf, 1999).

Regiony Rossii v 1999 (Moscow: Gandalf, 2000).

Roy, Purabi, S. Datta Gupta and Hari Vasudevan (eds.), *Indo-Soviet Relations 1917-1947: Select Documents from the Archives of the Russian Federation*, 2 vols. (Calcutta: Asiatic Society, 1998, 2000).

Sachdeva, Gulshan, 'Indo-Russian Trade and economic Relations: Present Realities and Future Possibilities', in Shamsuddin (ed.), *India and Russia, Towards Strategic Partnership* (Delhi: Lancer's Books, 2001).

Sampurnanand, *Memoirs and Reflections* (Bombay: Asia Publishing House, 1962).

Sapir, Jaques, *Les bases futres de la puissance militaire russe* (Paris: EHESS, Groupe de la sociologie de la Defense, Cahiers d'etudes strategiques, no. 16, 1993).

———, *La culture technologique: le cas des materiels militaires sovietiques* Compiegne, UTC, Cahiers de Recherches, no. 3, 1990).

Sardesai, S.G., *India and the Russian Revolution* (Bombay: Communist Party Publ., 1962).

Sareen T.R., *Russian Revolution and India, 1917-1921* (Delhi: Sterling Publishers, 1977).

Saunders, C.T. (ed.), *Economics and Politics of Transition* (London: Macmillan, 1992).

Sen, Mohit, *The Indian Revolution* (Delhi: PPH, 1970).

Sen, Pronab, 'Rupee-Rouble Exchange Rate', *Economic and Political Weekly*, 24 March 1990.

Sen, Samir K. *Military Technology and Defence Industrialization: The Indian Experience* (Delhi: Manas Publications, 2000).

Sharma, R.K. (ed.), *The Economics of Indo-Soviet Trade* (Bombay: Allied Publ., 1999).

Shmelev, N.P., 'Sotsializm I Mirovaia Ekonomika', *IMEMO*, no. 10, 1976.

Sidhu, S.S., *The Steel Industry in India* (Delhi: Vikas, 1983).

Sobell, Vladimir, *The Red Market* (Aldershot: Gower, 1984).

Statisticheskii Ezhegodnik 2000 (*Mezhdugosudarstvennyi Statisticheskii Komitet SNG*, Moscow, 2001).

Sokolov, Evgenii, 'Energeticheskaia Bezopasnost' Rossii', *Nezavisimaia Gazeta, Stsenarii*, no. 3, 1998.

Sokolov Iurii A., 'Commercial Banking in Russia', *Russian and East European Finance and Trade*, March–April 1996.

Srinivasan, N., *The Iron and Steel Industry of India* (Calcutta: TISCO, 1982).

Starr, Richard F., *The New Military in Russia* (Annapolis, Maryland: Naval Institute Press, 1996).

Szekely, J., *The Future of the World Steel Industry* (New York: Marcel Dekker Inc., 1976).

Tamozhennaia Statistika Vneshnei Torgovli Rossiiskoi Federatsii 2005, 2 vols. (Moscow: Federal'naia Tamozhennaia Sluzhba, 2006).

Tamozhennyi Tarif Rossiiskoi Federatsii (Moscow: Soft. Izd. 2006).

Usmani, Shaukat, *Peshawar to Moscow* (Benares: Swarajya Publication, 1957).

——— *I Met Stalin Twice* (Bombay: K. Kurian, 1953).

Vajda, Imre, *The Role of Foreign Trade in a Socialist Economy* (Budapest: Corvina Press, 1965).

Valkenier, E.K., 'New Trends in Soviet Economic Relations with the Third World', *World Politics*, April 1970.

——— 'The USSR, the Third World and the Global Economy', *Problems of Communism*, July–August 1979.

——— *The Soviet Union and the Third World: An Economic Bind* (New York: Praeger, 1983).

Vasudevan, Hari, '"Revolution" and "Transition" in Central Eurasia 1988-1996: The Making of Russian Foreign Policy' in Bhaskar Chakrabarty (ed.), *Exploring Regional Security: South and Central Asia* (Kolkata: K.P. Bagchi, 2003).

Vedomosti Ş"ezda Narodnykh Deptatov RSFSR I Verkhovnogo Soveta RSRSR (Moscow).

Veselovskii S., V. Potapov and O. Salkovskii, *Insane Squandering* (Moscow: Progress, 1988).

Vladimir Putin, President of the Russian Federation, Official Visit to India, December 2002 (Moscow: RIA, 2002).

Wedel, Janine R., *Collision and Collusion* (London: St. Martins, 1998).

——— 'The Harvard Boys do Russia', *The Nation*, 1 June 1998.

Zumbrennen, C. and Jeffrey P. Osleeb, *The Soviet Iron and Steel Industry* (New York: Croom Helm, 1986).

Zevin, Leon and Tadeush Teodorovich, *Soviet Union and Developing Countries. Economic Cooperation, Principles and Practice* (Delhi: Allied, 1988).

Zimarina, N.P. (ed.), *Russkii Rubl'* (Moscow: Progress Akademia, 1994).

Zhavoronkov, S., V. Mau, D. Chernyi and K. Ianovskii, 'The Deregulation of the Russian Economy', *Problems of Economic Transition*, September 2002.

Index